A HISTORY OF PHILOSOPHY
Volume 3
From Bolzano to Wittgenstein

A HISTORY
OF
PHILOSOPHY

Volume 3

From Bolzano to Wittgenstein

ANDERS WEDBERG

CLARENDON PRESS · OXFORD

1984

Oxford University Press, Walton Street, Oxford OX2 6DP

London Glasgow New York Toronto
Delhi Bombay Calcutta Madras Karachi
Kuala Lumpur Singapore Hong Kong Tokyo
Nairobi Dar es Salaam Cape Town
Melbourne Auckland

and associate companies in
Beirut Berlin Ibadan Mexico City Nicosia

Oxford is a trade mark of Oxford University Press

Published in the United States by
Oxford University Press, New York

First published in 1966 in a Swedish edition
entitled Filosofins Historia: Fran Bolzano till Wittgenstein

British Library Cataloguing in Publication Data
Wedberg, Anders
  A history of philosophy.
  Vol. 3: From Bolzano to Wittgenstein
  1. Philosophy—History
  I. Title   II. Filosophins histeria. English
  190.9   B72
  ISBN 0-19-824641-2
  ISBN 0-19-824693-5 Pbk

Typeset by Joshua Associates (Oxford)
Printed in Great Britain
at the University Press, Oxford

Contents

I

The Past 150 Years

The critical portraits of a number of philosophers and philosophical movements presented in this book do not give a coherent and comprehensible picture of the development of philosophy during the last 150 years. If I could, I would draw a map of this development and mark on it the positions of those systems of thought that I shall study in detail in the chapters that follow. Instead, however, I shall consider the development from a number of successive points of view, in a rather unsystematic and unavoidably superficial manner. I shall roughly indicate some directions in which "the winds of doctrine", one after the other and also in part simultaneously, have swept across the fields of philosophy.

1. PHILOSOPHY AND NATURAL SCIENCE

A. *Transcendental philosophy and its outgrowths*

The first of the philosophers whose ideas will be presented in this book, Bernard Bolzano (Chapter II), was active during the period when transcendental philosophy was still, on the whole, dominant in that part of the world which spoke German or was oriented towards Germany. And Germany was undoubtedly the great philosophical power of the time. In the eyes of transcendental philosophy, the external world was never truly real. Kant had taught that reality in space and time, which was the domain of empirical science, was nothing but a system of phenomena, or appearances within some minds—whether this mind should be understood as Kant's own, or that of any human being, or as a non-individual "general consciousness' (*Bewusstsein überhaupt*). What was more than a phenomenon, according to Kant, was the mind in which phenomena appear, on the one hand, and those "things in themselves" (*Dinge an sich*) that manifest themselves to the mind through the phenomena, on the other hand. The truly real was thus something beyond the horizon of science. This conviction was one of the most fundamental elements in transcendental philosophy.

Hence it is not astonishing that the imaginative world explanations that the transcendental philosophers boldly painted had practically no contact with the natural sciences of the time—save to the extent that their visions seduced several contemporary scientists with philosophical leanings. The transcendental systems had many properties that gave them a strong appeal. The mind, the soul, was nothing ephemeral in that infinite space that had once filled Pascal with fear. On the contrary, it was part of the truly real, and was more real than the infinite universe in space and time. In the worlds of transcendental philosophy the mind did not have to shiver. Nor did life appear to be without meaning. To an ambitious pupil the final examination constitutes the aim and meaning of school. Life, history, the evolution of the world, acquired meaning in a similar manner within the systems of the transcendental philosophers. They described an evolution, passing through a number of well-defined stages and finally reaching its desirable conclusion. (Schopenhauer, who, in spite of his contempt for transcendental philosophers, had a strong kinship to them, was an exception here. He promised no happy end. His pessimistic view of life, however, aroused no general interest until toward the end of the last century.)

As in our own days for psycho-analysis, Marxism, or existentialism, to adopt one of the transcendental systems was to learn a jargon, which enabled one to make profound comments upon most subjects of discussion. Since those ideal or spiritual realities which philosophy dealt with fell beyond the limits of empirical science, philosophical arguments were evidently subject to criteria of validity other than those of science.

Hegel created his own dialectical logic. Philosophy and science have perhaps never been as isolated from each other as they were during the era of transcendental philosophy.

The year of Hegel's death, 1831, is usually considered the end of that era. Inside and outside Germany, however, Hegelianism has remained a spiritual power far into our own century. "Idealistic" and "spiritualistic" movements of various descriptions ("critical idealism", "absolute idealism", "personalist idealism", etc. etc.) have shown a strong vitality. The conceptual apparatus of Hegelianism has been preserved in Marxism as well as in existentialism.

B. *The idea of immanence and the critique thereof*

The epistemological conviction which was the starting-point for transcendental philosophy was a version of an idea which has been one of the most fundamental and most persistent themes of post-medieval western philosophy, viz. the idea that consciousness is somehow locked up within itself. This idea, which was foreign to medieval scholasticism, entered philosophy in the seventeenth century largely through the resumed study of the ancient sceptics. Let us call it the idea of immanence. Hume stated it in the words that I never perceive anything but my own perceptions. Schopenhauer said that the world is my idea or representation (*Vorstellung*). The idea of immanence can be varied almost indefinitely. It was revived at the end of the nineteenth century by the many neo-Kantian schools that emerged, especially in Germany, at that time, by the so-called immanence philosophers and, to some extent, also through empiricist critique of science (cf. E). In many modern existentialists (e.g. Jaspers, Sartre), the idea of immanence also plays an important role. From the various versions of this idea, one can draw conclusions entirely different from those drawn by transcendental philosophers. They saw in it a philosophical demotion of that reality with which empirical science is concerned. At a later time, for example in some forms of neo-Kantianism, and in existentialism, it has been a threat to the communication between science and philosophy. But in the radical form of empiricism, developed by, for example, Ernst Mach and the logical empiricists of our own time (who at the outset toyed with the idea), the idea has been combined with an intense interest in science and a rejection of 'metaphysics'.

The reaction against the sort of idealistic speculation, alienated from science, of which the transcendental philosophy of the early nineteenth century is an extreme example, began very early. Bernard Bolzano was an acute and indefatigable critic of the many obscurities and sophistries to be found in Kant and Hegel. But since the enemy was tough, the same battle had to be fought many times over. There was born a more esoteric philosophical, and also a more scientific (often popularly scientific), reaction against idealism. The esoteric reaction especially took for its target the central idea of immanence. Such criticism was levelled from various points of view by Bolzano in the 1820s and 1830s, by Brentano and his school toward the end of the last century, by Moore and Russell in Cambridge during the first decades of our century, by the American realists (the "new", and the "critical"), by Hägerström and Phalén in Uppsala at the same time, by Wittgenstein in the 1930s and 1940s, and in our days it has been restated by the Oxford philosophers. I shall return to this critique in section 3.

C. *Scientific world pictures in the nineteenth century*

The second kind of reaction, often combined with the first, was to take the reality of the external world as an indisputable fact and to accept contemporary scientific theory as a set of fragments of the true world picture, fragments which were often, somewhat naïvely, thought to admit of completion through fairly self-evident extrapolations. Those who reacted most violently against idealism saw in the results of science a more or less consistently materialistic worldview. To these belonged, as is well known, Marx and Engels and their many followers. In many cases the reaction took the form of belief in the sort of mechanistic, deterministic view of which so many variants occurred in the seventeenth and eighteenth centuries.[1]

Consciousness is at once the stumbling-block and the *raison d'être* of materialism. The most radical materialists (like Ludwig Büchner in the 1850s) either denied its existence

[1] The question, posed by Leibniz's monadology, whether (a) a mass particle in its essence is a system of forces, or (b) the notion of force is an auxiliary mathematical term in the description of motions, was also kept alive in the nineteenth century. The physicist Faraday, e.g., leaned toward (a), while, for example, Karl Pearson, biologist, statistician, and philosopher, advocated (b), in *The Grammar of Science* (1892). The notion of energy, which increased in importance through the law of conservation of energy (formulated in the 1840s by Mayer, Joule, and Helmholtz), was proposed by Wilhelm Ostwald (1853–1932), chemist and monistic philosopher, as a new key to the essence of reality.

outright or declared it to be a neuro-physiological process. Others were satisfied with defending some sort of monistic world-view in which mind and matter were thought to be united as intimately as possible. Monadological ideas in the spirit of Leibniz as well as panpsychistic ideas in the spirit of Spinoza had many adherents in the nineteenth century.

During the latter half of the century, the scientific world-view was thought to include the evolutionist idea which claimed support from Darwin's doctrine of the development of species (1859) and which received its classic expression in the 'synthetic' philosophy of Herbert Spencer (1820–1903). One believed in 'evolution', whether it was a biological evolution toward 'higher' forms of life (e.g. Nietzsche's superman), or the development of society and culture toward greater happiness and justice (e.g. toward some form of socialism), or even some sort of cosmic evolution. This evolution was usually thought, as a matter of course, to be a change from worse to better. When a scientific world-view was combined with evolutionism, in the eyes of many it made existence as gloriously meaningful as the evolutionist, transcendental philosophy had once made it.

The sort of world-view which I have characterized here by the vague words "scientific", "materialistic", "monistic", "mechanistic", "deterministic", had its heyday during the latter part of the century. But thoughts have a long life, and something of the same view can be found in many philosophers of our century. When Hägerström and Phalén in Uppsala broke loose from the bewitchment of idealism, it appeared to them that the self-evident alternative was what Hägerström called an "enlightened materialism". Wittgenstein's talk in the *Tractatus* of natural science, or even of mechanics, as a "complete description of the world" is to be seen as a remnant of the same climate of opinion. In the 1930s Wittgenstein still occasionally spoke as if material objects were all that there is. The so-called scientific world-view of logical empiricism, sometimes condensed into the formula that the language of physics is a universal language, is a more sophisticated expression of the same outlook. The "pan-somatism" (the doctrine that bodies are all that exists) of the Pole Tadeusz Kotarbinski (b. 1886) is still another branch of this tradition. When behaviourism is not only a programme for research but also a doctrine, the doctrine that mental life does not exist or is merely a form of behaviour, behaviourism, too, is an offspring of eighteenth-century materialism. In the form of so-called logical behaviourism, behaviourism was an important ingredient in early logical empiricism, and it is a pattern of thought that the later Wittgenstein and the Oxford philosophers fall back upon again and again.

D. *The dissolution of the mechanistic world-view in science*

The nineteenth-century adherents of a "mechanistic", "deterministic", "scientific" world-view argued roughly as follows:

(i) The natural sciences give (or are on their way toward giving) a correct picture of the world.

(ii) They describe the world as a "mechanistic", "deterministic" (perhaps even "material") system.

(iii) Hence, the world is such a system.

Within science itself, and particularly physics, a development has taken place which has made the premisses (i) and (ii) of this argument appear more and more unrealistic. Parallel with this scientific process, philosophical epistemology and philosophical criticism of science have, from other points of view, undermined especially premiss (i), something that will be discussed in section E.

The development within science, with which we are concerned here, is, I think, so familiar to the reader that I shall not go into details. According to the mechanistic conviction, the laws which prima facie do not belong to mechanics ought to be derivable from purely mechanical hypotheses about the nature of phenomena. (The kinetic gas theory is a classical realization of this ideal.) It was within the theory of electricity that the ideal first began to wither away. By his electromagnetic theory Maxwell succeeded in explaining the known phenomena; but attempts to give to his equations a mechanical or even an intuitive interpretation did not succeed. The theory of relativity later led to a break with those notions of space and time which had been inherited from the ancient atomists, Euclid and Newton, and which are accepted as the self-evident framework in the classical mechanistic philosophy of nature. Quantum physics has put in doubt the idea of the particle structure of matter as well as the belief in a universal determinism. Neither electromagnetic theory, nor the theory of relativity, nor quantum mechanics, admits of the kind of intuitive interpretation which made classical mechanism so pleasing to thought. The equations of the theories are coupled to experience in a definite manner, but they do not seem to give us any picture of what the world is like.

E. *The empiricist critique of science*

The intellectual climate has been influenced in a parallel direction by the evolution of philosophical epistemology. This evolution contains several distinct lines of thought which, however, have all converged towards a critique of (i) in the above argument. This philosophical critique of science has been inspired by ideas in classical British empiricism, and also by ideas in Kant, and it has been carried out not least by the physicists who have also been philosophers.

Roughly speaking, the empiricist critique can be said to have centred upon two questions: (a) What is natural science about? Or what should it be construed as talking about? (b) How, and to what extent, can theories of physics be verified or falsified by experience?

Ernst Mach (1838–1916), professor first of mathematics, then of physics, and finally of philosophy, approached question (a) in a manner that rather resembles Berkeley's critique of the Newtonians at the beginning of the eighteenth century. According to Mach, science is a method of describing what is directly observable, our sense-impressions or sensations (*Empfindungen*), in consonance with the principle of intellectual economy. Seriously to believe in the existence of the non-observable entities that occur in physical theory (absolute space, absolute time, the atoms, etc.) is to fall into metaphysics, the word being used here in a pejorative sense. To work with non-observable entities is justifiable only if they are understood to be a sort of fiction or symbolic aid. It is to be recommended only if these fictions serve the economy of thought.

Mach desired simultaneously (1) to limit physics to the

observable and (2) to identify the observable with sensations. Many philosophers and some physicists have followed him on this very radical road. Although many physicists have agreed with Mach on thesis (1), most of them, I think, have been less willing than philosophers to underwrite also thesis (2). Wherever the line between the observable and the non-observable is drawn, a position in the spirit of Mach seems to lead to a conclusion in his spirit: physical theory countenances much that has the character of fictions or symbolic aids. (A peculiar proposal that has sometimes been put forward is that what is observable in physics is just the pointer readings.)

Positions close to that of Mach were taken at about the same time by the philosopher Richard Avenarius (1843–96), and by the physicists Ludwig Boltzmann (1844–1906), Heinrich Hertz (1857–94), and Pierre Duhem (1861–1916).

Mach's view had its closest historical parallel in the views of Berkeley and Hume, but he himself considered his doctrine to be identical with Kant's when the thing in itself is set aside, thus identifying Kant's "phenomena" with his own "sensations". Several neo-Kantians during the latter half of the nineteenth century also advocated views that pointed in the same direction as Mach's. On the basis of sense-physiological considerations Hermann Helmholtz (1821–94), physiologist, physicist, mathematician, and neo-Kantian philosopher, arrived at the conclusion that scientific theories are systems of signs, which should be judged by their usefulness. The neo-Kantian F. A. Lange (1828–75) and his pupil Hans Vaihinger (1852–1933) put forward similar thoughts with a more sceptical accent. According to Lange, science is a grandiose fiction (*Dichtung*), and according to Vaihinger's at one time much debated fictionalism, the whole structure of scientific theory is imbued with fictions. The neo-Kantian Hermann Cohen (1842–1918), the founder of the so-called Marburg school, held the reality of physics to be a mathematical structure that we correlate intellectually with experience.

The opinion that scientific theory is, in some sense, an instrument and that it should be judged by such criteria as "intellectual economy", "usefulness", "applicability" was also nourished by the new biological view of man that was inspired largely by Darwin's theory of biological evolution. With greater emphasis than clarity this view was defended by American pragmatism, founded by Charles Saunders Peirce (1839–1914), mathematician, logician, physicist, and philosopher, and William James (1842–1910), psychologist and philosopher. The view was also an ingredient in the philosophical doctrines of Friedrich Nietzsche (1844–1900) and Henri Bergson (1859–1941).

Also, the second of the above-mentioned questions, the problem (b) of verification and falsification, became the object of increased critical awareness toward the end of the century. The significance of the hypothetico-deductive method, introduced for good in science by the seventeenth-century physicists, was now reconsidered. (As Duhem has observed, the method can in a sense be traced back all the way to Plato.) It was especially two Frenchmen, the mathematician, physicist, and philosopher Henri Poincaré (1854–1912), and the physicist, historian of science, and philosopher Pierre Duhem, who formulated the new ideas. That a general theory cannot be definitively proved on the basis of experience, is an old insight —even if it has sometimes been obscured (e.g. by John Stuart Mill's doctrine about the methods of induction). Poincaré and Duhem pointed out that neither can it be definitively refuted by experience. If from the theory T we deduce the experiential statement E, and if experience shows E to be false, then it might seem that T has been refuted as definitively as anyone can wish. The French thinkers pointed out that, in the derivation of E from T, we usually invoke also a number of theories other than T, say T', T'', . . . The negative experiment hence shows, not the falsehood just of T, but the falsehood of the entire conjunction: T, and T', and T'' and . . . . Some part of this conjunction must be false, but we do not know which. The fundamental theorem of Euclidean geometry, that the sum of the angles in a triangle is 180°, cannot possibly be refuted, for example by optical triangulation. A negative outcome refutes Euclid only if we presuppose *inter alia* that light rays are propagated rectilinearly.

Suppose, quite generally, that a physical theory asserts certain quantities $q_1, q_2, . . .$ to fulfil the condition:

(i) $f(q_1, q_2, \ldots) = 0$.

Through pointer-readings on our instruments we test (i) in a particular case. We interpret the readings as saying:

(ii) $q_1 = a_1, q_2 = a_2, \ldots$,

and by calculation we find:

(iii) $f(a_1, a_2, \ldots) \neq 0$.

Our very interpretation (ii) of what the instruments show builds on the assumption of a number of theories other than (i). The outcome (iii) is *a priori* a reason for us to give up any one of these other theories just as much as (i).

Both Poincaré and Duhem made a distinction between different levels of scientific theory, on the one hand the experimental laws (or hypotheses) and on the other hand the theoretical principles: the former are somehow closer to experience than the latter. The theoretical principles are, on the view of Poincaré, a free creation of human thought, they have the character of "conventions" and even of "definitions" (on this issue, Poincaré is not very clear); according to Duhem, they are a "symbolic construction".

The trend of thought that has been sketched here can be characterized schematically as involving the following items:

(a) An attempt to distinguish sharply between what is observable in the field of science, especially physics, and what is not so.

(b) A demand that physical theory should not advance any (seriously intended) hypotheses that go beyond what is observable.

(c) A rather strong tendency to identify, in the spirit of phenomenalism, the observable with our "experiences", our "observations", or even our "sensations".

(d) The view that physical hypotheses cannot be definitively proved or refuted by experience.

(e) The view that the choice of physical theory (including that of physical geometry) is, in a fundamental sense, a matter of convention.

(f) The view that theories should be judged from the point of view of economy of thought, with regard to their simplicity and usefulness: the best theory is that which combines the greatest simplicity with the strongest explanatory power.

(g) The idea that the mathematically formulated laws of theoretical physics (and possibly of other fields) should be looked upon as mere formulae, which, by means of special physical rules of inference, are coupled with statements about the observable; thus a rejection of the search for intuitive (*inhaltliche*) models.

As they are spelled out here, these ideas are exceedingly vague, and they can be made more precise in many different ways. Obviously, they signify a break with the older, more naïve mode of thought according to which it was possible to read a picture of the world into the results of natural science, especially those of physics. The philosophical ideas have developed in pace with the development of science itself, although it is difficult to define exactly the role they might have played in science. (Einstein has pointed to Mach as one of his sources of inspiration.) These ideas have also exerted a deep influence upon the entire empiricist/epistemological discussion in our century. Logical empiricism (Chapter VI) is in essence an attempt to give more precise and systematic shape to these ideas, by utilizing the resources of mathematical logic. In my view, the attempt has not led as yet to any even remotely satisfactory result. No real clarity has yet been reached even on the fundamental distinction between what is observable and what is not.

In logical empiricism, empiricism has sometimes been wedded to a nominalism, giving an even sharper edge to the ideas sketched here. According to a modern version of nominalism, given its most precise formulation by the Americans Goodman and Quine, all 'abstract' entities are fictions. Classical mathematics is not nominalist: it deals with a swarm of abstract entities such as numbers, functions, sets, etc. From a strictly nominalistic point of view, classical mathematics therefore appears to be, in large part, a fictive theory or a mere symbolic calculus; and the same must then be also true of the physics that builds on this mathematics. Similar consequences also ensue from finitism, the view that no actual infinity exists, argued most forcefully by the great German mathematician and logician David Hilbert (1862–1943). One might of course arrive at a fictionalist interpretation of a theory, or of parts of a theory, without assuming philosophical views of a scope as large and as ambitious as some sort of radical empiricism, nominalism, or finitism.

F. *Three philosophical reactions*

Those who seek a world picture and who have experienced the previously indicated ideas as a part of the truth have reacted in several distinct ways. I wish to distinguish schematically three principal reactions. (They can occur in the same thinker; in Bertrand Russell, for example, all three seem to be discernible.)

1. *The positivist reaction*

In Mach himself the empiricist epistemology constituted a sort of world picture. All that can be said with good sense about reality can be said through a description of the observable, the sensations. To try to say something more will be to admit metaphysical ghosts. This reaction, which I shall call the positivist reaction, is found in many thinkers other than Mach. It is, as we shall see, one aspect of Russell's thought, which, however, is too many-faceted to be characterized as positivist.

In Wittgenstein's *Tractatus* positivism is also present, although it is there interwoven with so many other strands of thought that the positivist pattern is obscured. Rudolf Carnap and other logical empiricists have defended positivist standpoints, often with a dogmatic insensibility to other modes of thought. In the later Wittgenstein, the author of the *Philosophical Investigations*, there is a sort of positivism between the lines. A basic tendency of the book is to banish from the philosophy of language such occult entities as 'mental processes' and Platonic word meanings; the philosopher should stick to what is directly observable, the words and the behaviour connected with them. What most profoundly distinguishes the positivism of the later Wittgenstein from the positivism of the philosophers of science is mainly two things: he has lost interest in scientific theory, he wishes to stick to a straightforward "phenomenological" description of the observable, and he considers unimproved ordinary language to be a perfectly adequate instrument for the description. A similar brand of positivism is found in many of the so-called Oxford philosophers. (Both the later Wittgenstein and the Oxford philosophers have objected to Mach's identification of the observable with sense impressions.)

What the extreme positivists (if I rightly understand them) would like to say is something like this: "Only what (in one sense or another) is observable exists—the rest are chimeras, imaginings, fictions, myths, empty symbols." The positivist Quine puts the point as follows, our assertions about the external world are a complex though expedient system for correlating experiences with experiences:

> Physical objects are conceptually imported into the situation as convenient intermediaries—not by definition in terms of experience, but simply as irreducible posits comparable, epistemologically, to the gods of Homer. . . . in point of epistemological footing the physical objects and the gods differ only in degree and not in kind.

The same holds for "atomic and subatomic entities", for forces, energy, and matter. Also the classes and classes of classes and so on up, which are the substance of mathematics, are, epistemologically, "myths on the same footing with physical objects and gods".[2]

But can a strict positivist really speak with good conscience in the manner of Quine? Are not Quine's statements themselves statements that go beyond the observable, and, hence as unverifiable as those of the despised metaphysics?

A positivist like Carnap answers "yes" to this question: if the assertion *A* is metaphysical nonsense, so is not-*A*. The fundamental positivist conviction thus becomes something which cannot be expressed in words; indeed, which must not even be thought. Carnap can give expression to this conviction only by means of a proposal: "Speak only of the observable—if necessary (or if convenient) with the help of the sort of symbolic aids which already Mach accepted." Carnap does not put it so naïvely, but this is the import of his proposals for a "universal" empirical language. A non-positivist

---

[2] W. V. O. Quine: *From a Logical Point of View*, Cambridge, Mass., 1964, pp. 44–5.

may wonder, "But if the non-observable exists—and why should it not—would it not be interesting to find out about it, to say something plausible about its nature?" In reply a positivist of Carnap's severe cast can only repeat his proposal. In support of the proposal he might possibly argue, as Carnap did, that "meaningful speech" should be defined as such speech as the proposal recommends. But a definition is not an argument. Extreme positivism thus becomes a rather paradoxical intellectual standpoint.

If the positivist—like Mach, Carnap, and Quine—allows terms referring to unobservables to be introduced, as fictions or symbolic aids, into the description of the observable, then the distinction between positivist and non-positivist becomes somewhat ethereal. The two can speak exactly alike, affirm the existence of precisely the same things. While the positivist will make the mental reservation that these things are fictions, the non-positivist may seriously believe in their existence. Carnap at times expressed the idea that exactly the same theory can be presented either in a correct empiricist or in a reprehensible metaphysical spirit. The distinction appears truly subtle. Does the spirit matter so much? And how does it manifest itself?

2. *The sceptical reaction*

Philosophers have always sought certainty, and they have always been prone to extreme doubt. The positivist tries to take his stand on the certainty of the observable. But, obviously, the ideas discussed in E can also induce a sceptical attitude. There are many reasons for the repudiation, by modern analytical philosophers, of attempts to construct a general world-view. One reason is the ever-growing awareness of how difficult it is to formulate statements which have the intended generality and simultaneously fulfil reasonable demands as to clarity and plausibility. Another powerful reason is the situation in modern science and the empiricist critique of science. As is well known, the sceptical attitude was, often and articulately, voiced by Bertrand Russell— who nevertheless from 1914 onwards had his own metaphysics.

3. *The metaphysical reaction*

When Kant limited the scope of science to empirical phenomena in space and time, he was guided, *inter alia*, by his
wish to make room for religious belief. Radical empiricism
has sometimes been associated with a similar aim. The French
physicist Pierre Duhem was a practising Roman Catholic,
and in his eyes the empiricist critique of science had the
welcome effect of referring metaphysical questions to another
forum than science.

This pattern of thought recurs in many philosophers.
According to Bergson's philosophy of intuition, for example,
the core of reality is disclosed to us, not through science,
but through intuition and through the inner experience of
duration (*la durée*) and the vital leap (or urge, *l'élan vital*).

Another, more "rationalist" metaphysical reaction is also
possible. One can—roughly speaking—attempt to construct a picture of the world which does not sidestep science
but which, on the contrary, gives an interpretation of the
scientific theories of the day. Russell's neutral monism in
The Analysis of Mind (1921) and *The Analysis of Matter*
(1927) is intended as such an interpretation. I do not believe
that neutral monism is adequate, but it exemplifies a type of
philosophizing with which I am in sympathy.

On the borderline between religious and rationalist metaphysics lie systems like those elaborated by Samuel Alexander
(1859–1938) in *Space, Time and Deity* (1920) and by
A. N. Whitehead, mathematician, logician, physicist, and
metaphysician (1861–1947), in the highly cryptic *Process
and Reality* (1929).

2. THE PROBLEM OF CONSCIOUSNESS

A. *A cluster of problems*

"Consciousness" as used in the title of this section is a general term covering well-known states of affairs like the following:

> I see a white paper.
> I hear the music very well.
> I think the bush looks like a bear.
> (i) I am thinking about Alfred de Musset.
> I was just thinking about Apollo.
> I saw the Eiffel Tower in my dream.
> I remember how blue the water was in the Mediterranean.
> I have a pain in my little toe.

Consciousness in this sense naturally presents a virtually unlimited number of problems, including all those studied by modern psychology, psychophysics, and neurophysiology. By "the problem of consciousness", however, I wish to indicate a group of questions with which none of these respectable disciplines is much concerned, but with which philosophers (including earlier, more introspective and more speculative psychologists) have seriously occupied themselves.

The questions I have in mind are vague and difficult but they are connected with virtually all other philosophical questions and are thus of fundamental importance in philosophy. During the period discussed here, they have been a central theme in the philosophical debate.

Let us consider the state of affairs:

> (ii) I am thinking about Alfred de Musset.

If grammar is not misleading (which many, for respectable reasons, think it is), the statement says that a certain relation indicated by the words "am thinking about" obtains between two entities, myself and the French poet Musset, who died in 1857:

> (ii*) *I* --- am thinking about --- *Alfred de Musset.*

Interpreted in an analogous fashion the statement:

(iii) I saw the Eiffel Tower in my dream.

says, that the relation indicated by the words 'see in my dream' obtained between myself and the Eiffel Tower;

(iii*) *I --- saw in my dream --- the Eiffel Tower.*

Let us, for the sake of brevity, use the phrase "relations of consciousness" to designate the sort of relation which seems to be involved in (ii) and (iii), and which also seems to be involved in all the other situations under (i).

Every relation of biological kinship can be expressed by means of a small number of basic concepts, for example, the three, 'man', 'woman', and 'parent of'. The state of affairs:

(iv) x is the paternal grandmother of y,

can, for example, be expressed as follows:

(iv*) x is a woman and is a parent of a man who is a parent of y.

When I speak of "the problem of consciousness", I am primarily thinking of the following question:

(P1) How could the relations of consciousness be systematically explained on the basis of some set of fundamental concepts?

(P1) is not formulated very precisely, but it will serve as a first attempt to direct the attention of the reader in the intended direction. I have only vaguely intimated what I mean by "relations of consciousness". An attempt at solving (P1) must go hand in hand with an attempt at demarcating this category in a sharper manner.

When speaking of the "problem of consciousness" I am also thinking of the question:

(P2) How should a systematic theory of the relations of consciousness, possibly together with certain other related concepts, be framed?

The history of philosophy and of introspective, "analytical" psychology is full of ideas which can be interpreted as tentative suggestions and fragmentary contributions to solutions of (P1) and (P2). These may be questions on which general agreement is as difficult to reach as on the question about the existence of God, the creation of the universe, or the law of excluded middle in mathematics. If one were to define a "scientific question" as one on the solution of which it is possible to reach general agreement, then (P1) and (P2) are perhaps not "scientific". But it may be held to be the privilege, and one of the tasks, of the philosopher to deal with questions which (according to the definition just mentioned) lie on or beyond the borders of "science"— borders which we know are constantly shifting. In what follows I shall merely give some glimpses of one line of thought of the past 150 years.[3]

B. *The doctrine of immanence revisited*

The doctrine of immanence previously mentioned (p. 3) is not sufficiently precise to deserve to be called a theory of consciousness. But it has been, and still is, a very influential opinion, or family of opinions, concerning consciousness. It could be expressed along the following lines:

(Im) If S (I, you, . . .) has a relation of consciousness to something O, then O exists in S's consciousness, and hence not outside of S's consciousness.[4]

If the expression "O exists in S's consciousness" is taken simply as a synonym for "S has some relation of consciousness to O", and the expression "O exists outside of S's consciousness" as a synonym for "S has no relation of consciousness to O", then (Im) becomes a tautology. Like so many celebrated thoughts, (Im) oscillates between a trivial and a far from trivial significance. It is largely from its trivial

---

[3] Unfortunately, there does not exist (as far as I know) a critical–analytical history of philosophical theories of consciousness during the period under discussion.

[4] The doctrine of immanence has often been held in some weaker form. To make (Im) express a given weaker form of the doctrine, one should replace the phrase "a relation of consciousness" with "one of the relations of consciousness $R_1, R_2 \ldots$", where $R_1, R_2 \ldots$ are those relations of consciousness for which the doctrine in question makes the supposition of immanence.

interpretation that (Im) derives its persuasive power, but it is the non-trivial interpretations that give to (Im) its importance.

The non-trivial meaning of (Im) is actually very elastic. Let us use M as shorthand for "the consciousness of S", C to denote the collection of everything to which S stands in a relation of consciousness, and U to denote the total universe (everything there is). Diagram (A) is useful for illustrating the elasticity of (Im);

(A)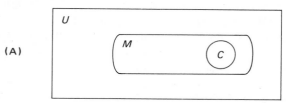

in this diagram, (Im) is expressed by the fact that area C is contained in area M. But (Im) in itself, when not interpreted trivially, says nothing about the extent of M. The more narrowly the boundary of M is drawn, the stronger (Im) becomes and the greater is the risk that (Im) will be false or absurd.

The following assertion, which is often encountered in the history of philosophy and which, I think, "common sense" endorses,

(v) Physical reality falls outside M,

implies that the boundary of M must be drawn rather narrowly. When (v) is combined with (Im) one reaches the conclusion that S cannot have any relation of consciousness to any physical object. (v) is only one of many similar assertions which give rise to similar negative conclusions. One such assertion is, for example:

(vi) Other minds fall outside M.

By virtue of (Im), then, S cannot have a relation of consciousness to any other mind. The wider the limits of M are drawn, the greater, *a priori*, is the likelihood of (Im) being correct and the greater also the risk that it will become a triviality. We have already observed one way in which (Im) can be trivialized. We simply *define* "to be in M" in such a way that C

is by definition in *M*. Another, even more radical way to trivialize (Im) is to define *M* so that *M* coincides with *U*: "everything there is exists in my consciousness"; "the world is my representation" (Schopenhauer).

Not merely through its elasticity but also through its emotive force, the doctrine of immanence reminds one of political ideologies—like, say, the following: "the property of the state is owned by all; the more the state owns, the more each one of us owns". (Im) can provide a feeling of power, as in Wittgenstein's *Notebooks 1914–16*. But (Im) can also induce a feeling of unreality, of life's being a dream. To abandon (Im) is to break with a way of experiencing life as much as to change an opinion.

C. *Some thoughts in Bolzano and Frege*

In the nineteenth century Bolzano was one of the first to suggest a theory of consciousness which broke radically with the doctrine of immanence. Bolzano's theory starts from a study of what happens when we understand linguistic expressions. When, for instance, I understand the phrase "the author of the *Prior Analytics*", I have according to Bolzano a "subjective representation", corresponding to a "representation-in-itself" that constitutes the significance of the word. The representation-in-itself has Aristotle for its "object". While the subjective representation is part of my mental life and has its natural causes and effects, the representation-in-itself is, on Bolzano's view, something which exists neither in space nor in time: it is, in contemporary jargon, a Platonic entity. According to Bolzano, to think about Aristotle is to be aware of a representation-in-itself having Aristotle for its object. The situation:

(vii)   *S* is thinking about Aristotle,

is thus thought by Bolzano to be analysable as follows:

(viii)   There is a representation-in-itself *r* such that *S* is aware of *r* and *r* has Aristotle for its object.

If we also explicitly take into account the so-called subjective representation, the analysis becomes even more complex:

(ix) There is a subjective representation ρ and a representation-in-itself *r* such that ρ is a part of *S*'s mental life and ρ corresponds to *r* and *r* has Aristotle for its object. Besides reality in space and time, there is, according to Bolzano (as according to Plato), a sphere of ideal entities to which representations-in-themselves belong. When I, who am a part of space and time, think about Aristotle, who is also a part of space and time, this event involves, so to speak, a detour into the ideal sphere. His view could be illustrated by diagram (B).

(B)
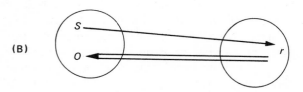

The single arrow symbolizes that *S* (that is me) conceives the representation-in-itself *r* (the meaning of the phrase 'The author of the *Prior Analytics*'). The double arrow indicates that *r* has *O* (Aristotle) for its object.

In Bolzano's view situations occur where the representation *r* has no object, for instance:

(x) I was thinking about Apollo.

The mythological name "Apollo" stands for a representation-in-itself, but since there is no god Apollo, this representation has no object. From Bolzano's point of view (x) appears misleading: it holds out the prospect of a relation between me and the god Apollo, whereas actually there is only a relation between me and a representation-in-itself. It can also occur that both *r* and its object *O* belong to the ideal sphere, for instance when *r* is identical with the representation-in-itself expressed by '$\sqrt{5}$', and $O = \sqrt{5}$.

Frege had little interest in psychology as such, but his semantical theory of "sense" (*Sinn*) and "reference" (*Bedeutung*) implies a view about consciousness nearly identical with that of Bolzano. Frege's "senses" are ideal entities that constitute the meanings of linguistic expressions—they thus play much the same role as representations-in-themselves do in Bolzano. Where Bolzano says that a representation-in-itself has an object, Frege says that a sense refers to something. If one applies Frege's conceptual scheme to (vii), the following analysis results:

(xi) There is a sense s such that S apprehends s and s refers to Aristotle.

Thus, with appropriate changes in terminology, the previous diagram can also illustrate an aspect of Frege's theory.

Bolzano's theory of consciousness denied fundamental presuppositions of German transcendental philosophy, and it formed the basis for his attempt to liberate logic from psychology. For Bolzano, the object of logical study is the ideal sphere to which representations-in-themselves belong. Something similar is true of Frege, who saw his arch-enemy in "psychologism", the tendency to transform logic into psychology which played a prominent role in German philosophy in his time.

D. *Husserl*

Edmund Husserl (1859–1938), the founder of phenomenology, formulated a theory of "intentions" which was partly inspired by the views of Bolzano and Frege. According to Husserl, (vii) can be analysed roughly as follows.

(xii) There is an intention i such that S experiences i and Aristotle is the object of i (i is intentionally directed towards Aristotle; i intends Aristotle; etc.).

Husserl's (often awkward) terminology must not be allowed to obscure the profound agreement with Frege. What Frege calls the "sense" (*Sinn*) of a linguistic expression, Husserl calls its reference (*Bedeutung*) and identifies it with an "intention". What Frege calls the "reference" (*Bedeutung*) of the expression is described by Husserl as the object intended through the intention.

At the same time, there are points on which Husserl, in the *Logical Investigations* (*Logische Untersuchungen*, 1900) clearly differs from Bolzano as well as from Frege. Husserl does not, for example, give his intentions the "Platonic" status which Bolzano's representations-in-themselves and Frege's senses are supposed to possess. Like all contents of experience, the intentions of a person are for Husserl parts of his mental life, his stream of experience (*Erlebnisstrom*).

Husserl's doctrine—I am only dealing with his position in the *Logical Investigations*—can probably be interpreted in several different ways. One is the following: All "mental life" (or "psychic life", or "consciousness") consists in experiencing something. What is experienced Husserl calls "contents of experience" ("immanent contents of experience", "experiences"). Contents of experience are either intentional ("intentional acts", "acts", "intentions") or non-intentional. What characterizes an intentional content is, metaphorically speaking, that it points beyond itself; it points, so to speak, in a certain direction, and it may or may not be the case that in that direction there exists an object toward which it points. When I think of Cologne Cathedral, the content is an intention pointing toward the cathedral; when I think of the Tower of Babel, the content is likewise an intention but one pointing in a direction where perhaps there is nothing to be pointed at. A content of experience is non-intentional if it lacks this property of pointing beyond itself. Such a content is called by Husserl a "sensation" (*Empfindung*). If I have understood him correctly, he denies intentionality of all that is sensory, intuitive, e.g. red, round, bitter, etc.

In normal mental life, contents that themselves lack intentionality are often fused with intentions. This occurs in the normal understanding of (one's own) language: one's image of a word is "animated" by an intention directed toward what is referred to by the word. (The Husserlian description of certain forms of aphasia would be that the word images have ceased to be accompanied by their appropriate intentions.) This animation is also characteristic of normal perception: what is sensed (the sense-datum of British philosophy) is animated by an intention pointing beyond it. When I see an apple, I sense only an aspect of it, but an intention so to speak completes what is sensed into a solid object and specifically an apple. (Here too, a disease may involve the dissociation of sensation from intention, thereby making normal perception impossible.)[5]

[5] Husserl's ideas have obvious points of contact with experimental investigations

E. *Brentano and the tradition of act psychology*

The views of Bolzano, Frege, and Husserl discussed above deal with the object side of consciousness, that of which one is conscious. Let us now turn our attention the other way, to the subject side, and reconsider the situation:

(vii)   *S* is thinking about Aristotle.

One can ask quite naïvely: What is it which bears the relation of thinking about to Aristotle? The question may seem pointless, since the answer is already given by (vii): the person *S*. But the question concerns one aspect of the old metaphysical problem of 'body and mind'. Is it, roughly speaking, *S*'s body, some physical part of his body, or some physical process in his body, etc., which primarily bears the relation in question to Aristotle? Or, is it some "psychic" factor joined to *S*'s body, say his "inner ego", his "mind", or his "consciousness" which primarily bears the relation? Descartes formulated sharply a position of the latter kind. Many of the philosophers who oppose Cartesian dualism, can be interpreted as spokesmen for a position of the first kind. The opposition between the Cartesians and their opponents is as clear, or as obscure, as the distinction between physical and psychical.

The Austrian philosopher Franz Brentano (1838–1917), like Bolzano a Roman Catholic theologian with a problematic relationship to his church, developed a point of view with deep roots in Aristotelian-scholastic speculation, and in doing so founded the so-called act-psychological tradition.[6] The classical document of this tradition is Brentano's *Psychology from an empirical standpoint* (*Psychologie vom empirischen Standpunkte*, 1874). Through many students and students' students, and through the intellectual stimulation which radiated from their writings, Brentano has deeply influenced philosophy in many areas and in many countries. Husserl was one of Brentano's pupils, and via phenomenology Brentano is among the ancestors of modern existentialism

concerning abstract (imageless) thinking and understanding of language which were undertaken at the turn of the century by the so-called Würzburg school of psychology (Külpe, Messer, Bühler, and others).

   [6] In Ockham's doctrine about the *intentiones animae* we met an interesting medieval predecessor to modern act psychology.

—although the apples (Heidegger, Sartre, etc.), have fallen far from the tree. Via his pupil, the psychologist Carl Stumpf (1848–1936), Brentano belongs to the ancestry of Gestalt psychology. The Gestalt psychologist Max Wertheimer and Wolfgang Köhler were both students of Stumpf. Alexius Meinong (1853–1920), another pupil of Brentano, founded the Austrian school of "object theory" (*Gegenstandstheorie*) and "value theory" (*Werttheorie*), which in its turn influenced Moore and Russell. Another student of Brentano's was Kasimir Twardowski (1866–1938), the father of modern analytical philosophy in Poland.

The tradition of act psychology, inaugurated by Brentano, is so complex and rich that any brief synoptic summary must be misleading. However, some basic thoughts of Brentano's can be expressed as follows: The state of affairs:

(xiii) The person S is thinking about Aristotle at time *t*, is to be analysed as:

(xiv) There is an act of consciousness (a "thought", an "idea", a "perception", etc.), say *a*, such that S has *a* at *t* and *a* is intentionally directed toward (is a thought *of*, an idea *about*, a perception *of*, etc.) Aristotle.

All relations of consciousness are thought to admit a similar analysis. The word 'act' suggests an activity and someone who performs it, but these associations are not intended by the terminology of act psychology.

Brentano's analysis (xiv) exhibits a formal analogy with Bolzano's (viii), Frege's (xi), and Husserl's (xii). But Brentano's views lie, it seems to me, on a different level from those of the other three. Bolzano's representation-in-itself, Frege's sense, and Husserl's intention are entities, which I am aware of, experience, or apprehend. Brentano's act, on the other hand, is that *through which* I am conscious of, experience, or apprehend something. (In Brentano, the situation is complicated by his assumption that a person who, for example, is thinking of Aristotle is always simultaneously aware of this act of thinking. This presumed fact is interpreted by Brentano as signifying that every mental act, whatever it "primarily" intends, is "secondarily" directed towards itself.)

The following schematic theses are an attempt to summarize some main points in Brentano's act psychology:

(B1)   That a person S at time t has a relation of consciousness to an object O, means that S at t has an act of consciousness a which intends O.

(B2)   Each act of consciousness intends something. A person cannot be conscious without being conscious of something.

(B3)   That towards which an act is directed need not exist. One can think about Apollo as well as about Aristotle.

(B4)   Distinct acts (for example, in the same person at different moments, or in different persons) can intend the same.

(B5)   Acts which intend the same can have distinct "act-qualities". An act with O for its object may be a representation (*Vorstellung*) of O, a judgement (*Urteil*) about O, or joy about O, etc.

(B6)   A person can have an act at one moment and not have it at another moment. An act cannot, however, intend an object at one moment and fail to intend it at another. The intending of an object by an act resembles, in this respect, the fact that $2 + 2 = 4$.

(B7)   An act can, but need not, be intended by another act. To observe one's own mental life is to make one's acts into objects of immediately succeeding acts.

(B8)   Acts are not "physical".

(B9)   The mental life of a person is the system of all the acts the person has throughout time.

It was mentioned above that Brentano took the act of thinking of Aristotle to have Aristotle as its "primary" object and itself as its "secondary" object. Differing from Brentano on this score, many act-psychologists (such as G. E. Moore and the young Bertrand Russell) have insisted on the following thesis:

(B10) An act is always distinct from what it intends. The awareness of red, for example, is something other than the red of which one is aware.

(B2) and (B3) involve a kind of paradox. "Given an act", the doctrine seems to say, "there is always an object which the act intends, but this object need not exist: in other words, there is an object which does not exist." One way out is to assume that existence is a property belonging to some but not to all objects, that there are non-existing as well as existing things. Existence (*Dasein*) is understood in this way by Bolzano, and Frege similarly distinguishes between "real" (*wirkliche*) and "unreal" (*unwirkliche*) objects. Both primarily had in mind the distinction between "concrete" objects, occurring in time (or in time and space), and what are now often referred to as Platonic entities. Their distinction could save us from paradox when analysing a situation like:

(xv) The person *S* is thinking of the number π.

It can plausibly be said of the number π that it is something even though it does not exist in time and space. But how should we handle (x)? We cannot very well maintain that Apollo himself *is* something, although something which is not endowed with existence in time and space. Or, how can we get rid of the paradox in the case of:

(xvi) The person *S* is thinking about a square circle,

supposing that a situation could occur which would be adequately described in this manner? Alexius Meinong distinguished not only between existing and non-existing entities, but also among the non-existing, between subsisting and non-subsisting ones. He would have said that π is a non-existing but nevertheless subsisting object, while a square circle is an object which neither exists nor subsists but which nevertheless *is* both square and circular.

Bolzano's distinction between a representation-in-itself and its object, and Frege's distinction between a sense and its object, are evidently relevant for the treatment of these puzzles. Brentano himself tried to clarify them by assuming that the statement "the act *a* intends *O*" is only apparently relational.

What are the "acts" postulated by act psychology? If, for the moment, we disregard the problem about non-existing objects, act psychology in Brentano's sense apparently allows an interpretation which renders it rather trivial. As a synonym for:

(xvii) The person *S* is in the manner *q* conscious of *O*, we could agree to use:

(xviii) S has the property of being conscious of O in the manner q.

Then the following definitions could be introduced:

(D1) a is an act of consciousness = df There is an object O and a manner q such that a is the property of being conscious of O in the manner q.

(D2) a intends O = df There is a manner q such that a is the property of being conscious of O in the manner q.

(D3) a has the act-quality q = df There is an object O such that a is the property of being conscious of O in the manner q.

(B1) and (B2) follow directly from these definitions. (B3) is, I acknowledge, a problematic point. (But it might be argued that the problematic nature of (B3) is not substantially increased by construing (B3) in agreement with (D1)–(D3).) Under the same interpretation, (B4) and (B5) describe well-known facts, and (B6), too, is apparently correct. The same may be argued to hold for (B7). (B8) and (B9) can be taken as definitions or corollaries of implicitly understood definitions. (B10), finally, appears obvious on the basis of the above definitions: the property of being aware of O cannot be the same as O any more than the property of sitting on a chair can be the chair.

Even if act-psychologists of Brentano's type sometimes appear to become bogged down in such trivialities, obviously they intended to say something important. But what? When Brentano tries to clarify what he means by an "act", he says that an act is a "representation of something", an "awareness of something", an "experience of something", and so on.

He thus appeals to our understanding of these common expressions. It is difficult to suppress the question whether act psychology might not rest on a misconstrual of them. Of course, we usually understand very well what is meant by assertions like:

(xix) The person S has an awareness of O.

But (xix) might merely be a more roundabout way of saying what is more simply and philosophically more adequately said by:

(xx) *S* is aware of *O*.

In other words, the claim, implied by (xix), that the relation between *S* and *O*, asserted by (xx), is mediated by a third entity, an awareness, could be rejected as false.

Looked upon from the perspective of economy of thought, act psychology may seem to assume an unnecessarily large burden. By postulating a middle term, the act of awareness, act psychology replaces the original problem, understanding the relation (xx) between *S* and *O*, by the two problems of understanding the relation between *S* and the act and that between the act and *O*.

F. *The Hume–Mach tradition*

Hume said that when "I enter most intimately into what I call *myself*, I always stumble on some particular perception or other, of heat or cold, light or shade, love or hatred, pain or pleasure. I can never catch *myself* at any time without a perception, and never can observe anything but the perception."[7] We can translate "perception", as used here by Hume, as "what is directly apprehended". Had Hume been acquainted with act psychology, he ought, I think, to have considered its acts to be as impossible to catch, and hence as non-existent, as the perceiving self.[8]

Hume represented a position which differs radically from act psychology, and he inaugurated a tradition which was represented most forcefully in the nineteenth century by Ernst Mach in *The Analysis of Sensations* (*Die Analyse der Empfindungen*, 1886) and in the twentieth century by William James, the American neo-realists (E. B. Holt, R. B. Perry,

[7] D. Hume, *A Treatise of Human Nature*, Bk I, Part IV, Sect. VI (ed. Selby-Bigge, 2nd edn., Oxford, 1978, p. 252).

[8] In Hume's *Treatise*, Book I, Part III, Sect. VIII (Selby-Bigge, p. 106), there is, however, a remarkable passage which runs counter to the dominant trend in Hume's philosophy and to what I here label the Hume–Mach tradition in philosophical psychology. "In thinking of our past thoughts we not only delineate out the objects of which we were thinking, but also conceive the action of the mind in the past mediation, that certain *je-ne-sais-quoi*, of which it is impossible to give any definition or description, but which everyone sufficiently understands."

et al.), and, not least, by Bertrand Russell after he took leave of act psychology with *The Analysis of Mind* (1921). Carnap's *The Logical Structure of the World* (*Der logische Aufbau der Welt*, 1928) also belongs to this tradition. One may justifiably speak of a Hume–Mach tradition in philosophical psychology.

A person's being conscious of something, say *O*, at a certain time consists on the act-psychological interpretation in the occurrence at that time of a mental act that is distinct from *O* but directed toward *O*. According to act psychology, the person's being conscious of *O* at a given time does not imply the existence of *O* at that time, or at any time whatsoever, for that matter. A fundamental assumption of the Hume–Mach tradition, on the other hand, is, I believe, the following thesis:

(HM1) That a person *S* at a time *t* directly experiences something *O*, is the same as that *O* itself occurs at *t* within the system of entities that constitutes *S*'s "field of immediate experience" ("phenomenal field", etc.).

The word "directly" in "directly experience" is essential. If I think about Napoleon at 11.13.07 a.m. on 3 May 1972, this does not, according to (HM1), imply that Napoleon is part of my field of experience at that moment. Within the Hume–Mach tradition, as within act psychology, a distinction has frequently been made between what is "directly" apprehended (perceived, experienced, etc). and what is apprehended only "indirectly", in some manner or other. According to many British empiricists, we directly apprehend sense-data in external perception, while the physical objects themselves are at most perceived in some different fashion, through the aid of the sense-data. On this view, the emperor Napoleon is clearly excluded from the range of the directly apprehended. In 1921 Russell formulated (HM1) in this paradoxical way: 'The occurrence of the content of a thought constitutes the occurrence of the thought."[9]

Another view characteristic of the Hume–Mach tradition is the thesis:

(HM2) A person's mind is nothing but the system of all

---

[9] B. Russell, *The Analysis of Mind*, 1921, p. 17.

the entities ("perceptions", "elements", etc.) which constitute his "field of immediate experience".

Hume says:

> The mind is a kind of theatre, where several perceptions successively make their appearance; pass, repass, glide away, and mingle in an infinite variety of postures and situations. . . . The comparison of the theatre must not mislead us. They are the successive perceptions only, that consititute the mind; nor have we the most distant notion of the place where these scenes are represented, or of the materials, of which it is composed.[10]

In William James, in Mach, in Russell, and in several other thinkers of the Hume–Mach tradition, a third idea also plays an important role:

(HM3) There is a set of "neutral elements", elements which in themselves are neither "physical" nor "psychical", and of which physical objects as well as minds are ultimately built.

(HM3) is a part of a general metaphysics, and, as such, it is not an essential part of that theory of consciousness which I refer to as the Hume–Mach tradition.

From one point of view, the Hume–Mach tradition advocates a view that, by its denial of the problematic acts, is more economical than act psychology. But the doctrine has its own problems and difficulties, amply discussed in the literature.

(a) How can one explain, and remain consistent with the doctrine, the fact that we are somehow conscious of things of which we are not directly aware, that we think of Aristotle, the number π, and the interior of the sun? One possible expedient would be to incorporate something like Husserl's intentions into the Hume–Mach view. Another possibility, tried by Russell and others, is to introduce a behaviouristic explanation here.

(b) If what is directly apprehended at a certain moment exists at the moment, mustn't it be assumed to exist somewhere in space? But where? Making room for the directly apprehended (sense-data, for instance) in space and time,

---

[10] D. Hume, op. cit., Book I, Part IV, Sect. VI (Selby-Bigge, p. 253).

apparently forces us to adopt some extremely unorthodox
theory of space and time.

G. *Behaviourism*

Behaviourism is both a research programme and a philosophical theory (or a family of such theories). The programme
demands that in describing animals and men the psychologist
should talk only of their bodily behaviour. The theory says
that there is nothing but behaviour to be described by the
psychologist. Both as a programme and as a theory, behaviourism has a long ancestry in the history of philosophy and
psychology.

It is intimately related to the materialistic and mechanistic
world views which have been among the great themes of
western thought ever since Greek atomism. Descartes regarded
animals as automata, and man appears in his theory as a
machine which usually functions automatically but of which
now and then the soul takes control. In the eighteenth
century, Descartes's theory was transformed, for example by
De la Mettrie in *Man and Machine* (*L'homme machine*,
1748), into an all-out theory of man as a mechanical machine.
The experimental theory of conditioned-reflexes, developed
at the turn of the century by the Russians Ivan Pavlov and
Vladimir Bechterev, was supposed by many to provide a
general scheme for explaining human behaviour. Modern
behaviourism, inspired by the work of Pavlov and Bechterev,
is primarily associated with the name of the American
psychologist J. B. Watson. In several writings, published in the
1910s and 1920s, he articulated his view. He said:

For the behaviorist, psychology is that division of natural science
which takes human behavior—the doings and sayings, both learned
and unlearned, of people as its subject matter. It is the study of what
people do from even before birth until death.[11]

The behaviorist has nothing to say of consciousness. How can he?
Behaviorism is a natural science. He has neither seen, smelled nor
tasted consciousness nor found it taking part in any human reactions.[12]

[11] J. B. Watson, *Psychology from the Standpoint of a Behaviorist*, 3rd edn.,
Philadelphia and London.

[12] J. B. Watson, *The Ways of Behaviorism*, New York and London, 1928, p. 3.

As a philosophical theory, behaviourism occurs in two versions. One version denies the existence of consciousness. One could cite passages from Watson which imply this version. The so-called logical behaviourism, popularized around 1930 by the logical empiricists, insists that it does not deny consciousness. What it explicitly maintains is only that every statement of psychology (for example every statement that a relation of consciousness obtains) can be "translated" into a statement of physics. The significance of this claim depends on what is required of a "translation". It is not always easy to see clearly how logical behaviourism differs from older types of behaviourism. The closer the method of translation is meant to join the translation to what is translated, the smaller becomes, figuratively speaking, the distance between logical behaviourism and the behaviourism which denies consciousness.

Positions in philosophy on psychological, semantical, and epistemological questions have been strongly influenced by behaviourism. Logical empiricism is the trend in modern philosophy which has staked most on a systematic behaviourism. Also, many philosophers who cannot be described as consistent behaviourists reveal a strong behaviourist component in their thinking: Bertrand Russell (from *The Analysis of Mind*, 1921, onward), Arne Naess (*Erkenntnis als wissenschaftliches Verhalten*, 1936), the later Wittgenstein, and Gilbert Ryle (*The Concept of Mind*, 1949), in common with many other contemporary Oxford philosophers, can be cited as examples. Watson wished to treat thinking as essentially movements or innervations in the larynx. The linguistic philosophy of the later Wittgenstein joins intellect and language almost as closely.

3. ANALYTICAL PHILOSOPHY

A. *Analysis and speculation*

It is common to distinguish between philosophical analysis and philosophical speculation. While speculative philosophy tries to achieve some kind of total view of reality, to attain some sort of intimate contact with the essence of things and persons, analytical philosophy, to quote Wittgenstein in the *Tractatus*, aims at making thoughts clearer. When the analytical philosopher is confronted with a statement, his first question is usually concerned not with its truth or falsehood but with its meaning. The latter question is closely connected with such other questions as, for example: What statements follow from the given statement, and from what statements does it follow? How can it be verified or falsified? How should the concept which it involves be suitably defined? How can it be expressed in some more or less formalized language? And so on.

One and the same philosopher may practise philosophical analysis as well as philosophical speculation. Depending on the proportion between the roles which the two play in their thinking, philosophers may be arranged along a scale. There are still naïvely speculative philosophers to whom the analytical questions seem pointless or bewildering, and they can be placed at one end of the scale; however, I doubt whether there are any purely analytical philosophers who could be placed at the opposite end. Philosophers in whose work analysis, in one form or another, plays a dominant role are customarily called "analytical philosophers". All the philosophers discussed in this volume belong in that category. But in each of them, there is, in addition to analysis, a strong element of what must be called speculation. Indeed, it is difficult to imagine a non-trivial philosophical analysis without a speculative component.

Generation after generation of modern analytical philosophers have regarded themselves as philosophical revolutionaries wiping the slate clean of earlier philosophies and laying the foundation for something entirely new: a self-critical, strictly scientific philosophy. As far as I can see, this belief has always been a flattering illusion. Philosophical analysis is nothing new, we can trace it back to Socrates, Plato, and Aristotle, and reflections of an analytical character can be found in the work of nearly all the great philosophers. (I am aware that this verdict, coming from me, verges on a tautology.) What has happened in modern philosophy is not the advent of something radically new, but the development and intensification of something which was always there. New realms of thought have been subjected to analysis, and new methods of analysis have been created. The many contemporary schools of analysis have joined in a discussion which has sharpened criticism and stimulated the imagination. Modern analytical philosophy, however, does not present the picture of a steady evolution toward greater clarity and self-criticism. In the eyes of a wiser posterity, many analytical attempts will no doubt appear as failures. Theses and antitheses of our day will probably come to be united into syntheses which now lie beyond the horizon. This book is, however, written in the belief that analytical philosophy has a future.

Those who set philosophical analysis and philosophical speculation against each other usually characterize the two by means of one or more of the following pairs of opposite attributes:

Analysis	*Speculation*
To study thought or language.	To study reality beyond thought and language.
To refine and sharpen our instruments for the description of reality.	To use the instruments.
To separate the given into its constituent parts.	To create something new
To make proposals concerning concept formation and theory construction (proposals that may or may not turn out to be fruitful).	To present theories that are correct or incorrect.
Does not intrude upon the domain of the special sciences.	Does so intrude.
Is relatively free of theoretical risks.	Is not so.

A moment's reflection will make it appear highly doubtful whether all these dichotomies coincide. In B to H some of the thinkers discussed in this volume will be reviewed and for each of them I shall try to clarify what sort of philosophical analysis his work exemplifies and how it combines analysis and speculation. A thorough-going discussion of, for example, the status of Frege's semantic methodology could fill an entire volume, and the following comments will necessarily be summary. If they point at all in the right direction, philosophical analysis as we meet it in the thinkers here discussed is a highly complex and problematic enterprise which has often brought the analysts into contact with the most controversial and difficult questions of the philosophy of language, psychology (phenomenological and behaviouristic), formal logic, ontology, and metaphysics.[13]

B. *Gottlob Frege*

Gottlob Frege (Chapter III) is generally considered one of the great pioneers of modern philosophical analysis. Bertrand Russell once (1914) hailed Frege as the thinker who had given "the first complete example" of the application of the logico-analytical method.[14] Frege's work has several facets. Let us first take a brief look at his analysis of the concept of number, (cf. sections 12 and 13) which Russell presumably had in mind.

This analysis is the first systematically elaborated example in philosophy of what might be called *reductive theory interpretation*. Frege considered a set of "arithmetical truths" which we can call A. (This is a very indefinite characterization of the set of A but it can be sharpened at will.) The concept of number appeared problematic to Frege: What are numbers? How do we know that they satisfy our arithmetical theory? On the other hand, he saw a rock of theoreti-

[13] The words "ontology" and "metaphysics" are vague and often misused.In keeping with a usage which seems to be rather widely accepted today, I shall make the following distinction between these expressions. By an ontological theory, I mean a theory about the most general categories, under which everything that is (in the widest sense of this expression) can be subsumed. Such theories occur for example in Frege (section 11), Russell (section 17), and Wittgenstein (section 24). By a "metaphysical theory", I mean a theory which tells us what is to be put into the categories of a presupposed ontology. I would label different forms of materialism (cf. section 32, C) and phenomenalism (cf. section 34) as metaphysical. An ontological theory is usually compatible with several different metaphysical standpoints as, for example Russell's thinking clearly exemplifies.

[14] B. Russell, *Our Knowledge of the External World*, 1926, preface.

cal security in logic; and in logic he included a theory of the extension of concepts, which in his interpretation became a special case of a more general theory of "courses of values" (*Wertverläufe*), cf. section 11, C) which his contemporary Georg Cantor developed into set theory. Frege wanted to show how the arithmetical concepts of *A* can be interpreted as logical concepts so as to transform the truths of *A* into logical truths. In other words, Frege wanted to reduce arithmetic to logic.

"Reduce" has a connotation which may mislead in this context. Talk of reduction may give the impression that arithmetic, before it was interpreted by Frege, was a theory independent of logic and that Frege allowed it to be absorbed by logic. As long as Frege believed in his logicist interpretation of arithmetic (toward the end of his life he abandoned it for a geometrical interpretation), he might have objected that numbers had all along been the kind of logical entities which he described them as being. Without taking a stand on such a difficult question, one can defend the talk of reduction in the following manner. Leaving aside what numbers "really are"—does the question have any meaning?—arithmetic had, before Frege, been regarded as an independent theory beside logic. If we accept Frege's logistic interpretation, our picture of the situation is simplified: instead of two theories set side by side, we get only one theory, logic, of which arithmetic is a subordinate part. The reduction affects, if not the theories themselves, at least our way of looking at them.

In this connection the word "reduction" can also evoke the idea that Frege's interpretation is a form of intellectual parsimony, that our theoretical solvency is improved by the intellectual reorganization he recommends. In fact Frege himself entertained this idea, and Russell later stated it in strong terms. On this point, too, care is required. Talk of intellectual thrift would be justified if the theory to which Frege reduced arithmetic—logic with set theory—was less problematic than arithmetic. But today no one, I think, is prepared to make this assertion.[15]

[15] Logical empiricists, such as Carnap and Hempel, have sometimes regarded Frege's logicism as an "explication", i.e. a transition from something that is less

Reductive theory interpretation has, since Frege showed the way, been a common form of philosophical analysis. The form was not completely new when Frege first tried it. In mathematics it has a long lineage. Descartes's so-called "analytical" interpretation of geometry (analysis here signifies the theory of real numbers) can be considered as an informal reductive interpretation, reducing geometry to the theory of real numbers. During the last century, reductive theory interpretation became a common phenomenon in mathematics. The theory of complex numbers was reduced to the theory of real numbers, the latter to the theory of rational numbers, and so on. In philosophy, too, there were precursors (although logically very primitive ones) of reductive theory interpretation: think of materialism, and nominalism.

Is a reductive interpretation of a theory to be classified as analysis or speculation? The answer must be "both", or "it depends". When two theories T and T' are both given, to deduce T from T' (if that is possible) is a purely logico-deductive and hence "analytic" task. When T alone is given, to create a more comprehensive theory T' and then from it to deduce T is obviously something more complex. Clearly, this is exactly what Frege did. According to a common notion, theory creation goes beyond what can be accomplished by mere analysis. Then why is Frege's logicism usually classified as analysis rather than speculation? Theory reduction also occurs in the sciences, outside philosophy. Why is Frege's reduction of arithmetic to logic so often considered an outstanding example, not only of analysis, but of philosophical analysis?

The questions propounded in the previous paragraph do not admit of strict answers. However, the following comments seem pertinent. Frege's logic offers a unified method by which, for a very large number of statements S, one can find an equivalent transcription S^*. This transcription is formulated in a standardized logical language which makes the

clear (exact, etc.) to something that is more so. This view is not plausible. According to what standard can our common pre-Fregean, and pre-Russellian, handling of the natural numbers: 0, 1, 2, ... be said to be less clear than Frege's and Russell's logic?

logical relations among statements stand out more clearly than they do in ordinary language. The method partially realizes something which has long been striven for in philosophy, and it is without doubt a contribution to the analytic activity of "making thoughts clearer" (cf. sections 37 and 38). Now, that S^* is an equivalent transcription of S depends on the meanings of S^* and S. The meaning of S^* is at least partially determined through Frege's axiomatic theory for the logical concepts occurring in S^*. The connection between the method of transcription and the logical theory may seem to justify us in referring to the theory, too, as philosophical analysis. On the other hand, Frege's logical theory is something highly speculative, in the current sense of the word. It is, for example, intimately tied to his doctrine of ontological categories. Also, it contains the beginning of a general set theory, the most speculative branch of abstract mathematics. It is truly difficult here to discern with any confidence where the boundary runs between analytically decomposing what is given and speculatively creating something new.

Frege's semantic doctrine (sections 14 and 15), about the "sense" and "reference" of linguistic expressions, is perhaps even more difficult to classify from the present point of view. It can be understood to be a linguistic theory with a strong empirical component, consisting in observation of linguistic usage, intuitive understanding of language, and perhaps also a certain amount of introspection. With but a slight change of emphasis the doctrine can also be seen as a semi-abstract axiomatic system, establishing conditions which the following two relations have to fulfil:

The expression x has the sense y.
The expression x has the reference y.

The axiomatic system should be conceived of as accompanied by the recommendation that these two semantic notions be used in describing given languages. The recommendation would be based on the supposition that a description in these terms has certain specifiable theoretical advantages. From a third point of view, Frege's semantics can be interpreted as an attempt to clarify semantic ideas with a long history in philosophy.

C. *George Edward Moore*

G. E. Moore (Chapter VIII), one of the founders of the so-called Cambridge school, represents a style of thought that is essentially different from Frege's. On first acquaintance, analysis *à la* Moore may seem worlds apart from analysis *à la* Frege. In his analysis, Moore wanted to find definitions of the form:

$$\text{Brother} = \text{male sibling,}$$

where the right side (the *analysans*) is to be synonymous with the left side (the *analysandum*), but should at the same time possess a more refined grammatico-semantic structure. What Moore as analyst actually accomplished was usually something much less: tentative sketches of, and ingenious critical reflections on, such definitions. According to Moore's methodological theory, analysis consists in distinguishing the constituent parts of a complex content of thought, for example a concept or a proposition. On his view, successful analysis demands rigorously concentrated attention on the content, careful "inspection" of it. Moore was primarily interested in analysing certain propositions which he took to be truths of "common sense", truths that are indubitable and known by every man, along with analysis of concepts involved in such propositions. When sketching the *analysans* for a given *analysandum*, he freely used whatever terms seemed appropriate for the task at hand.

Although the distance is truly enormous between Moore's informal and Frege's rigorously formalized procedure, there is also, on closer view, an interesting similarity between them. Moore practised his analysis on particular common-sense truths such as "This is a pencil", but he was interested in the particular only as a representative of an entire class of such truths. Let *C* be a class of such common-sense truths as Moore wanted to clarify through analysis, that class which Moore took "This is a pencil" to represent. Moore expected analysis to reveal such a truth as having a significance, as fitting into the framework of the correct metaphysical theory, say *M*, though what *M* was he did not know. The relationship in Moore's thought between *C* and the (unidentified)

M is parallel to that between arithmetic and logic, in Frege's philosophy. There is also a further common trait. Moore foresaw that the analysis of *C* might in the end turn out to be extremely "Pickwickian", i.e. that the truths of *C* might be found to say something totally different from what they prima facie seem to say. Analysis might reveal "This is a pencil" to be a truth about Russellian "sensibilia" (cf. section 22), Leibnizian monads, or something equally remote from everyday thought. Is not Frege's analysis of the concept of number a remarkable example of an analysis which must be classified as Pickwickian in Moore's sense? The simple lesson, taught in elementary school, that 5 + 7 = 12, becomes, in Frege's analysis, a complex statement about infinite sets of finite sets.

In Moore, as in Frege, there is no sharp boundary, or no boundary at all, between analysis and speculation.

D. *Bertrand Russell*

Bertrand Russell (Chapter IV), who learned from Moore and Frege, often said that he considered the "logical-analytic" method as the most fruitful, or even as the only scientific, method in philosophy. Considering Russell's works as attempts to apply the method, however, one may well feel doubt as to what the method meant for him. He proposed theories in all fields that interested Frege, and what was said above about the analytic elements in Frege's philosophy holds in principle for Russell's philosophy as well. Russell's reduction of arithmetic to logic is similar to Frege's, and it has the same methodological status as Frege's (cf. section 18). Russell's logic is, like Frege's, based on an ontology, although a different one from Frege's (cf. section 17). Russell's semantics, differing from Frege's on important points, has a methodological status just as difficult to ascertain as that of Frege's semantics (cf. section 19). Frege spoke of the desirability of a language which would mirror the structure of the thoughts it expressed. Especially during the 1910s, under the influence of his discussions with Wittgenstein, Russell believed himself on the way to developing such a language, and his ideas on the topic grew into an abstract and complex metaphysics and epistemology, the so-called philosophy of logical atomism (cf. section 20).

Russell wanted to apply what he considered to be Frege's method, and what I have called reductive theory interpretation, in areas other than mathematics. The most grandiose, as well as, I think, the most fantastic, of these applications, is his analysis of "our knowledge of the external world", first formulated in the book *Our Knowledge of the External World as a Field for Scientific Method in Philosophy* (1914). The "scientific method", referred to in the title, is Frege's reductive method. A metaphysical theory of the sort for which Moore sought in vain is boldly sketched here, a sketch which Russell was later to alter several times during his long career as a philosophical author.

E. *Tractatus Logico-Philosophicus*

The type of analysis, found in Wittgenstein's *Tractatus* (Chapter V), does not require many words of comment here. Although the doctrines of the *Tractatus* concerning language and the world (sections 24 and 25) are often considered as exemplars of analysis, 'speculative metaphysics' appears a more adequate classification. The sections of the *Tractatus* to which the word "analysis" best applies are those in which the author's ideas about logic are set forth. Wittgenstein's philosophy of language, akin to Russell's during his period of logical atomism, exhibits a methodological ambiguity that will be more carefully discussed in section 26.

F. *Rudolf Carnap and logical empiricism*

Logical empiricism, the foremost spokesman of which has been Rudolf Carnap (Chapter VI), is one of the contemporary movements in philosophy which has explicitly placed logical analysis on its programme: it has even, not infrequently in highly polemical terms, urged the identification of legitimate philosophy with such analysis.

Logical empiricism entered the philosophical world with a number of semantic and epistemological theses, which were intended as weapons against "traditional philosophy". Some of them were: "Metaphysical sentences are meaningless";

"Sentences that are neither analytical nor contradictory are meaningful only if they are empirically verifiable" (cf. sections 30 and 31); "Any scientific statement must be capable of expression in a universal empiricist language"; "Statements about other minds can always be translated into statements about other people's behaviour" (cf. section 32); "knowledge *a priori* is exclusively concerned with analytic truths" (cf. section 33); etc. The long discussion to which these theses gave rise brought to light how indefinite their intended methodological status was. Sometimes they were put forth as definitions (terminological proposals or corollaries thereof), sometimes as inductive generalizations from linguistic and epistemological observations, and sometimes as a kind of "deeper insight" into the nature of language and knowledge.

As practised by logical empiricists, analysis has not infrequently been of a highly speculative kind. An especially clear example is Carnap's first major work, *The Logical Structure of the World* (*Der logische Aufbau der Welt*, 1928). It belongs to the same epistemological tradition as Russell's *Our Knowledge of the External World*. It is an attempt to create a formalized universal phenomenalistic language. For any given legitimate scientific concept (term) A, there is, Carnap maintained, an expression B of the formalized language, such that:

(i) All that falls under A also falls under B, and conversely;

and, in view of (i), the definition:

(ii) $A = B$

can be accepted as "materially adequate". Only a small sample from the total "scientific" vocabulary is actually defined in this manner in the book. With regard to most of the presented definitions, it is easily seen that the justifying assumption (i) is a mere hypothesis. Conceptual analysis and the framing of hypotheses thus go hand in hand here. The claim that the formalized language of the book is universal involves a hypothesis of a higher order: viz. that hypotheses of type (i) can be formulated and confirmed in sufficient quantity to justify definitions of all the concepts for which science will ever find legitimate use. Can this higher order hypothesis be entertained except on the basis of a conviction that, roughly speaking, the formalized language allows us to speak about everything there is to speak about? This conviction is a belief about the world as much as about language and science. The desire to create a universal language for science was to remain one of the basic motives of Carnap's philosophical thought.

In *Logical Foundations of Probability* (1950) Carnap defines his problem as that of giving what he calls an "explication" of a certain "logical" concept of probability, viz. that which occurs in an assertion like "Quantum mechanics is more probable relative to the experimental data known today than it was relative to the data known twenty years ago." The "explicandum" involved in this statement, the intuitive concept of probability, is more or less imprecise. The task is to substitute for it an exact concept, the "explicatum". Carnap's demands upon a good explication are: (i) the explicatum can be used in place of the explicandum in most cases where the latter has hitherto been employed; (ii) the explanation of the explicatum is given in an exact form; (iii) the explicatum is a scientifically fruitful concept; and (iv) the explicatum is as simple as (i)–(iii) will allow. Explication in this sense is, of course, a normal component of all scientific research, and it is obviously an aspect of research which cannot be isolated from its other aspects. Possibly labour could be divided so that the philosopher provides a battery of alternative *explicata* for a given *explicandum*, leaving it to the working scientist to make his choice among them. With regard to the "logical" concept of probability, Carnap views the situation in exactly this way. Carnap has often stressed that philosophical analysis, understood as explication, must be carried out in the most intimate contact with the sciences.

Explication, as understood by Carnap, acquires a quite distinct character through his ideas about what precise concept formation implies. According to Carnap, a term acquires a precise meaning by being incorporated in a language with precisely formulated rules. On the question as to which rules must be precisely stated, Carnap took different successive stands. During his syntactical period (*Logical Syntax of Language*, 1934) he demanded only that it be precisely stated what combinations of signs are sentences of the language, and what combinations of sentences are correct inferences. During his semantical period (beginning with *Introduction to Semantics*, 1942), he added the demand that the significance of the sentences be stated in exact "semantical rules". Frege's interpretation of arithmetic through logic is mentioned by Carnap as an outstanding example of an explication which satisfies this requirement. Still later Carnap demanded that one state precisely the "valuation rules" for the language, i.e. the rules determining when a sentence of the language should be accepted as true or rejected as false.

Carnap sometimes seems to take the so-called observation language as a philosophically unproblematic datum, and to consider the field of philosophical explication as limited to its superstructure, the so-called theoretical languages (or "the theoretical language"). In order to clarify a theoretical language L, one ought to state, beside its rules of sentence formation and of inference, combinatorial rules determining which combinations of sentences from L and sentences from the observation language constitute correct inferences from one language level to the other. These rules Carnap has occasionally called "rules of correspondence".

If the explication of a concept (term) is understood to mean its incorporation in a language where literally all concepts obtain their well-defined places. Carnap's search for a universal language is thus rooted in his very conception of explication.

G. *Formalization*

No contemporary trend in philosophy has emphasized the philosophical value of formalization as much as logical empiricism. However, formalization is an activity which does not commit its practitioners to any particular philosophical position. It is practised today by many philosophers who do not otherwise endorse the logical empiricist creed.

The interest in formalization among contemporary philosophers has rendered the very concept 'philosophy' even less definite, if possible, than it was before. When is formalization part of philosophy, and when is it part of mathematics, theoretical physics, biology, psychology, linguistics, jurisprudence, and so on? I am fortunate in not being obliged to give an answer. People who see themselves as philosophers, as well as people who see themselves as mathematicians, physicists, etc., work today with the formalization of theories from nearly all fields of research. There are areas where formalization occurs and which seem to be markedly 'philosophical', for example, the logic of 'ought', value theory, and the logic of knowledge and belief ('know' and 'believe' as in "I know that . . ." and "I believe that . . ."), the logic of questions, and so on. But formalization tends to blot out the specifically philosophical character of the problems, and to attract to them investigators who do not regard themselves as philosophers, who sometimes are just "professional formalizers". Modal logic (the logic of necessity, possibility, and impossibility), for example, began as a purely philosophical study (with C. I. Lewis in the 1910s) but soon became one of the borderlands between philosophy and mathematics. Something similar happened with the non-Aristotelian many-valued logic which was first proposed on purely philosophical grounds (Lukasiewicz, 1922), but was later employed by theoretical physicists (Birkhoff and von Neumann, 1936).

When is formalization a tool for analysis and when is it speculation, the framing of hypotheses, etc.? If someone formalizes a previously given theory, for instance Aristotle's theory of the syllogism or Newton's mechanics, the formalization can appropriately be regarded as a type of analysis. When a new theory is set forth in a formalized garb, the designation "analysis" seems misplaced. It is sometimes difficult to draw the boundary between the two sorts of formalization: the new formalized theory can be a more or less amended version of an older (unformalized) theory.

Of traditional philosophical interest is some of the work on theory reduction, which occurs in connection with formalized theories. A reduction of a theory T to a theory

T' of the sort which Frege undertook, implies that the basic concepts of T are defined in T', and that, by the aid of these definitions, the theorems of T are shown to be theorems also of T'. In formal semantics, founded by Tarski, a procedure has been developed which may also be called theory reduction, although of a different sort: we can here speak of semantic theory reduction. Semantic reduction of a theory T to a theory T', presupposes that one can speak in T' about T as a formal structure (a system of sign combinations). The reduction then consists in defining T' the concept:

(iii) The sign combination x is a true sentence of T'

or some analogous semantic concept. Possibly, also, (iii) is provable in T', whenever the sign combination x expresses a truth in T.[16] Although the semantic variety of theory reduction is widely practised today, unfortunately little work has been done toward achieving a deeper understanding of its methodological significance. In itself, a definition of (iii) merely fixes a certain distribution of truth-values over the sentences of the language in which T is formulated. What tacitly understood presuppositions lead us from this distribution to an improved understanding of the meanings of these sentences? There is overwhelming evidence in the literature that such improved understanding is usually the aim of the reduction.

Theory reduction is of special interest when it apparently opens the possibility of simplifying our world-picture in some fundamental way. Frege and Russell desired to reduce arithmetic to logic and set theory. Russell and Carnap wished to reduce physics to a theory about sense-data. In *Principia Mathematica* Russell wished to reduce the theory of sets (and of certain other so-called extensional objects) to the

---

[16] When arithmetic is reduced, in the Fregean sense, to a theory T' the sign combination:

(a) $2 + 2 = 4$

turns out to be provable in T'. Such need not be the case if arithmetic is semantically reduced to T'. Although (a) is not provable in T', the statement:

(b) "$2 + 2 = 4$" is a true arithmetical sentence

may then be found to be provable there.

theory of properties (and other so-called intensional entities). Moved by opposite philosophical convictions, later thinkers have been interested in reducing the intensional to the extensional. The current interest in nominalism has led to various attempts at reducing non-nominalistic theories to nominalistic ones.

H. *The later Wittgenstein*

In the *Philosophical Investigations* (*Philosophische Untersuchungen*, 1953), Wittgenstein gave the classic expression to a new type of philosophical analysis, a type to which much of the work of the so-called Oxford school of linguistic philosophy belongs (Chapter IX). Wittgenstein here develops his ideas in opposition to a view of language which is often encountered in philosophy, and which he had met in Frege, Moore, and Russell. According to this view, the majority of expressions in language are connected with something which constitutes their "meaning" or "sense", something which they "stand for" or "designate". To understand an expression is to be aware of this entity connected with it. The difference between the various theories which are forms of this view are doubtless as important as the similarities. Wittgenstein, however, is inclined to treat them alike. One of his many striking aphorisms against what he is attacking reads as follows:

We forget that we *calculate*, operate with words, and in the course of time translate them sometimes into one picture, and sometimes into another. It is as if one were to believe that a written order for a cow which someone is to hand over to me always had to be accompanied by an image of a cow, if the order was not to lose its meaning.[17]

According to Wittgenstein's view, the meaning of words and sentences consist in their (actual or potential) use, in the manner in which they are tied, by the rules of the language, to each other and to our observations, feelings, actions, etc. The synonymy of two expressions, their identity of meaning, will hence signify that they are used in an identical manner. From this point of view, to give an analysis of an expression

---

[17] L. Wittgenstein, *Philosophical Investigations*, Oxford, 1958, Part I, §449.

A, in Moore's sense, is to find another expression A^* used in the same manner as A. The later Wittgenstein is not interested in analysis *à la* Moore, although he never systematically developed reasons why not. It is a reasonable guess that he thought pairs of expressions with the same use to be rare in a language, and that he did not think the contemplation of such a pair provided any deeper understanding of the use of either of them. The kind of clarity he sought, could be better achieved, he assumed, by direct consideration of the way in which the problematic expression is used, by noting the rules according to which it functions in language (its "logical grammar").

Whereas Carnap wished to create clarity by constructing languages with clearly formulated rules, the later Wittgenstein hoped to come to see clearly by bringing to light the rules of the language that we already use. That the rules of this language have not been clearly understood, is, according to Wittgenstein, the main source of our philosophical problems, problems which he does not want to solve, but to free us from.

Philosophical analysis as conceived by the later Wittgenstein seems to be an empirical study of language of essentially the same kind as that occurring in linguistics. This judgement is not refuted by the fact that the analyst, working in the spirit of the later Wittgenstein, points out features of linguistic usage in which the professional linguist is not usually interested. For, at the same time, linguistic analysis as practised by the later Wittgenstein is marked by a speculative, not to say metaphysical, bent. It is easy to overlook this aspect since Wittgenstein's metaphysics remains so vague and inexplicit, and since it is a metaphysics which pretends to be wholly anti-metaphysical. The metaphysics which Wittgenstein turns against is that which distinguishes between body and soul, between physical objects and sense data, or between concrete things and abstract entities. The anti-metaphysics with which his own description of language is leavened is vaguely materialistic, behaviouristic, a kind of naïve realism, and nominalistic. An empirical description of language which simultaneously contains a metaphysics, even if a vague one, may seem like a paradox. But is it? For how could one describe at all what words mean or designate, without making assumptions as to what there is for words to mean or to designate?[18]

[18] The Norwegian Arne Naess has made an interesting and important attempt at once to "trivialize" philosophical analysis and to give it a firm empirical foundation by using methods borrowed from the behavioural sciences (questionnaires and statistical analysis of the replies). Even though many so-called "analytic" theories in philosophy no doubt contain elements for whose testing such methods are relevant, I hardly think that the methods of Naess will give us the answers to those questions in which analytic philosophers are most profoundly interested. Naess's most important contribution to the development of analytic philosophy is, I think, his sharpening of the demands for methodological awareness, especially with regard to the distinction between logical analysis and empirical research, and especially in the fields of the philosophy of language and epistemology.

II

Perfection and Innovation:
Bernard Bolzano

4. BERNARD BOLZANO AND HIS *WISSENSCHAFTSLEHRE*

The Bohemian Bernard Bolzano (1781–1848), mathematician, philosopher, Catholic theologian and preacher, was a late representative of the philosophy of enlightenment, an intellectual descendent of Leibniz. He lived in a time when transcendental philosophy and Hegelianism dominated the German-speaking philosophical world and in a society where reaction against the political ideas of the French revolution prevailed. In temperament, method, and point of view he was in sharp opposition to the intellectual fashions of his time. Critical of the imaginative syntheses which were the strength of the romanticists, he focused on minute and step-by-step investigations. He was as much a mathematician as a philosopher, and in philosophy as well as in mathematics, he sought rigorous definitions and proofs. In both theory and practice, he adopted as the principle of morality the common good. He understood this principle to include equality and justice, the abolition of class privileges and of national antagonisms. Although Bolzano inspired, both morally and intellectually, a circle of younger Bohemians, he lacked university affiliation during most of his productive lifetime. Because of his political views he was removed in 1819, by a decree of the Emperor, from the professorship in the philosophy of religion which he had held in Prague since 1805. He spent the remainder of his days as a private scholar. Because of the censorship, he had difficulty in publishing his works in Austria. Several were printed anonymously or outside the Austrian empire, and many remained unpublished.

Bolzano was ahead of his time on many intellectual frontiers—in some instances, very far ahead. His posthumous work, *Paradoxes of the Infinite* (*Paradoxien des Unendlichen*, 1851), anticipates ideas in Cantor's set theory, both by its unhesitant acknowledgement of the existence of infinite sets and by its insight that a set is infinite if and only if it can be put in one-to-one correspondence with a proper subset.

In mathematical analysis Bolzano was an early constributor to the creation of solid logical foundations and the elimination of appeals to geometrical intuition. But his greatest contribution was in philosophy, especially in logic and epistemology. Unfortunately, his ideas did not become generally known at a time when they could have advanced the development of philosophy. Only in our own time has his greatness received general recognition, and important notions more completely developed after his time and independently of him are now being discovered in his writings. His major work, the *Wissenschaftslehre*, was published in 1837 in four volumes (with a total of more than 2,000 closely reasoned pages). Some of the ideas of this work will be discussed here.

Bolzano's definition of "theory of science" will hardly arouse a modern reader's interest. The "theory of science" comprises, he says, the rules which ought to be followed when the total realm of truth is divided into the fields of the separate sciences and when the results of scientific investigations are stated in a textbook. The delimitation of the different sciences is primarily a problem of organization, the solution of which depends on local and temporal circumstances. How a textbook ought to be most suitably written also depends upon a multitude of conditions which can scarcely be systematically foreseen. Neither issue seems to be of central philosophical importance. However, Bolzano does not reach his own specific 'theory of science' until the fourth volume. In the first three volumes he lays the foundations, by developing, first, the "fundamental theory" in which scepticism in its different forms is refuted; second, the "elementary theory" which involves an original logical doctrine; then an epistemology; and finally, a heuristics. In the "elementary theory" he advances his Platonistic view about ideas-in-themselves and propositions-in-themselves, his original logic of variation, and his puzzling view concerning the objective order of truth. In his epistemology he studies human knowledge as a mental phenomenon given in the form of "judgements": how it arises through "mediation" and how it is related to truth. His heuristics, which provides rules for the search for truth, contains among other things a detailed discussion of causal analysis. The first three volumes constitute the philosophical core of the *Wissenschaftslehre*.

Into Bolzano's logico-epistemological system, are woven themes and ideas that can be followed far back in the history of philosophy. They are formulated by him with a sophistication that, I think, surpasses that of most, if not all, previous philosophers. His work stands out as the most mature fruit of the two traditions, post-medieval European empiricism and rationalism, to which it belongs. Simultaneously, his work is rich in new ideas which anticipate future developments. This is especially true of his logical doctrines. The trend in modern semantics represented by Church and Carnap, which derives from Gottlob Frege's ideas in the 1890s, has stimulated interest in the semantics of Bolzano. The latter is on many scores an interesting alternative to Frege's semantics. Quantification theory, first formulated with clarity by Frege, is anticipated in Bolzano's logic of variation. Tarski's set-theoretical concept of "consequence" has a precursor in Bolzano's concept of "derivability". Bolzano's logical definition of probability is an interesting forerunner of modern definitions such as Carnap's. And one could go on.

Of course, much in the *Wissenschaftslehre* appears antiquated today, 150 years after its conception. Time has been hard on Bolzano's psychological theories, especially those concerning the "mediation" of judgements. But even if everything he wrote were equally antiquated, the work would occupy a distinguished place in the world's philosophical literature. I know of no earlier and few later philosophical writings which are composed throughout with such clarity and precision, such dialectical acumen and such attention to earlier and contemporary literature. To turn from, for example, Kant's *Critique of Pure Reason* to Bolzano's work is like coming from a jungle to an open and well-planned community. Clarity prevails not only in the general organization of the work but also in every detail. Hardly any concept is introduced without a thorough explication with illuminating examples or, whenever possible, a concise definition.

Hardly any assertion is made without an account of his reasons for it. Conceivable objections are answered. Throughout Bolzano gives attention to other writers who have dealt with the same topics, whether or not their points of view agree with his own. His prose, disdaining all literary embellishments, advances with a quiet and somewhat heavy matter-of-factness. To read the *Wissenschaftslehre* is also to receive a lesson in intellectual morality.

On the other hand, in Kant's writings many echoes and voices are heard—unclear, ambiguous, but stimulating—and in the distance many bewildering and enticing perspectives appear. Bolzano's theory of science is unequivocal but at the same time less suggestive. Through its straight avenues blows only a steady, dry wind of clarity. It seems that clarity must often be purchased at that price.

5. THE REFUTATION OF SCEPTICISM

Even in his scientific writings the theologian Bolzano felt responsible for the spiritual well-being of the reader. Scepticism—the claim that there is no truth, or that truth, if it exists, is unknowable—was regarded by Bolzano as a dangerous, although generally curable, disease. A primary aim of the first section of the *Wissenschaftslehre*, the "fundamental theory", is to refute scepticism. Bolzano's interest in this rebuttal was partly based upon the Cartesian tradition that philosophy must begin without presuppositions. "The philosopher", he says, "is not entitled to assume that anything whatsoever is already known or settled." Thus he must not assume the existence and knowability of truth. In content, Bolzano's critique of scepticism does not belong to those of his accomplishments which point ahead. Scepticism, in the sense in which he takes it, is scarcely one of the more fertile themes in philosophy. However, his refutation is interesting because of its form.

Bolzano distinguishes two varieties of scepticism. The first consists in maintaining "There is no truth", or "No proposition is true". He is of the opinion that this kind of scepticism can be rigorously refuted. The second variety consists in denying the assertion "I can acquire knowledge of at least one true proposition." Doubt of this kind, which he calls "total" or "complete", cannot be refuted as definitely as doubt of the first sort. But Bolzano thinks that he can advance reasons which will bring about a change of mind among the majority of "complete" sceptics.

A. *The existence of truth*

Bolzano's refutation of the first form of scepticism is a new version of an argument which occurs in Aristotle and Sextus Empiricus. To start with he sets out to prove:

Thesis I. At least one proposition is true.

His proof takes the form of *reductio ad absurdum* of the opposite assumption. Let us suppose:

(i) No proposition is true.

Bolzano observes that since (i) is a proposition, (i) cannot be true. But, that (i) is not true is the same as the negation of (i), which is the same as Thesis I. Consequently, (i) is an impossible supposition and Thesis I is thereby proven.

Following Aristotle, Bolzano next wants to prove:

Thesis II. There are infinitely many true propositions.

He offers at least two different presumptive proofs for this thesis, one in the *Wissenschaftslehre* and another in the *Paradoxien des Unendlichen*. The latter proof, which most closely resembles Aristotle's, is the simpler. Bolzano states the proof as follows:

The set of all propositions-in-themselves or all truths-in-themselves [cf. below section 6, A] can easily be seen to be infinite. For if we consider an arbitrarily chosen truth, for example, the assertion that there is a truth, or any assertion whatsoever, and label it *A*, we find that the proposition expressed by the words "*A* is true" is distinct from *A*, since it has *A* for its subject. The same law which makes it possible for us to derive from *A* another and distinct propositon, which we can label *B*, also makes it possible for us to derive from *B* a third assertion *C*, and so on without end. The set of all these propositions, in which each has its predecessor as its subject and asserts the truth thereof, constitutes a set of elements (each element a proposition) which is greater than any finite set.[1]

[1] *Paradoxes of the Infinite*, § 13.

As is easily seen, Bolzano has not accounted for all the premisses on which the proof rests. Let us indicate the proposition "*A* is true" with the symbol *tA*. The series which Bolzano considers is of the form: *A, tA, ttA, tttA,* . . . The "law" which Bolzano invokes says that to every proposition *A* there corresponds a distinct proposition *tA*. But this "law" is not sufficient to guarantee that the series is infinite. Although *A* ≠ *tA*, it might be the case that *A* = *ttA*, so that the series would have only two members: *A, tA*. Bolzano must assume also that *B* (= *tt* . . . *tA*) is different from *C* (= *tt* . . . *tA*) if the number of *t*s in *B* is different from the number of *t*s in *C*. In other words, he must assume that his series is isomorphic with the series of numbers: 1, 2, 3. . . . But then the proof becomes a *petitio principii*.

The proof for the same thesis in the *Wissenschaftslehre* is a *reductio ad absurdum* of the opposite thesis. If we suppose:

(ii) There are not infinitely many true propositions,

then, since there is at least one true proposition (Thesis I), we must be prepared to accept for some *n* ≥ 1:

(iii) There are exactly *n* true propositions, $A_1, . . . , A_n$.

From (iii) then follows:

(iv) In addition to $A_1, . . . , A_n$, there are no true propositions.

But now consider:

(v) (iv) is a true proposition.

"On the basis of the form alone of the proposition [(iv)]" we realize, Bolzano claims:

(vi) (iv) is not identical with any of the propositions $A_1, . . . , A_n$.

From (v) and (vi) follows:

(vii) There is at least one true proposition in addition to $A_1, . . . , A_n$.

Thus, (ii) leads to the contradictory assumptions (iv) and (vii), and, hence, must be false.

B. *The knowability of truth*

Bolzano's attempt to convert the "total doubter" reminds one of classical attempts found, for example, in St. Augustine and Descartes. Even if a person adopts the attitude of the total sceptic, he must "feel in his mind" that:

(viii) I have ideas,

is true. Feeling that, he also feels:

(ix) I know I have ideas.

Being aware of (ix) he must give his assent to:

Thesis III. I know the truth of at least one proposition.

If I know the truth of a given proposition A, I can always come via further reflection to the insight: *I know* the truth of A. The assertion that I know the truth of A is an assertion different from A itself, we can call it kA. Similarly, when I know the truth of kA, I can come to know the truth of a third assertion kkA, and so on indefinitely. Via this process the sceptic can be brought to realize:

Thesis IV. I can come to know the truth of any number of propositions.

However, Bolzano acknowledges that there may occur cases of scepticism so severe that not even this medicine will cure them.

A very different form of scepticism was in the focus of philosophical interest during Bolzano's lifetime—that for which Kant made himself the spokesman in the *Critique of Pure Reason*, and which maintains the existence of certain frontiers beyond which human knowledge cannot pass. This scepticism, too, was combated by Bolzano. Since his criticism of Kant is intimately interwoven with his theory of knowledge, the discussion of it will be deferred until section 9.

6. SEMANTICS

A. *Propositions: uttered, apprehended, and in themselves*

A proposition is something that is neither true nor false; and a science according to Bolzano, is a body of true propositions. The concept 'proposition' is therefore of central importance for his theory of science.

Bolzano distinguishes (1) propositions which are uttered;

(2); propositions which are thought; and (3) propositions-in-themselves (also called objective propositions). An uttered proposition is any utterance (*Rede*) by means of which something is maintained or asserted, i.e. any utterance which is either true or false "in the usual sense of these words". The two word-combinations "God is omnipresent" and "A square is round" are examples of uttered propositions, whereas the phrases "the omnipresent God" and "a round square" are not. There are also propositions which are not formulated in words but which are simply thought by someone, and these propositions Bolzano calls "apprehended propositions". The nature of a proposition-in-itself is indicated in the following passage:

> Just as in the expression "an uttered proposition" I obviously distinguish the proposition itself from the uttering thereof, so also in the expression "an apprehended proposition" I distinguish the proposition itself from the apprehension thereof. What one must necessarily mean by the word *proposition* in order to make this distinction, what one means by a proposition when one can still ask whether someone has or has not uttered it, thought or not thought it, is precisely what I call a *proposition-in-itself* and what I understand by the very word *proposition* when, for the sake of brevity, I use it without the addition "in-itself". In other words, by *proposition-in-itself* I mean any assertion whatsoever that something is or is not; regardless of whether that assertion is true or false, is formulated in words by anyone or not, nay, even whether thought or not.[2]

In support of this notion Bolzano cites a long list of logicians of the past, including Aristotle and Leibniz. Obviously Bolzano is considering a threefold schema:

(1) the combination of words itself, for example the three words "God is omnipresent";

(2) the thought that is expressed by the words and that occurs in the mind of him who utters them;

(3) that which is stated, i.e. the actual or possible state of affairs, which constitutes the content of the thought.

What Bolzano calls the proposition-in-itself is (3). I understand him to mean that (1) is an uttered proposition and (2) is an apprehended proposition.

(I must acknowledge, however, that Bolzano's manner of

[2] *Wissenschaftslehre*, §19.

expression occasionally invites other interpretations. Let *P* be a proposition-in-itself, *e(P)* its linguistic expression, and *t(P)* the thought which has *P* for its content. While I above interpreted Bolzano's terminology in such a manner that *e(P)* is an uttered proposition, and *t(P)* an apprehended proposition, the interpretation that *P* + *e(P)* is the uttered and *P* + *t(P)* the apprehended proposition can also be defended. According to an arguable third interpretation, the uttered propositions are those *P*s for which there is an *e(P)*, and the apprehended propositions are those *P*s for which there is a *t(P)*. However, on the whole, the ambiguity seems to be of a harmless sort.)

The following Table illustrates Bolzano's conceptual scheme.

Propositions	True	False
Uttered	Uttered truths	Uttered falsehoods
Apprehended	Apprehended truths	Apprehended falsehoods
In-themselves	Truths-in-themselves	Falsehoods-in-themselves

Bolzano is more interested in the second column than in the third. He never—as far as I have noticed—coined the phrase "falsehood-in-itself" (which I have introduced as a counterpart to "truth-in-itself") although the things for which it stands undoubtedly form part of his universe of discourse.

But are there propositions-in-themselves? That there are uttered propositions, in the sense of true or false utterances, and that there are apprehended propositions, in the sense of true or false thoughts, is unquestionable. But propositions-in-themselves, as described by Bolzano, are considerably more difficult to comprehend. A suggestive attempt by Bolzano to make us see what they are is the following:

The quantity of blossoms which a certain tree standing in a specific place bore during the past spring is a stateable number, even if no one knows it; a proposition which states that number is thus for me an objective truth (a truth-in-itself), even if no one is aware of it.[3]

With regard to propositions-in-themselves, as on so many

[3] *Wissenschaftslehre*, § 25.

other points, Bolzano is a decided Platonist. In the spirit of Plato he distinguishes between what exists in time and what exists independently of time. In his terminology only that which occurs in time (at one or another moment, or perhaps at all moments) has "existence", or "reality" (*Dasein, Wirklichkeit*). Of truths-in-themselves or, more broadly, of propositions-in-themselves we cannot assert these predicates. To say of a proposition-in-itself that it exists "forever" (i.e., at every moment) is as absurd as to say that it sprang into existence at a certain moment and ceased to exist at a later moment.

B. *Ideas: uttered, apprehended, and in themselves*

A proposition, according to Bolzano, is something complex. The parts of a proposition which are not themselves propositions he calls "ideas". To them as well he applies the distinction between linguistic expression, subjective thought, and objective thought content, which he made with regard to propositions. In the proposition-in-itself, "Caius has prudence", the idea-in-itself (or the objective idea) "Caius" occurs. This idea-in-itself is the content of the subjective idea which occurs in my mind when I, for example, consider the proposition in question. The idea-in-itself is distinct from the subjective idea: it is something objective which many subjective ideas occurring in different minds, or at different moments in the same mind, can intend. The idea-in-itself Cauis is also distinct from the word "Caius". The word is obviously in a sense arbitrary; the same idea could just as well be represented by another word. Bolzano seems to hold that every meaningful linguistic expression which can occur in an uttered proposition, but which is not itself an uttered proposition, stands for an idea-in-itself. In the sentence "Caius has prudence", not only "Caius" but also "has" and "prudence" each stands for an idea-in-itself. No more than propositions-in-themselves do ideas-in-themselves exist. Ideas-in-themselves have the same independence of time as the propositions-in-themselves of which they are parts. It makes no sense to enquire whether an idea-in-itself exists or does not exist at any one moment.

C. *Ideas and their objects*

An idea-in-itself is distinct from its object or objects. The relation which may hold between an idea-in-itself *i* and an entity *x* where:

x is an object for *i*,

is scarcely satisfactorily clarified by Bolzano. But the *Wissenschaftslehre* gives many presumptive examples of this relationship. The question asking how many objects a given idea-in-itself has, must receive one of the following answers: (1) none; (2) exactly one; (3) more than one. Examples of empty (*gegenstandslose*) ideas, i.e. of the kind for which (1) holds, are "$\sqrt{-1}$", 'nothing', and 'golden mountain'. According to Bolzano, who did not acknowledge the existence of complex numbers, there is no number which multiplied by itself yields the product -1; neither does there exist anything which is nothing or a golden mountain. Examples of singular ideas (*Einzelvorstellungen*), i.e. of the kind for which (2) holds, are 'Caius' and 'the totality of all Greek philosophers'. There is only one person who is Caius (when "Caius" is used as the name of a definite person) and only one sum total of all Greek philosophers. A general idea, i.e. one for which (3) holds, is for instance 'Greek philosopher'; Socrates, Plato, Aristotle, and so on, are all its objects. A given entity is usually (if not always) an object of many distinct ideas. Bolzano, for example, is an object of all these ideas: 'Bohemian philosopher', 'author of the *Paradoxien des Unendlichen*', and 'one of the best logicians of the nineteenth century'.

Bolzano's doctrine of ideas-in-themselves and their objects contains, at least implicitly, a semantics which reminds one of the theory of the Stoics, and which foreshadows features of Frege's view. Bolzano's threefold scheme:

(i) linguistic expression—idea-in-itself—object,

is nearly identical with that of the Stoics, a historical fact of which Bolzano himself was well aware. The scheme also bears an important likeness to Frege's:

(ii) linguistic expression—sense—reference.

7. THE LOGIC OF VARIATION

Bolzano's logical doctrines differ in two important respects from current logical theory. First, Bolzano develops his theory without the aid of any symbols other than the customary use of letters as variables. Although the issue is one of the linguistic clothing of thought, this point is quite important. Even the relatively simple logical theorems which Bolzano develops frequently become extraordinarily complicated and lengthy in his German formulations. It would have been practically impossible for him to state more advanced results in the same manner. Second, Bolzano makes no attempt to state his theories in an axiomatic form. However, his original and interesting definitions make him a precursor of several modern developments.

His most important logical creations are what one may call his logic of classes and what I shall call his logic of variation. Bolzano's logic of classes is inferior to the algebraically formulated theory of classes which George Boole gave in *The Mathematical Analysis of Logic* in 1847—only ten years after the *Wissenschaftslehre*. The basic ideas of the logic of variation will now be presented.

A. *Fundamentals of the logic of variation*

The logic of variation deals with the propositions-in-themselves and ideas-in-themselves, not with sentences and expressions of language, or judgements and thoughts as psychological phenomena. In the proposition-in-itself:

> (i) The man Caius is mortal,

we can consider the idea-in-itself 'Caius' as "variable". This means that we compare (i) with the sentences which result when "Caius" is replaced by, for example, "Sempronius", "Titus", "triangle", etc. Then we get the propositions:

> (ii)   The man Sempronius is mortal,
> (iii) The man Titus is mortal,
> (iv)   The man triangle is mortal, etc.

Of these variants of (i) the first two are "objective" (*gegenständlich*) while the third is "non-objective" (*gegenstandslos*). We may bypass the question how Bolzano explains this distinction. In the logic of variation only "objective" variants are considered, so that when variants are spoken of in what follows, I shall always presuppose that they have the "objectivity" to which Bolzano alludes. (This notion of "objectivity" (*Gegenständlichkeit*) must not be confused with the one entering into the notion of an "objective proposition" (*objektiver Satz*).) Since Bolzano rejects anomalies like (iv), he can establish that all variants of (i) with regard to the concept 'Caius' are true: every man is mortal. If we take instead the proposition:

(v)   The man Caius is omniscient,

and still regard 'Caius' as the variable idea, we find that all its variants are false since no man is omniscient. The proposition:

(vi)   The being Caius is mortal,

has some true and some false propositions among its variants. For Bolzano, the theologian:

(vii)   The being God is mortal,

is one of the false variants.

In his logic of variation Bolzano studies properties of, and relations among, propositions, which depend on the truth and falsity of their variants. In the above-mentioned example, borrowed from Bolzano, only *one* idea is considered to be variable, and that idea occurs only *once* in the original proposition. However, one can regard several ideas as variable, and each one of them may occur several times.

The basic approach, adopted in the logic of variation, is original and fruitful. The logic of variation anticipates, as many writers have stressed, modern quantification theory, which was formulated in a precise manner for the first time by Gottlob Frege in his *Begriffsschrift* (1879), as well as the "theory of models" which has developed within our century's semantics, its basic concepts receiving their first explicit formulation from Alfred Tarski. A more accurate comparison reveals that the logic of variation cannot be identified with either of these two theories.

It might seem as if Bolzano's assertion:

(viii) Every variant of the proposition "The man Caius is mortal", with reference to the idea 'Caius', is true,

could be taken to be synonymous with Frege's quantified assertion:

(ix) It holds for all x that x is mortal,

assuming mankind to be the range of variation of x. But that interpretation is inadequate since the idea whose variation is considered can have linguistically hidden occurrences in the proposition in which it is varied. Let us consider another example:

(x) Every variant of the proposition (p) "$0 \leqslant 3$ and $4 = 2 + 2$" with regard to the idea '3' is true.

What are the variants of (p) with regard to '3'? Let us suppose that we can restrict ourselves to the consideration of the non-negative integers: 0, 1, 2. . . . It might be assumed that propositions of the form:

(xi) $0 \leqslant n$ and $4 = 2 + 2$,

are exactly all the variants of (p) with respect to '3'. If, and only if, all propositions of the form (xi) are true (they are!), then so is the following Fregean sentence:

(xii) For all x it holds that $0 \leqslant x$ and $4 = 2 + 2$,

provided that the variable x ranges over the non-negative integers. It might thus seem that Bolzano's (x) says the same as Frege's (xii). But is that really the case? If, for instance, the concept '4' was identical with the concept '3 + 1', then the proposition (p) would be identical with the proposition:

(xiii) $0 \leqslant 3$ and $3 + 1 = 2 + 2$.

The variants of (p) with regard to '3' would then be, not the propositions of (xi), but propositions of the form:

(xiv) $0 \leqslant n$ and $n + 1 = 2 + 2$.

In that case Bolzano's (x) would say the same, not as Frege's (xii), but as Frege's:

(xv) It holds for all x that $0 \leqslant x$ and $x + 1 = 2 + 2$, still assuming that the non-negative integers form the range of variation of x. Whereas (xii) is trivially true, (xv) is trivially false.

The attempt to identify Bolzano's logic of variation with Frege's theory of quantification thus fails because there may be lingustically hidden occurrences of the ideas varied. For similar reasons Bolzano's logic of variation cannot be regarded as a theory of models in the sense of Tarski.

The observation through which we have realized the difference between Bolzano's and Frege's ideas simultaneously discloses what is perhaps the greatest weakness in Bolzano's presentation of his logic of variation: the lack of a criterion determining when ideas-in-themselves, or propositions-in-themselves, are identical with each other, and when not. Without such a criterion, the directive to replace one idea by another throughout a given proposition remains indefinite. As we have just seen, the question as to what are the variants of (p) with regard to '3' will receive different answers depending on whether or not the idea '4' is identical with the idea '3 + 1'. Strangely enough, I have not been able to find a discussion of this central (but perhaps not insoluble) issue in the *Wissenschaftslehre*.

B. *Analytic propositions*

With the aid of his logic of variation, Bolzano attempted to clarify certain concepts which were used in logic and epistemology long before his time and many of which are still used today. His most interesting clarifications concern the following concepts: analytic proposition, consequence, and probability.

While Kant usually thought that the analyticity of a judgement implied its truth, Bolzano uses "analytic" in a way which allows false as well as true propositions to be analytic. In order to avoid bewilderment one must keep in mind that the counterparts of Kant's "analytic judgements" are to be found among Bolzano's *true* "analytic propositions". In the *Wissenschaftslehre* §148 Bolzano first gives a definition of "analytic" or "analytic in the broader sense", which he later refines to a definition of "logically analytic" or "analytic in the narrower sense". It is Bolzano's notion of a true and logically analytic propositions which comes closest to Kant's notion of an "analytic judgement".

The letters p, q, r, will here represent propositions-in-themselves. The letters $a, b, c,$ will stand for ideas-in-themselves. The letters A, B, C, will designate finite sequences of such ideas. "Substitution" will mean the replacement of one such finite sequence by another. By "p is a variant of q with respect to A" I shall mean that p can be obtained from q by substituting some sequence B for A. (Let A be the sequence 1, 2, 3; B the sequence 2, 5, 7; and C the sequence 2, 5, 2. If one substitutes B for A, the proposition "1 + 2 = 3" is, at least prima facie, transformed into the proposition "2 + 5 = 7". If one substitutes C for A then the former proposition is transformed into "2 + 5 = 2". The sequence *for* which substitution occurs must not, for obvious reasons, contain any repetition of the same idea. On the other hand, the sequence which is substituted for another can very well, like C in our example, contain repetition.) With this terminology we can briefly express two of Bolzano's preliminary definitions as follows:

Def. 1. p is universally valid with respect to A = df every variant of p with respect to A is true.

Def. 2. p is universally invalid with respect to A = df every variant of p with respect to A is false.

All variants of (i) with respect to the idea 'Caius' are—as we have seen—true. (i) is therefore universally valid with respect to 'Caius'. We also saw that all variants of (v) with respect to 'Caius' are false. Thus (v) is universally invalid with respect to that idea.

Bolzano's definition of "analytic" (or "analytic in the broad sense") can be stated as follows:

Def. 3. p is analytic = df p is universally valid or universally invalid with respect to at least one idea occurring in p.

The parallel preliminary definition of "synthetic" (or "synthetic in the narrower sense") reads:

Def. 4. p is synthetic = p is not analytic.

Since (i) is universally valid with respect to the idea 'Caius', (i) is a true analytic proposition. (v), which is universally invalid with respect to the same concept, is also analytic, but false. The propositions:

(xvi) God is omniscient,
(xvii) The interior angles of a triangle equal two right angles,

are examples of true synthetic propositions.

Kant thought that an analytic proposition is one that follows from the laws of logic ("the law of contradiction"). Bolzano's true analytic propositions do not generally have that characteristic. The true analytic proposition (i), which states that the man Caius is mortal, is not demonstrable within pure logic. Kant would surely have classified (i) as "synthetic *a posteriori*". Bolzano himself is aware of the discrepancy between definitions 3 and 4 on the one hand and Kant's intentions on the other. After developing the above-mentioned ideas in paragraph (1) of § 148, he continues:

(2) Some very general examples of analytic propositions, which are also true, are the following: *a* is *a*; *a* which is *b* is *a*; *a* which is *b* is *b*; every object is either *b* or not *b*; and so on . . .

(3) The examples of analytic propositons, which I have just quoted are different from those in paragraph (1) in that logical insight alone is required in order to realize the analytic nature of the former, since the concepts which constitute their unchangeable part all belong to logic; while to judge the truth or falsity of propositions of the kind which are mentioned in paragraph (1), other insights are required since concepts extraneous to logic are involved. This distinction is certainly somewhat vague, for the class of those concepts which belong to logic is not so sharply delineated that it could never give rise to dispute. Occasionally it may nevertheless be useful to attend to this distinction; and thus one could call propositions of the kind mentioned in paragraph (2) *logically* analytic or analytic in the narrower sense; the propositions in paragraph (1) could be called analytic in the broader sense.

In accordance with these quotations we can state the following definition:

Def. 5. *p* is logically analytic = df *p* is universally valid or universally invalid with respect to a sequence which includes exactly all those concepts occurring in p which do not belong to logic.

As a companion to definition 5 one can introduce:

   Def. 6. p is logically synthetic = df p is not logically analytic.

Bolzano thus proposed an explication of the concepts "analytic" and "synthetic" that is reminiscent of explications that have been given in our time, independently of him. It is interesting to notice that Bolzano was aware of one of the most obvious difficulties of this approach: the vagueness of the notion "concept which belongs to logic".

C. *Consequence*

In modern logic, we are accustomed to distinguish between the relation of consequence and that of derivability. To say that a statement is derivable from certain other statements, is to say that it can be reached from them by a step-by-step procedure where at each step a given rule of inference is applied. Derivability, hence, is relative to a system of rules of inference. To say that a statement is a consequence of certain other statements, is to say that the truth of these other statements would necessarily imply its truth. Unlike derivability, consequence is not relative to a system of rules of inference.

   Bolzano's "derivability" (*Ableitbarkeit*) corresponds to the modern notion of consequence. The idea of a formal system was unknown to Bolzano, and the modern notion of derivability is entirely absent from his logical speculation. Thus Bolzano's definition of derivability can be considered as an attempt to clarify the idea of consequence. In the same way as Bolzano recognizes two senses of analytic ("analytic in the broader sense" and "logically analytic"), so he recognizes two senses of derivable: "derivable (in the broader sense)" and "logically derivable". It is the latter notion which comes closest to what present-day logicians usually mean when they say that one proposition is a consequence of certain other propositions.

   The letters p, q, r, . . . have been used to represent propositions. The corresponding capital letters, *P, Q, R, . . .* will now be used to represent sets of propositions (a single proposition being considered as a limiting case of a set). In order to state Bolzano's definitions briefly it is helpful to introduce the following conventions. A set of propositions *P* is said to be true if every proposition in *P* is true, and false if at least one proposition in *P* is false. *P + Q* will mean the set of propositions which results when one conjoins *P* and *Q*. "*B* gives a true variant of *P* with respect to *A*" will mean that one obtains nothing but true propositions if one substitutes *B* for *A* in every proposition which occurs in *P*. Two of Bolzano's definitions can now be stated as follows:

Def. 7. *P* is consistent with respect to *A* = df There is some *B* which gives a true variant of *P* with respect to *A*.

Def. 8. *P* is derivable from *Q* with respect to *A* = df (i) The set of propositions *P + Q* is consistent with respect to *A*, and (ii) every *B*, which gives a true variant of *Q* with respect to *A*, also gives a true variant of *P* with respect to *A*.

Bolzano now makes approximately the same observation which he made earlier concerning the preliminary definition 3 of "analytic", and then sharpens the concept "derivable (in the broader sense)" to "logically derivable":

Def. 9. *P* is logically derivable from *Q* = df *P* is derivable from *Q* with respect to a sequence which contains exactly all concepts occurring in *P + Q* which do not belong to logic.

This concept of logical derivability is closely related to, although not identical with, the model-theoretical concept of consequence which Tarski proposed in the 1930s.

D. *Logical measures*

Bolzano makes an interesting attempt to introduce measurement into logic. Let us suppose that the number of variants of a given set of propositions (or a single proposition) *P* with respect to a sequence of ideas *A* is finite. If the number of existing men is finite, then the proposition "The man Caius is a Roman" fulfils this condition relative to the idea 'Caius'. One can now compare the number of true variants of *P* with respect to A with the total number of variants of P relative to A. If all the variants are true, P is universally valid. If none of the variants are true, P is universally invalid. But when neither of these extremes occurs, Bolzano still wishes to speak about "the validity of P with respect to A". Bolzano's definition of this notion runs:

Def. 10. If the number of true variants of P with respect to A is m and the total number of variants of P with respect to A is n ($n > 0$), then the validity of P with respect to $A = m/n$.

In general both m and n are infinite, and the fraction m/n thus has no meaning. Bolzano proposes several methods—which I shall not discuss here—by means of which the infinite numbers might be reduced to finite ones. It is easy to see that in Bolzano's spirit one could introduce a concept "logical validity", which would be related to Bolzano's "validity" as his logical derivability is related to his derivability. The definition, which does not occur in the writings of Bolzano, could read:

Def. 11. The logical validity of P = df The validity of P with respect to a sequence of ideas which contains exactly all the ideas occurring in P which do not belong to logic.

In order that P be derivable from Q relative to A, it is required by definition 8 that every B which gives a true variant of Q relative to A also gives a true variant of P relative to A. But this is an extreme case. The opposite extreme is the case that every B which gives a true variant of Q relative to A gives a false variant of P relative to A. Between the two extremes lie all those cases where some of the Bs which give true variants of Q relative to A give true variants, and the others false variants, of P relative to A. In these intermediate cases Bolzano still wishes to say that P has a certain "validity" or "probability" in relation to Q and relative to A. Bolzano's definition of probability can be spelled out as follows:

Def. 12. If the number of true variants of $P + Q$ relative to A is m and the number of true variants of Q relative to A is n ($n > 0$), then the probability of P in relation to Q with reference to A is $= m/n$.

If the numbers *m* and *n* are infinite, the fraction *m/n* again has no meaning, and again Bolzano thinks that in some cases the infinite numbers can be reduced to finitude. However, the proposed method of reduction does not always work, and Bolzano therefore distinguished between what he calls *determined* probability, which can be numerically measured, and *undetermined* probability, which is not measureable. Obviously the determined probability, like the determined validity, is always a number somewhere between 0 and 1. It is easily seen also that if all probabilities are determined, they together satisfy the basic postulates of the calculus of probability.

Bolzano's concept of probability (definition 12) can, of course, be narrowed down to a concept of logical probability in the same way as his concept of validity (definition 10) was narrowed down to a concept of logical validity (definition 11). (The logical probability of *P* in relation to *Q* is the probability of *P* in relation to *Q* with respect to a sequence containing all ideas in *P* + *Q* which do not belong to logic.

The study of logical measures has been intensified in recent time, largely because of Carnap's investigations into the concept of probability. The prevailing present-day ideas on this issue show an intimate relationship with the ideas which Bolzano presented 150 years ago.

8. THE OBJECTIVE ORDER OF TRUTHS

A. *Three motives for the doctrine of the*
   objective order of truths

In addition to the relation of derivability (or logical derivability), Bolzano introduces a relation which he calls "*Abfolge*" and which I shall call "(objective) founding". This relation is something of a puzzle. Bolzano gives no definition of it, and he supposes that it is what he calls a simple concept, in which no parts can be distinguished. The meaning he gives to the concept is not easy to grasp. However, I believe that one can distinguish at least three different motives behind Bolzano's supposition that there is such a relation. (As a synonym to the phrase "*A* is founded upon *B*", we shall in the sequel also use the mode of expression, "*B* is a ground (foundation) for *A*".)

The first motive is connected with the Platonic–Aristotelian ideal of science. The ideal involves belief in the existence of a hierarchical order among truths, which—at least, within certain limits—is uniquely given: certain truths are, in an absolute sense, basic propositions or axioms, while all other truths are, in an absolute sense, derived propositions. Bolzano speaks of an "objective order" of truths, and he thinks that a truly scientific presentation of a given set of truths ought to follow this objective order. Bolzano's concept 'derivable' (or 'logically derivable') is clearly incapable of establishing such an order, since, if for no other reason—as Bolzano explicitly states—every truth is (logically) derivable from other truths. Hence, there must exist another relation which creates the order. I venture to propose the hypothesis that Bolzano was guided by the following idea when he postulated the concept of objective founding:

(M1) There is a relation of founding such that some truths are not founded by others and that upon these non-founded truths all the other truths are founded.

The second motive which I believe can be ascribed to Bolzano, is connected with his interpretation of the causal nexus. According to a common view, which we have earlier met in Hume, the assertion that something A is the cause of something B, implies an assertion that the connection between A and B is, in a sense, 'necessary'. Bolzano was probably guided by this common view when he formulated the definition:

(*Def.*) A is the cause of B = df The truth "B is (exists)" is founded upon the truth "A is (exists)" or upon the latter together with certain other truths.

If we wish to apply the concept of causality as it is usually applied, it would obviously be absurd to replace in this definition "founded upon" with "(logically) derivable from". This lesson can be drawn from Hume. If the definition is not to collapse, Bolzano must look around for a notion of founding which is distinct from derivability. Bolzano's theory of the founding relation, thus, was probably inspired also by the idea:

(M2) There is a relation of founding such that the definition (Def.) is correct.

As a third motive one can point to Bolzano's assumption that between certain particular designated propositions there exists a founding relation which is not also a relation of derivability. The highest principle of morality can, according to Bolzano, be formulated in the words:

(i) One ought to do (to will) A.

From such a principle, plus a proposition of the form:

(ii) X is necessary in order for A to occur,

one can, Bolzano assumes, infer every subordinate moral truth:

(iii) One ought to do X.

The highest moral principle (i) cannot itself be inferred in this manner. But nevertheless, there are objective grounds for (i)—among them is the proposition "A is possible". But according to Bolzano the relation between (i) and its objective grounds is not one of derivability. In other words:

(M3) There is a relation of founding which obtains, for example, between the highest principle of morality and its objective grounds.

It is interesting to compare this third idea with Hume's celebrated pronouncement that an author in moral philosophy is guilty of a fallacy when he passes from assertions about what *is*, to assertions about what *ought* to be. Bolzano agrees with Hume in so far as he denies that (i) is (logically) derivable from its grounds. But he modifies Hume's position by claiming that (i) is none the less founded upon truths which do not contain the specifically moral concept 'ought'.

(M1)–(M3) are fused in Bolzano so that he supposes that in all three cases he is dealing with the same relation.[4]

---

[4] A Bolzano scholar, Professor Jan Berg (München), author of *Bolzano's Logic* (1962), has informed me that in his study of Bolzano's unpublished manuscripts he has found my hypothesis about the three motives well confirmed.

B. *Some properties of the founding relation*

Bolzano makes a multitude of general assertions about the founding relation. As I have often done previously, I find it natural to cast my account in the form of a series of numbered propositions, where, thus, I am responsible for the enumeration. My account will be highly selective. I will restate only those assertions of Bolzano's which I think that I have understood, and I shall ignore some apparent contradictions. (The letters p, q, r will as before be used to stand for propositions-in-themselves. P, Q, R retain their function of standing for sets of such propositions. Whenever convenient, a single proposition may be taken as a limiting case of such a set.)

(F1)   If P is founded upon Q, then P is a truth and Q is a set of truths.

The founding relation is distinct from the relation of derivability in that the former applies only to true propositions.

(F2)   If P and Q are foundations of exactly the same truths, then P is the same set of truths as Q.

(F3) If P is founded upon Q and Q is founded upon R, it is never the case that P is founded upon R.

Thus, in constradistinction to (logical) derivability, founding is not transitive.

Starting from a given truth p we may seek its grounds, i.e. those truths upon which it is founded. Let us assume that q, r, s are the grounds of p. We can then go on and seek the grounds for each one of q, r, and s. And so on. In this way we obtain a logical tree:

$$\frac{\overline{t\ u}\qquad\overline{v\ w}}{\underbrace{q\qquad\hat{r}\qquad s}_{p}}\qquad (x)$$

The curved line over the sign for a proposition shows, in Bolzano's notation, that the proposition is not founded upon any other truth. If p itself were a truth of this kind, then the logical tree would be reduced to:

$$\hat{p}$$

We can now restate one of Bolzano's definitions as follows:

(D1) q is an auxiliary truth for p = df There is a logical tree for p in which q occurs above the line marked (x).

In this terminology one of Bolzano's fundamental assumptions about founding reads as follows:

(F4) No truth is an auxiliary truth for itself.

If we interpret a "logical tree" as a kind of proof, a violation of (F4) would imply that the proof is circular. Bolzano's own reason for (F4) is similar: to follow a logical tree for p from above downwards is a way of coming to know p, but knowledge of p cannot be a means of acquiring that same knowledge.

From (F4) one can derive the several further assumptions about founding which Bolzano makes:

(F5) No truth is founded upon itself.

(F6) If p is founded upon Q and Q is a set of truths, p does not belong to that set.

If counterexamples to any of these assumptions were to occur, we would get a tree of the form:

$$\frac{\ldots p \ldots}{p}$$

which is ruled out by (F4).

Bolzano's next definition is:

(D2) p is a basic truth = df There is no Q upon which p is founded.

The question whether there are basic truths, Bolzano thinks he can answer affirmatively by pointing to the supposed basic truth "There is something". If I have not misunderstood him, his inclination to believe that there are basic truths is one of the motives for the entire theory of founding. Bolzano also thinks that there is a multitude of basic truths.

C. *Finite and infinite logical trees*

Let us now make the simplifying terminological convention that a "tree" must be in a certain sense complete: if a proposition occurring in the tree has any foundation, a foundation for it is included in the tree.

In an obvious sense one can speak about "lines" in a logical tree. In a tree beginning (from below) with (S) there are one or more lines which begin with each one of the sequences of propositions: $p\,q\,t$, $p\,q\,u$, $p\,s\,v$, $p\,s\,w$. There is also a line which consists only of two propositions: p and $\hat{r}$. A line in a tree is obviously finite, if and only if it concludes with a basic truth. We can call a logical tree infinite, if it contains an infinite line. One can now ask whether there exists any infinite tree. Bolzano's answer is affirmative. There are "truths such that not only do they have a ground, but the truths which constitute the ground also have grounds, and this continues into infinity." As a proof he points to the supposed fact that the causal chains in nature run endlessly backward in time. Here Bolzano's position is influenced by (M2).

One can also ask whether every truth has some finite tree. In the *Wissenschaftslehre* Bolzano hardly presents an unambiguous answer to this question. The opinion that there are several basic truths, he justifies by saying: "I do not understand how all the truths which there are could stem from a single truth as consequences, and consequences of these consequences." This statement seems to imply that every truth has some logical tree, all the lines of which end in basic truths, thus some finite tree. Here Bolzano's motive (M1) comes to light. But other arguments of Bolzano's can be cited as evidence for the opposite view.

Obviously a basic truth has only finite trees in the trivial sense that a basic truth is itself its only tree. Bolzano thinks that there is also another important category of truths, all the trees of which are finite. These are the so-called conceptual truths, i.e. truths which do not contain any "intuition" but are composed solely of "concepts". The distinction between "intuitions" and "concepts" derives from Kant. In Bolzano's view all truths of pure mathematics are conceptual truths, and he denies that any historical truth is conceptual. On the basis of certain assumptions which he makes, he can maintain that any tree for a conceptual truth is finite. The assumptions are:

(h1) Every conceptual truth is constructed from a finite number of simple concepts.

(h2) If p is a conceptual truth and q is an auxiliary truth for p, then q is also a conceptual truth; and the simple concepts, which occur in q, are at most as many as the simple concepts which occur in p.

(h3) The number of truths which are such that the number of simple concepts which constitute them is not larger than a certain given number, is finite.

From these assumptions it follows—as is easily seen—that every tree for a conceptual truth is finite.

In a perfect scientific exposition, according to Bolzano, the truths are presented in the "objective order" represented by their logical trees. Bolzano's just-mentioned view on the trees for conceptual truths specifies this ideal. In mathematics and generally in any exposition which involves only conceptual truths, one ought to go from simpler propositions (containing fewer simple concepts) to more complex propositions (containing a larger number of simple concepts). This is a thought which can be traced back to Plato's teaching about the dialectical "downward way", a teaching expressing both a mystical–religious view and a directive of scientific methodology. The mystical side was developed further by the NeoPlatonists and their many followers in the Middle Ages and in more recent times, who have seen the world's multiplicity as an emanation from an underlying unity. The methodological side recurred in sharpened form in such modern rationalists as Descartes and Leibniz. Bolzano belongs to this rationalistic tradition.

9. EPISTEMOLOGY

Bolzano's epistemological investigations are concerned with classical questions such as: How do we acquire knowledge?

How certain is our knowledge? Are there any limits to human knowledge, and if so, what? What is new in Bolzano's epistemology is the careful deliberation with which he introduces his concepts and formulates his questions, and the clear distinction he maintains between the theory of human knowledge, on the one hand, and such disciplines as logic and metaphysics, on the other.

In discussing the epistemologies of Hume and Kant we have seen that the fundamental aims of their theories of knowledge are unclear. When Hume accounts for how we acquire our knowledge about "matters of fact" and our knowledge about "relations of ideas", is he exploring genetic psychology, is he formulating methodological recommendations, or are his explanations to be understood as parts of a definition of "knowledge"?

On this point Bolzano's epistemology is, in principle, perfectly unambiguous. It is explicitly meant to be genetic psychology, and more precisely, a psychological theory about the causal relations between the judgements made by *one* person. But Bolzano lived long before psychology had become an empirical science, and his approach to the psychology of knowledge is purely speculative and in many respects rather conventional. His procedure can, in its essentials, be described as consisting in the reorganization, and translation into his own conceptual framework, of assumptions encountered in older epistemologies. Bolzano's translation shows, I think, that the genetic–psychological approach cannot do justice to what we may call "the intentions of classical epistemology", whatever these might have been. (In "classical epistemology"—a deliberately vague term—I include also many of the epistemologies of today, for example the empiricists of our age.) Ideas of classical epistemology which seem to contain some kernel of important truth—although ones that are difficult to spell out clearly —are transformed through his translation into a sometimes grotesquely schematic psychology. Although Bolzano's clarifications were not successful, let us not shut our eyes to his merit in (probably) being the first in the history of philosophy to attempt clarification in this area. His lack of success can be seen as an exhortation to epistemologists in the classical style either to find better conceptual clarifications or to break radically with many time-honoured patterns of thought.

A. *Fundamental concepts and problems*

While a truth-in-itself is something objective, which is independent of human life, knowledge of a truth-in-itself is a phenomenon tied to a conscious mind. Bolzano defines "knowledge" as "true judgement". To make a judgement is to believe a proposition-in-itself, and the judgement is true if the proposition is true. While truths-in-themselves as well as falsehoods-in-themselves are (so to say) elevated above the world of "existence", true judgements like any other psychological phenomena are integrated in a temporal and causal context.

Among the factors which together constitute the sufficient and temporally proximate cause of our making the judgement J, there may be certain other judgements made by us, for example $J_1, \ldots, J_n$. Designating this entire set of judgements $(J_1, \ldots, J_n)$ by K, we can then say that J is "mediated" by K. Epistemology, for Bolzano, is a theory which builds upon logic (including the logic of variation and the theory of the objective order of truths), but which is distinct from logic in that it considers the causal relation of mediation between judgements. On the basis of this relation we can introduce a number of other concepts.

Def. 1. J is a mediated judgement = df J is a judgement that is mediated by other judgements.
Def. 2. J is an immediate judgement = df J is not mediated.

Some of the problems which are in the focus of Bolzano's epistemological interest can now be phrased as follows:

Problem 1. What immediate judgements does a human being make?
Problem 2. What logical relations obtain between a given judgement and those judgements through which it is mediated?
Problem 3. How do we reach—or how could we reach —our most important items of empirical knowledge?

Problem 4. Are there any truths-in-themselves about which human beings can never acquire knowledge, mediated or immediate?

Bolzano's answers to questions 1–4 will be discussed below in sections B–E.

We already know that Bolzano, like Kant before him, distinguishes between *intuitions* and *concepts*:

Whenever we turn the attention of our minds toward the change which an external object presented to our senses, for example a rose, brings about in our mind, the closest and most direct effect of this act of attending is that an idea of the change arises within us. This idea is not empty. Its object, to wit, is the very change that happens in our mind and beyond that nothing, hence a single object. Therefore, we can say that this idea is a singular idea. On this occasion and through the continued activity of our mind, many other ideas, it is true, are brought about, among them also such as are not singular ideas, likewise entire judgements, especially concerning the change occurring within us, as when we, for example, say: This (which I see just now) is the sensation or idea Red; This (which I now smell) is a pleasant odour; This (which I feel just now when I touch a thorn with the tip of my finger) is a sensation of pain; etc. In these judgements the ideas *red, pleasant, odour, pain*, etc. have several objects. But the subject-ideas, which occur in them and which we designate by the word "this", are to be sure, truly singular ideas.[5]

In such considerations Bolzano finds a reason for defining an *intuition* as a simple idea with a single object. He maintains that this definition delineates approximately the same class of phenomena which Kant indicated with the term. *Concept*, he defines as an idea which neither is, nor contains as a constituent, any intuition. Bolzano's definitions of intuition and concept are not, I think, very illuminating. An intuition, he maintains, can never be reproduced, i.e. no two distinct subjective intuitions can occur which have the same intuition-in-itself for their content. Thus, we can never impart our own intuitions to another person, i.e. produce in him subjective intuitions with the same contents as our own. By contrast, concepts can be reproduced and shared.

In connection with the above distinction Bolzano develops

[5] *Wissenschaftslehre*, § 72.

the distinction between intuitional and conceptual propositions (judgements). A proposition (judgement) which is made up exclusively of concepts is called a conceptual proposition (judgement), and a proposition (judgement) which contains at least one intuition is called an intuitional proposition (judgement). On the basis of the relation of mediation and these new concepts, Bolzano frames his definitions of the classical concepts *a priori* and *a posteriori*. If we take a conceptual judgement and find the judgements by which it is mediated, and then those further judgements by which these mediating judgements are themselves mediated, and so on until we reach immediate judgements, it can happen that we encounter all the way only conceptual judgements. In that case Bolzano calls the judgement that was our starting-point an *a priori* judgement. On the other hand, if this judgement is itself an intuitive judgement, or if in tracing its mediation we at any point encounter an intuitive judgement, then it is an *a posteriori* judgement.

Def. 3. *J* is an *a priori* judgement = df *J* is a judgement which either is an immediate conceptual judgement or is all the way mediated through conceptual judgements.

Def. 4. *J* is an *a posteriori* judgement = df *J* is a judgement which is not *a priori*.

Like Kant before him, Bolzano now asks himself:

Problem 5. What *a priori* judgements occur in human knowledge?

While the words are identical with those of Kant, the question has received a new sense through Bolzano's subtle but also somewhat baffling definitions. Like Kant, Bolzano holds that there are synthetic as well as analytic judgements *a priori*. One of Bolzano's examples of a synthetic *a priori* judgement is the judgement that the concept 'horse' is not identical with the concept 'dog'. Like Kant, Bolzano thought that *a priori* judgements play an essential role in natural science, especially physics. In opposition to Kant, he considered arithmetic to be analytic. Although he did not take the geometry of his day to be *a priori*, he held that it should be possible to develop it in a purely conceptual manner, without recourse to our intuition of space, and thus to make it *a priori*—"so that it must also be acknowledged by those who do not associate any pictorial ideas with the words "line", "surface", and so on." But Bolzano did not undertake any systematic treatment of problem 5.

B. *Immediate judgements*

The previously mentioned incongruity between the aims and methods in Bolzano's epistemology seems to be especially blatant in his discussion of immediate judgements. Bolzano asserts that all our immediate judgements have the same highest degree of "reliability", which he also describes as "complete certainty". Error is impossible in the immediate judgements: as if the most foolish convictions could not arise "immediately"! Here, as in several other questions, he shows a sort of abstract, rationalistic optimism regarding human mental life. But it is an optimism which does not compel him to a definite opinion in any concrete case. An immediate judgement, in Bolzano's sense, can indeed never be incorrect, but Bolzano also affirms that we can never be certain of any judgement we make that it *is* immediate: it may very well be mediated through other judgements, although we are unconscious of the fact.

Regarding our immediate knowledge *a posteriori* Bolzano adopts a position which largely resembles what I earlier called Hume's subjectivistic view. Bolzano holds that there are two kinds of "perceptual judgement" (immediate intuitive judgement), which he, like Hume, regards as the ultimate basis of human empirical knowledge.

One kind are judgements of the form:

(i)   I experience the phenomenon (*Erscheinung*) *A*.

The subject *I* is here the being who makes the judgement, while the predicate is "a phenomenon that occurs in this being at the moment, for example, a present idea, a judgement just made, a given sensation, a decision or something of that sort".

The other kind are judgements of the type:

(ii)   This is an *A*,

where "this" indicates something which I am intuiting at the moment I utter (ii). "The subject-idea is here an intuition, just present in the being that makes the judgement, and which this being subsumes under a certain concept A saying, for example: This (which I intuit just now) is something red, a pleasant odour, or something like that."[6]

Judgements of kinds (i) and (ii) can be mediated, but some of them are immediate. The immediate judgements of these kinds, Bolzano calls judgements of perception or perceptual judgements. According to Bolzano they have a purely subjective bearing.

Thus I think . . . that we can not have immediate knowledge of the existence of a single [external] object, still less of its properties or changes, for example whether it is just now in motion or not. If we thus, for example, judge that here flies a bird, I consider this as a judgement reached by inference. But since we are unaware of the premisses on which it depends, in general we consider it to be a direct perception, and therefore assert that we do not infer the flight of the bird but directly see it.[7]

In addition to these judgements of perception, the ultimate basis of human knowledge contains also certain immediate conceptual judgements, that is immediate judgements *a priori*. As previously stated, Bolzano has not developed systematically this part of his theory.

C. *The mechanism of mediation*

The notion of founding, which establishes the objective order of truths, is primarily a relation between truths-in-themselves. But, in a simple way, the notion can be extended so as to become applicable also to judgements. We may say that the judgement J is founded upon the set of judgements K if the proposition-in-itself which is asserted through J is founded upon the propositions-in-themselves which are asserted through judgements belonging to K. In an analogous manner the concepts of derivation and probability, from the logic of variation, can be made to apply also to judgements. Bolzano's rationalistic optimism is further revealed in his theory of the mechanism of mediation, i.e. how human beings move

---

[6] *Wissenschaftslehre*, § 300.
[7] *Wissenschaftslehre*, § 400.

from given judgements to new judgements. When a judgement *J* is mediated by a set of judgements *K*, one of the three following relations always obtains according to Bolzano:

(1)   *J* is founded upon *K*,
(2)   *J* is derivable from *K*,
(3)   *J* has a certain probability in relation to *K*.

If we were to form a judgement *J* on the basis of certain other judgements *K* without any of these three relations obtaining, then Bolzano says, "the human mind would contain a certain faulty mechanism", and this he refuses to believe. Although he will not ascribe a faulty mechanism to the human mind, he allows that it is imperfect in its manner of mediating judgements. If a judgement *J* is formed on the basis of our immediate knowledge solely by use of relations (1) and (2), then *J* must be true. For immediate knowledge is true, and relations (1) and (2) always lead us from a true *K* to a true *J*. That we ever make mistakes is due to our occasionally deriving a conclusion merely with probability. That we do so, is due to an imperfection in our ability to survey carefully a large multiplicity. According to Bolzano, God never makes a merely probable inference.

These epistemological views would have immensely amused Voltaire who wrote *Candide* against Bolzano's master Leibniz! A sense of humour was probably not on the long list of Bolzano's virtues.

D. *How empirical knowledge is acquired or
could be acquired*

Section 303 in the *Wissenschaftslehre* carries the long-winded subtitle: "How we partly come to, partly could come to, our most general empirical judgements." Thus, Bolzano does not merely wish "to describe how such judgements actually are formed", but also wants to clarify "how they could and must be formed, if the reasonable man wishes to render to himself the most perfect account of this kind of judgement." From this point of view Bolzano studies first our judgements about our own mental life, then our judgements about our own bodies, and finally our judgements about the external world. What he attempts here is a type of "rational reconstruction", to use Carnap's phrase, of empirical knowledge. From a modern point of view, it is interesting to observe the importance which Bolzano attaches to the clarification of our judgements about spatial and temporal relations, as well as his view that judgements about spatial relations presuppose judgements about temporal relations. The details of Bolzano's reconstruction are too involved to be reproduced here.

E. *The limits of human knowledge*

The idea that there are infinitely many truths but that we, as finite human beings, are incapable of getting acquainted with more than a finite number of them, leads naturally to the question whether there are definite limits to our cognitive faculty, and whether we might be able to state these limits. Before we can give an answer to this question, we must first determine more exactly what we understand by such limits to our cognitive faculty and by a specification of these limits.[8]

With these words Bolzano opens his discussion of a question raised in Kant's critique of reason. The aim of stating the limits to our cognitive faculty must be, Bolzano says, to give us a criterion by which we can decide whether or not a given question transcends our cognitive faculty. Such a criterion would spare us the futile labour of attempting the impossible. If someone were to say that we cannot know anything except what is useful for us to know, he would not give us the desired criterion. For how can we decide whether or not something is useful for us to know? The statement of a limit to what our cognitive faculty could accomplish in the past and can accomplish in the present, would not do either. What is required, is the statement of a limit to what our powers of knowledge can ever accomplish also in the future.

But, a limit to *whose* knowledge? To my own? To that of all mankind? To that of all finite beings? Bolzano says that this indeterminacy must be overcome before a truly thorough discussion can commence.

What is meant by "knowledge"? Here "knowledge" cannot be the same as "true judgement", since anyone may by accident, as it were, make a true judgement about anything whatsoever. By "knowledge" we must here understand "true judgement, arrived at according to rules".

[8] *Wissenschaftslehre*, § 314.

In what terms could limits to our knowledge be stated? Bolzano tests several possibilities, all of which he eventually thinks himself forced to reject. First he enquires whether it is possible to assert, concerning some set K of truths, that they all lie beyond the boundary. How could such a set K be described? If the boundary applies also to *my* knowledge, obviously I cannot enumerate the members of K; $p, q, r, \ldots$, and know that just these propositions are both truths and inaccessible to knowledge. I cannot simultaneously know *both* that the proposition A is true *and* that I cannot know that A is true. Could one perhaps state some property which would characterize a set of unknowable truths? Could one assert, say, that all truths of a given form are unknowable? For instance, could I perhaps find a concept A about which I could know:

(a)   No truth of the form "All A are X" is knowable.

According to Bolzano, this is impossible. For (a) itself can be transcribed into a proposition of the form "All A are Y". (Bolzano's reader may wonder how.) Knowledge of (a), hence, would be a counterexample to (a) and thus falsify (a). Consequently, (a) can never assert a knowable boundary to our knowledge. Perhaps instead one could know concerning some concept A:

(b)   No truth of the form "All A are X" is knowable, unless X is already contained in the concept A.

But this proposition, too, according to Bolzano, can be brought into the form "All A are Y", and the Y here either is or is not contained in the concept A. If the former is the case, the statement (b) becomes a tautology and uninteresting. If the latter is the case, our knowledge of (b) would itself be a counterexample to (b).

Kant's attempt to indicate in his critique of reason, limits to human knowledge, can, according to Bolzano, be interpreted in the sense of (b). Kant maintains that the "transcendent" (*das Übersinnliche*, i.e. what transcends the reach of our senses) is beyond the scope of our knowledge. He thus, Bolzano thinks, asserts the following:

(c)   No truth of the form "All transcendent objects are X"

is knowable unless X is contained in the concept 'transcendent object'.

Bolzano hence finds that his general criticism of (b) applies to (c). In addition, Bolzano considers the concept "transcendent" as used by Kant to be too vague to be used in a precise discussion.

Could we then ever know concerning some set K of propositions that it transcends our powers ever to decide concerning any one of them whether it is true or false? How exceptionally difficult it would be, Bolzano says, to prove an assertion of this kind. That we have not succeeded in proving or disproving a given proposition heretofore is not a sufficient reason for asserting the proposition's undecidability in principle. Suppose that a purely conceptual proposition of the form "A has the property b" is at issue:

Who will be so deprecatory as to assert that we shall never have the fortune to understand that the two concepts A and b can, or that they cannot, be joined into a judgement, no matter how long we reflect upon both concepts, no matter how long and how thoroughly we compare them, not only with each other, but also with all related concepts, and so on? How many questions in the domain of purely conceptual truth was one for centuries at a loss to resolve and yet at last the means for the resolution were found? One may, for instance, recall the question whether the relation between the diameter and the circumference of the circle is rational, and hundreds of similar questions.[9]

The same situation exists in the case of empirical truths:

Even though a decision cannot be reached through mere reflection, but new experiences are required; even though these experiences until now have been unknown to us, indeed, even though we cannot even conceive how they could ever be made; yet they can occur in the future and teach us the answer to the question.[10]

Bolzano thinks that we are at a loss how to state a limit to our knowledge, "because there actually is none, since the sum of human knowledge allows of enlargement to infinity." Against Kant's intellectual resignation in favour of religious belief, Bolzano puts his confession to rationalistic optimism.

[9] *Wissenschaftslehre*, § 314.
[10] *Wissenschaftslehre*, § 314.

While Kant, the critic of reason, dismissed metaphysical speculation as an idle attempt to go beyond the impassable boundaries of knowledge. Bolzano thought himself able to give reasons for a world-view which on many scores is reminiscent of Leibniz's monadology. (In opposition to Leibniz, Bolzano maintains that the "simple substances" or "atoms" are literally in space, which he takes to be an objective reality.) Concerning some of the propositions which are parts of this world-view, Bolzano even dares to say that they are "truths which allow a proof as cogent and as clear as that of any mathematical theorem."[11]

[11] *Paradoxes of the Infinite*, § 50.

III

Logic and Arithmetic:
Gottlob Frege

10. GOTTLOB FREGE AND HIS WORK

The German mathematician and philosopher Gottlob Frege (1848-1925) has, directly and indirectly, exercised an enormous influence on the so-called analytical philosophy of our time. Since Frege's connection with philosophy was tangential, this fact may appear paradoxical. His interest was focused almost exclusively on the logico-epistemological foundations of arithmetic. Using Kant's terminology, but in opposition to Kant, he wished to prove conclusively that the propositions of arithmetic are "analytic *a priori*".[1] The doctrine that arithmetic is "synthetic *a priori*" is only a subordinate part of Kant's critique of reason, a part which, in Frege's own judgement, is not essential to the fundamental ideas of that critique. As far as geometry was concerned, Frege held that Kant was correct: geometry, in fact, is synthetic knowledge *a priori*. How, then, has Frege, through his attempt to correct Kant on one point, become one of the classical writers of modern philosophy? The question is prima facie the more intriguing since hardly any competent judge today would be prepared unhesitatingly to maintain that Frege's criticism of Kant is tenable.

Frege's so-called logicist interpretation of arithmetic, which he first put forth in 1884, and which was later to be reformulated by Russell and Whitehead in *Principia Mathematica* (1910–13), has played a large role not only in research into the foundations of mathematics, but also in philosophy in a more traditional sense. Within the logical empiricism of the 1920s and 1930s, logicism was often considered as a definitive philosophical insight, and as providing support for an

[1] It was primarily the theory for the non-negative integers, 0, 1, 2, . . . , which Frege had in mind, and he only carried out his programme in any detail for that theory. However, his thesis about the nature of arithmetic was intended to apply to the other kinds of numbers as well: negative, fractional, irrational, and complex numbers, and also the transfinite numbers discovered by Cantor.

empiricist epistemology. Logicism also acted as a source of inspiration, since for the first time, an ancient philosophical problem, the problem of numbers and our knowledge of numbers, seemed to have received an exact solution, and by the use of methods from which one could expect similarly exact solutions to many other difficult classical problems. Thus logicism stimulated the interest of philosophers in mathematical logic and its applications.

In fact, Frege's greatness is independent of the fortunes of logicism. Columbus sailed westward in order to reach India, but found America. It is still a matter of dispute how close Frege came to his India. But the discoveries which he made on the way are today indisputable in many essential respects. Kant justified his position, that $7 + 5 = 12$ is a synthetic proposition, in a rather impressionistic way: the idea of 12 is not contained, he said, in the idea of a sum of 7 and 5. Frege's view that the same proposition (and the entire family to which it belongs) is analytic is the conclusion of a very comprehensive theoretical system. The elaboration of this system occupied the greater part of Frege's life.

To show that the propositions of arithmetic are analytic is, for Frege, the same as showing that they can be derived from "general logical laws" with the help of suitable definitions. The best way to show that something is derivable is to derive it. Frege saw that his task was, first, to formulate the "general laws of logic", then to construct suitable definitions of the concepts of arithmetic on the basis of the concepts which occur in the laws of logic, and finally to accomplish the derivation.

A traditional mathematician is generally content in his proofs to trust his logical feeling at each separate step from given premisses to conclusion. At this point Frege sharpened the traditional mathematician's demand for exactness: he insisted that not only the axioms and the definitions but also the rules of inference must be specified in advance. This demand is a very natural development of the axiomatic ideal which mathematicians have pursued since antiquity. When, like Frege, one attempts to axiomatize logic itself, fulfilment of the demand becomes imperative. When the traditional mathematician moves from premiss to conclusion, he relies on a logic which he tacitly presupposes. If we were to proceed in the same manner in axiomatizing logic, we would run the risk of circularity, of assuming in advance what we were going to deduce. To state formal rules of inference for a theory formulated in unregimented ordinary language would be inordinately difficult, if not impossible. To develop manageable formal rules of inference one must first specify in a standardized language the assertions to which the rules are to be applied, where the very forms of the statements mirror their mutual logical relations. Such a language Frege calls a "concept language" (*Begriffsschrift*), today we call it a formalized language. Thus he had to develop a formalized languge sufficiently expressive to allow the formulation of the logic which he was considering. To create a formalized language for a given domain, is, as is easily seen, practically equivalent to analysing, from a uniform point of view, the statements which belong to that domain. The statement analysis which Frege undertook compelled him to develop certain ontological views about the kinds of entities which there are and which are referred to in the statements, and certain semantical views about how words and statements function in language.

Frege's interpretation of arithmetical propositions rests essentially on the concept of a 'set', and therefore the formalized logic whcih he used as a basis for his attempt to derive arithmetic, included a beginning of a formalization of set theory. Frege's derivation of arithmetic is thus the crowning point of a system of thought whose structure can be schematically indicated through diagram (C).

Let us take a brief glance at the different parts of Frege's work and attempt to form a preliminary idea of their significance in the recent history of philosophy.

Frege's ontology, his theory of the fundamental categories of entities which exist in *rerum natura*, has not in its entirety been taken over by later investigators in logic and the foundations of mathematics. This ontology unites ideas which today are utilised in formalized set theory and ideas which are developed today in type-theoretical predicate logic or functional logic. Frege's semantics, his doctrine concerning the sense (*Sinn*) and reference (*Bedeutung*) of linguistic expressions,

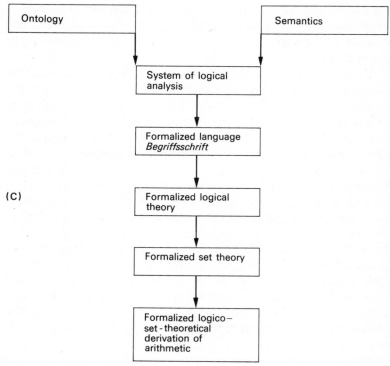

(C)

two distinct concepts for Frege, can be said to belong to the same tradition as the semantics of the Stoics and of Bolzano. Frege's position has inspired the semantical constructions of Rudolf Carnap, Alonzo Church, and others. Frege's ontology and his semantics are two parts of his work about whose validity or merits contemporary opinions widely differ. Although Frege's system of logical analysis is based on his ontology and semantics, some of its essential features remain invariant under strong variations in the ontologico-semantical substructure. By "a system of logical analysis" I mean, roughly speaking, a conceptual system with the aid of which assertions from a given domain can be articulated in a uniform manner.

The domain for which Frege's system was primarily intended was that of logic and mathematics. But as he indicated, his system is applicable well outside that field: as a matter of fact, it seems capable of extension so as to become applicable in any domain where logical precision is desirable. Frege's system of logical analysis contains the "truth-functional" sentential connectives (intended to replace, to a certain extent 'not', 'and', 'or', and 'if then' of ordinary language),[2] the universal quantifier "for all values of x" (designed to do the job of 'all', 'no', and 'some' of ordinary language),[3] a precise concept of function, the concept 'value-range for a function' (of which, according to Frege, the notion of a 'set', or the 'extension of a concept', is a special case), a precise concept 'that which',[4] a concept of identity, and the

[2] A sentential connective is a word or a phrase with which given certain sentences A, B, . . . , one can construct complex sentences containing A, B, . . . , as constituents. If A and B are sentences, then not-A, A and B, A or B, and if A then B are also sentences. The truth-value of these molecular sentences, according to Frege, can be determined through the truth-values of the constituent sentences in accordance with the following table.

A	B	not-A	A and B	A or B	If A then B
T	T	F	T	T	T
F	T	T	F	T	T
T	F	F	F	T	F
F	F	T	F	F	T

(The first line of the table states that if A and B are both true, then not-A is false, while A and B, A or B, and if A then B are true.) Ideas of this kind were already present, as we have seen, in the Stoic–Megaric logic in antiquity. In the nineteenth century one meets similar ideas prior to Frege, in Boole (1847) and McColl (1877), and after Frege in Schröder, Peirce, Peano, and several other logicians.

[3] The proposition "it holds for all x that x is material" means the same for Frege as "Everything is material". If, with Russell, we employ the symbolical abbreviation (x) instead of the phrase 'It holds for all x that', then the following are plausible examples of translations:

(x) (x is material)	Everything is material
(x) not-(x is material)	Nothing is material
not-(x) (x is material)	Something is not material
not-(x) not-(x is materal)	Something is material

After Frege quantification theory was independently developed by Pierce (1885) and Peano (1889).

[4] Frege introduces a function f with the properties:

(i) If x is a set whose sole element is y, then $f(x) = y$. Otherwise, $f(x) = x$.

This function partly fills the same role as the idiom 'that which'. Suppose that y is the only object which has the property E. According to our common manner of using the idiom 'that which', it then holds:

(ii) y = that which has E.

Now let us form the set of all objects which have the property E and call it S_E. y is the only element in S_E, and thus according to (i):

(iii) $y = f(S_E)$.

To this extent $f(S_E)$ can serve the same purpose as 'that which has E'. Frege was quite aware of the fact that the two expressions behave differently in other contexts.

notions of the truth-values 'the true' and 'the false'. Through its systematic strength and wide applicability, this system of logical analysis is epoch-making in the history of philosophy. Many features of Frege's system recur in most modern attempts to codify logic and mathematics precisely. Frege's theories of the sentential connectives and quantification have been especially durable. In fact, in the decades around 1879, the year of publication of Frege's *Begriffsschrift*, many starts in the same direction as his were made independently. It is thus plausible to suppose that the most important logical doctrines of Frege would have been developed around the end of the nineteenth century, even if Frege had never lived. However, this supposition does not diminish the value of Frege's contribution: he was still the first who had the intellectual power to articulate and systematize what others saw more or less dimly and incompletely.

Frege's system of logical analysis and his formalized language are so intimately connected that they represent two aspects of the same thing. (Of course, the language developed by Frege is only *one* among several conceivable ways of expressing his system of logical analysis.) In spite of many earlier attempts at formalization, especially within logical algebra (Leibniz, Boole, etc.), Frege, in his *Concept Language, a Formula Language of Pure Thought Imitating the Arithmetical* (*Begriffsschrift*, 1879), provided the first example of a strictly formalized and very expressive language. In *The Foundations of Arithmetic* (*Die Grundlagen der Arithmetik*, 1884) he informally sketched his theory of arithmetic, and in the *Fundamental Laws of Arithmetic* (*Grundgesetze der Arithmetik*, vol. I, 1893; vol. II, 1903), he presented the same theory deductively within his formalized language. What Frege achieved in the way of deductive theory can be summarized thus. He produced a strictly formalized logical theory containing a propositional logic (the classical two-valued), a logic of quantification (with quantification of variables for "objects" and "functions"), and a theory of identity. Besides this, he also provided a fragmentary set theory which, as we shall see, turned out, alas, to be inconsistent. With the aid of ingenious definitions of arithmetical concepts on a logico-set-theoretical basis he succeeded in deriving a representative selection of arithmetical theorems. Since Frege's set theory is inconsistent, the value of this derivation is naturally not unimpeachable. But his attempt at derivation forms the starting-point for a long and important tradition in the philosophy of mathematics.

No one prior to Frege had grasped or put into practice the idea of formalization with Frege's degree of clarity. In this area he is the great pioneer. Frege's thought is to a large degree technical and esoteric. To expound Frege's logic to the non-specialist would be tantamount to writing a slightly dated textbook in mathematical logic. In this chapter I shall merely consider some ideas of Frege's which can be stated without too cumbersome an apparatus of notation and symbols. In section 11, I shall state some of the philosophical assumptions with which Frege approached his major problem, the nature of arithmetic. In sections 12 and 13, I shall then present and critically consider some fundamental ideas in Frege's philosophy of arithmetic. In sections 14 and 15, I shall discuss his semantics.

11. FREGE'S PROBLEMS, AND HIS EPISTEMOLOGICAL ASSUMPTIONS

The two classical problems in the philosophy of mathematics which primarily occupied Frege were: (a) the problem of the nature of numbers; and (b) the problem of the nature of arithmetical knowledge or arithmetical truth. Proposed solutions to these questions have, as we have seen, played a large role in the history of philosophy ever since Pythagoras, Plato, and Aristotle. The two questions are closely interrelated, and in Frege the answers to them constitute two sides of the same coin. First we shall look at the form which (b) took for Frege, and the epistemological assumptions with which he approached it. Afterwards we shall glance at the ontological apparatus which he applied to (a).

A. *Analytic and synthetic*

Frege's manner of formulating the problem is, as was Bolzano's, largely inspired by Kant. Like Kant he works with the two pairs: analytic–synthetic; *a priori–a posteriori*. Like Kant he asserts that all analytic statements are *a priori*, and thus the question becomes for him, as for Kant, to which of the following three categories of statements do arithmetical truths belong:

analytic (*a priori*),
synthetic *a priori*,
synthetic *a posteriori*.

The thesis he wished to establish was that they belong to the first named category.

In Frege's thinking this Kantian question receives a complex technical import which we shall now try to describe. According to Frege, both the Kantian distinctions concern how one should justify belief in a proposition. They are therefore applicable only to those propositions which are actually true. If one collates different passages from Frege's writings (for example, the preface to the *Concept Language* and section 3 of *The Foundations of Arithmetic*) one gets approximately the following definitions:

(D1) The proposition *P* is *a priori* = df *P* is true, and there are propositions which: (i) are true; (ii) have the form of general laws; (iii) are evident and unprovable; and (iv) together with definitions constitute a sufficient basis for a proof of *P*.

(D2) The proposition *P* is analytic = df *P* is true, and there are propositions which fulfil (i)–(iv) above and which also (v) are of a general logical nature.

(D3) The proposition *P* is *a posteriori* = df *P* is true but not *a priori*.

(D4) The proposition *P* is synthetic = df *P* is true but not analytic.

According to these definitions, just as in Kant, all analytic propositions are *a priori*. If a proof does not ultimately rest on unprovable general laws (and definitions), Frege holds that among its ultimate grounds there must occur certain "individual facts", i.e. "unprovable truths lacking generality (*Allgemeinheit*), which contain assertions about particular objects".[5] Every proof of a truth which is *a posteriori* must therefore ultimately invoke some such "individual fact".

[5] Frege, G., *Die Grundlagen der Arithmetik* (Hildesheim, 1961), p. 4.

To show that arithmetic is analytic, in the sense of (D2), appears important to Frege for several related but not identical reasons: (1) We would obtain the answer to the question about the nature of arithmetical truth; (2) We would give to the truths of arithmetic the most secure foundation conceivable, since the truths of logic, in Frege's view, are the most certain of all; (3) We would get a new insight into the mutual dependencies of truths; (4) We would also gain from the point of view of economy of thought, arithmetic would not need to appeal to any primitive truths of its own besides those of logic.

In (D1)–(D4) Frege presupposes as known the concepts: 'true proposition', 'general law', 'proposition of a general logical nature', 'evident and unprovable proposition', 'definition', and 'proof'. Each and every one presents a complex problem, but reasons of space unfortunately forbid a more thorough discussion. I must restrict myself to some reflections on the concepts 'propositions of a general logical nature' and 'definition'.

Although Frege never draws any sharp boundaries for the conceptual apparatus of logic (or for its terminology), it is very obvious that he regarded a certain, more or less clearly delimited, conceptual apparatus (terminology) as specific to logic. In order to admit nuances of speech let us use 'proposition of a logical form' to indicate those propositions which can be formulated solely with the aid of the conceptual apparatus specific to logic, however the boundaries are eventually to be established. Certainly it was Frege's opinion that all the propositions which could be expressed in his formalized language were also propositions of a logical form. Whether the class of propositions that can be expressed in his language also exhausts the class of propositions of a logical form, is a question which Frege may reasonably be presumed to have left open. (Sometimes he even expressed doubt whether the conceptual apparatus which he employed in his formalized language was of a logical nature throughout. His doubt concerned the notion of a set which was so essential to his derivation of arithmetic and at the same time proved so difficult to handle.)

In clarifying (D2) one could conceivably proceed in different ways. One specification, (D2') results from interpreting (v) in (D2) as follows:

(v')   is a proposition of a logical form.

But it is by no means obvious that this interpretation accords with Frege's deeper intentions. It is conceivable that among propositions of a logical form Frege would wish to distinguish between those which are logical truths and those which are not. Perhaps the clarification (D2''), which is obtained when we replace (v) in (D2) with:

(v'')   is a proposition of a logical form and is a logical truth,

would be historically more correct. As we shall see later, the distinction between (D2') and (D2'') became important for Russell (and for many philosophers after him). Propositions which are of logical form and true need not according to Russell be logical truths.

An instance of this is Russell's so-called axiom of infinity. The statement that "arithmetic is analytic" in the sense of (D2') is conceivably weaker than the statement that it is analytic in the sense of (D2'').

In philosophical and other literature, 'definition' has a long series of distinct meanings. Frege uses the word in a very special and technical sense. His major view as regards definition is this:

Definitions are not actually creative and to my mind ought not to be; they merely introduce abbreviating designations (names), which could be dispensed with, were it not that the lengthiness [of our language] would otherwise create insurmountable external difficulties'.[6]

Although Frege chose a slightly different method, we can, without essentially distorting his thought, regard his definitions in the following way. Let us call those expressions of Frege's formalized language which do not contain any defined expressions, primitive expressions, or expressions in the primitive language. Frege's definitions can then be considered as rules, according to which expressions in the primitive language can be translated into another and more succinct language. The expressions in this other language, we

[6] Frege, G., *Grundgesetze der Arithmetik* (Hildesheim, 1962), vol. I, p. VI.

can call it the secondary language, borrow their meaning from the primitive expressions of which they are the translations. According to Frege, a legitimate definition must be a definition either of a proper name or of a function-name. A conceivable definition of a proper name would be, for example:

(a) $2 = \mathrm{df}\ 1 + 1$,

where the proper name "2" is the *definiendum* and the complex proper name "1 + 1" is the *definiens*. A conceivable definition of a function-name would be, for example:

(b) Even $(x) = \mathrm{df}\ x$ is an integer which is divisible by 2 without remainder.

From the point of view adopted here, (a) implies the rule that "2" can be replaced wherever it occurs in a sentence with the expression "1 + 1", and conversely. (b) implies the rule that an expression of the form "Even (—)" can be replaced by the expression "— is a number which is divisible by 2 without remainder" wherever it occurs in a sentence, and conversely. Frege's most basic demand upon a legitimate system of definitions is that every name in the secondary language shall be the translation of exactly one name in the primitive language. This demand we shall call the demand for unique translatability. The system of definitions presupposed in (D2) should be a system which yields unique translatability.

B. *Frege against psychologism*

In many respects Frege was a pronounced Platonist. His insistence that arithmetic shall be based on logic, strongly reminds one of Plato's demand that mathematics, the most important parts of which, for Plato, were arithmetic and geometry, ought to be based on dialectic. Frege's Platonist interpretation of the existence of logical and arithmetical objects will be presented in the following section, where we discuss his ontology. By means of some quotations I wish to show here how Frege regarded the laws of logic on which he wanted to base arithmetic. He considered "psychologism", the position which conceives of logic as a sort of psychology, to be one of his major theoretical enemies. The psychologistic bias leads, among other things, to the view that the laws of logic are a kind of psychological law of thought. The preface to the first volume of *The Fundamental Laws of Arithmetic* contains a spirited attack on psychologism:

To be true is not the same as to be held true, were it by one, were it by many, were it by all, and can in no wise be reduced thereunto. It is no contradiction that something is true which everyone takes to be false. By laws of logic I do not mean psychological laws for the being-held-to-be-true but laws for the being-true. If it is true that I write this on the 13th of July, 1893, in my study, while the wind is howling outside, it remains true even if all mankind would later consider it false. If the being-true thus is independent of whether it be acknowledged by anyone, the laws for the being-true are not psychological laws but boundary stones, which are rooted in an eternal ground and which can be flooded by our thought, it is true, but can never be dislocated.[7]

That the laws of logic shall be guides to our thought in its search for truth, is generally acknowledged but it is all too easily forgotten. The ambiguity of the word "law" is fatal here. In one sense, a law states what is; in another sense, it prescribes what ought to be. Only in the latter sense can the laws of logic be called laws of thought since they lay down how one ought to think. Any law which states what is, can be considered as prescribing that one ought to think in accordance with it, and is hence, in that sense, a law of thought. This is true of the laws of geometry and of physics as much as of the laws of logic. These deserve the name "laws of thought" with greater right only if the name is taken to imply that they are the most general laws which prescribe how it ought to be thought whatever thinking is done at all.[8]

It is possible to falsify the meaning of the word "true" in a worse way than when one wishes to include a relation to a judging subject? One objects that the sentence "I am hungry" can be true for one person and false for another. The sentence, I grant, but not the thought, because the word "I" signifies another human being in the mouth of the other, and hence, also the sentence, when pronounced by the other, expresses another thought. All indications of place, time, etc., belong to the thought whose truth is being dealt with; the being-true itself is independent of place and date. How does the principle of identity really run?

Perhaps like this: "In the year 1893 human beings are incapable of acknowledging an object to be distinct from itself", or like this:

[7] Frege, op. cit., pp. XV–XVI.   [8] Ibid., p. XVI.

"Each object is identical with itself". The former law speaks of human beings and contains and indication of date; in the latter law, neither human beings nor any date is spoken of. The latter is a law for the being-true, the former a law for human holding-to-be-true. Their contents are entirely dissimilar, and they are independent of each other so that neither of the two can be derived from the other.[9]

C. *Frege's ontology*

By Frege's ontology is customarily understood his doctrine concerning the fundamental categories under which everything in the universe can be subsumed. His basic dichotomy is:

object/function,

which is paralleled in language by the division:

proper name (name of an object)/function name.

Among objects Frege includes both "real" objects encountered in the world of the senses, and "unreal" objects which are accessible only to thought. To be "real", he claims, is to be capable of affecting, directly or indirectly our senses. Reality in this sense is a very special characteristic, which some objects have but which many others lack. From the point of view of logic the category "real object" is as special as the category "algebraic number" in mathematics. Among the unreal objects recognized by Frege are: sets, numbers, truth-values, thoughts (which constitute the "meaning" of declarative sentences), and so on.

What Frege says about unreal objects could have been said word for word by Plato. An unreal object like, for example, the number 5, exists at no place in the world of the senses. To that extent it resembles, according to Frege, our thoughts, which do not occur at any place: our thoughts do not exist within our skulls. But the number 5 is not anyone's thought about anything. 5 is an independent object, which is exactly the same for all who consider it. Nor is 5 something which man has created. "No more than the geographer can the mathematician arbitrarily create anything; even he can only discover what exists and give it a name."[10]

Wittgenstein tells us that: "The last time I saw Frege, as we

9 Ibid., p. XVII.
10 Frege, G., *Die Grundlagen der Arithmetik*, pp. 107–8.

were waiting at the station for my train, I said to him: 'Don't you ever find *any* difficulty in your theory that numbers are objects?' He replied: 'Sometimes I *seem* to see a difficulty —but then again I *don't* see it.' "[11]

If, from an object-name which contains another object-name as a constituent, we omit that constituent, the result is what Frege calls a function-name. If we, for example, in the name:

(i) $5 + 7$

omit '7', the result is the function-name:

(ii) $5 + (\ )$.

The parentheses indicate here that something has been omitted. Instead of merely omitting a name, Frege usually employs the more flexible notation of replacing it with a Greek letter. Instead of (ii) he thus writes:

(iii) $5 + \epsilon$,

where the Greek epsilon indicates that something has been omitted. Among functions Frege includes what he calls concepts. The concept 'dog' is for Frege the function:

(iv) ϵ is a dog.

The value of (iv) for a determined argument, for example Caro, is what the sentence:

(v)   Caro is a dog,

signifies. As we shall find when studying Frege's semantics, he holds that (v) is the proper name of a truth-value: of the True if (v) is true, and of the False if (v) is false. Concepts are thus functions whose values are truth-values.

To every function there corresponds an object which constitutes the value-range of that function. If two functions take the same values for the same arguments, they have the same value-range. The value-range of the function (iii), Frege designates by the symbolic expression:

(vi) $\grave{\epsilon} (5 + \epsilon)$,

[11] Anscombe, G. E. M., and Geach, P. T., *Three Philosophers* (Oxford: Basil Blackwell, 1961), p. 130.

This value-range being identical with, for example:

(vii) $\grave{\epsilon}(\epsilon + 2^2 + 1)$.

For Frege the notion of 'value-range' was more general and more fundamental than the notion of a 'set'. From the point of view of modern set theory it would be natural to identify the value-range (vi) with the set of all ordered pairs: $x, 5 + x$, where the first term is an arbitrarily chosen argument for the function (iii) and the second term is the value of that function for this argument. From the same point of view, the value-range of the function (iv), i.e.:

(viii) $\grave{\epsilon}(\epsilon$ is a dog)

would be the set which includes both all ordered pairs of the form: x, The True, where x is some dog, and also all ordered pairs of the form: x, The False, where x is not a dog. However Frege himself identifies the value-range (viii) with the extension of the concept 'dog', i.e., with the set of all dogs.

If Frege appears to be a whole-hearted Platonist in his views on unreal objects, there is simultaneously, paradoxically enough, a kind of nominalist tendency in his view on the second basic category, the functions. According to Frege, a function-name like (ii) or (iii), is incomplete (*ungesättigt*) and in need of completion (*ergänzungsbedürftig*). The completion which Frege has in mind consists in the replacement of what was omitted when the function-name was formed from the name of an object. The bare function-name cannot appear as the subject in a sentence. This theory leads to quite paradoxical results. Frege himself asserts:

(ix) (ii) is a function,

and in this assertion the function (ii) is the subject. According to his own theory, (ix) is thus an illegitimate statement. Frege endeavoured, without success, to find a way out of this difficulty. Frege's manner of thinking about functions, furthermore, brings him very close to the thesis that there are no entities, 'functions', which are named by the function-names. According to Frege's terminology, functions are not objects. The general concepts like 'dog', with which Plato populated his heaven, are considered by Frege to be functions and thus not to be genuine objects. Although both Plato and Frege dealt with a world of "unreal objects" which cannot directly or indirectly affect our senses, the position of the two philosophers diverged when it came to the question of what exists in that world.

12. THE NATURE OF ARITHMETIC

A. *The nature of numbers*

When Frege discussed the nature of numbers, he wished to capture the import which numbers have for the mathematician and also for the man in the street when he is counting. In his doctrine of ideas, Plato more or less consciously maintained that, within a given area of language, words have a constant meaning, the same for all persons who belong to the language community. Frege makes this Platonic contention explicit with regard to arithmetical concepts. If "one" meant different things to different persons, he says, then mathematicians would fall into insoluble differences of opinion:

. . . when one said "one times one is one" and the other said "one times one is two", one could merely note the difference and say: my "one" has one character, yours has another. There could be no dispute about who was correct or any attempt to convince; for the necessary common object would be lacking. Obviously this militates against the meaning of the word "one" and the meaning of the sentence "one times one is one".[12]

According to Aristotle's account in the *Metaphysics*, Plato assumed the existence of two kinds of abstract number concepts: the so-called mathematical numbers, and the so-called ideal numbers. The mathematical number 5 is a set of five abstract units (monads) and thus looks as follows:

$$u_1, u_2, u_3, u_4, u_5.$$

The ideal number 5, on the other hand, is the Platonic form in which any set containing precisely five distinct things participates, or the Idea of Five. In his *Foundations of Arithmetic* Frege sharply criticizes a series of views about the nature of numbers which remind one of mathematical number

[12] Frege, G., *Grundgesetze der Arithmetik*, vol. I, p. XVIII.

as discussed by Aristotle. The conception of the nature of numbers which Frege adopts, closely resembles the concept of ideal number which Aristotle ascribes to Plato and which is also discernible in Plato's dialogues.

Plato's concept of ideal number implies that the expression:

(i) I have 5 fingers on my left hand,

can be considered equivalent to the assertion:

(ii) The set of fingers on my left hand partakes of 5,

where "5" stands for the ideal number 5, or the Idea of Five. One possible interpretation of this Platonic "participation" is that it is a relation between an object and a set of which the object is an element. This transcription changes (ii) into:

(iii) The set of fingers on my left hand is an element in the set 5.

Frege was not, as far as I know, directly inspired by Plato, but the notion that (i) ought to be regarded as equivalent to (iii) is actually the starting-point for his logical analysis of the number concept. Since the two assertions:

(iv) M has five elements,
(v) M is an element in (the set) 5,

are taken to be synonymous, it follows that:

(vi) 5 is the set of all sets which have 5 elements.

What has been said about the non-negative integer 5 can be said about any other non-negative integer n, and we arrive at the result:

(vii) A non-negative integer n is the set of all sets that have n elements.

This is precisely the theory of the nature of numbers which Frege proposes, and which thus can be regarded as one possible elaboration of the Platonic theory of ideal numbers.

B. *Frege's definitions*

Let us designate the set of all sets which have exactly n elements by K_n. Frege's fundamental idea can then be concisely expressed in the equation:

(viii) $n = K_n$, for all non-negative integers n.

The special cases of this idea:

(ix) $0 = K_0$, $1 = K_1$, $2 = K_2$, and so on,

are, on Frege's view, truths about the numbers 0, 1, 2, and so on, but, of course, they are not definitions. Construed as definitions they would suffer from the most obvious and vicious circularity.

To define, for example, the numeral 0, is, on Frege's conception of the nature of numbers, to characterize in some way the set K_0. If the definition is to serve Frege's aim of deriving arithmetic from logic, the characterization must be made exclusively in terms of concepts taken from logic. Let us examine how Frege defines 0 and 1. The definitions follow a common scheme, which I shall first state.

Let us say that two sets are equinumerous if they contain exactly the same number of elements. In his definition of the relation of equinumerosity, Frege exploits an idea with which, for example, Hume was familiar and which Frege's contemporary Cantor systematically used in his set theory.

(D1)   The relation R correlates set M with set N = df Every element in M has R to some element in N, and to each element in N some element in M has R.

(D2)   The relation R is one-to-one = df It holds for all x, y, and z that if x has R to y as well as to z, then $y = z$, and if x as well as y has R to z, then $x = y$.

(D3)   The set M is equinumerous with the set N = df There is a relation R which is one-to-one and correlates M with N.

If M_n is some set with n elements, then because of (viii) the following holds:

(x) n is the set of all sets equinumerous with M_n.

In particular, it is true of the integers 0 and 1:

   (xi) 0 is the set of all sets equinumerous with M_0.
   (xii) 1 is the set of all sets equinumerous with M_1.

Thus in order to obtain purely logical definitions of 0 and 1, we need only look for two sets M_0 and M_1, which can be characterized in purely logical terms. Frege chooses the definitions:

   (D4) M_0 = df the set of all objects which are not identical with themselves.

   (D5) M_1 = df the set of all sets which are identical with 0.

According to the "law of identity" of classical logic every object is identical with itself, and thus no object is an element in M_0. Obviously, M_1 contains exactly one object, namely 0. If we combine (D4) with (xi) and (D5) with (xii), we reach Frege's definitions of 0 and 1.

In order to simplify the notation we can introduce the following abbreviations. The set M_0, the empty (null) set, is often indicated by Λ. $\{a\}$ is the set which contains a as its only element. By $E(M)$ we designate the set of all sets equinumerous with M. With these abbreviations, Frege's definitions of 0 and 1 can be put as follows:

   (D6) 0 = df $E(\Lambda)$.
   (D7) 1 = df $E(\{0\}.)$.

Let $\{a, b, c, \ldots, k\}$ be the set whose elements are exactly $a, b, c, \ldots, k$. A definition $\{a, b, c, \ldots, k\}$ could be formulated:

   (D8) $\{a, b, c, \ldots, k\}$ = df the set of all objects which are identical either with a, with b, with $c, \ldots$ or with k.

If one systematically extends the idea which is the basis of (D6) and (D7), one can represent the Fregean number series in the following way:

$$0 = E(\Lambda).$$
$$1 = E(\{0\}).$$
$$2 = E(\{0, 1\}).$$
$$\ldots$$
$$n + 1 = E(\{0, 1, \ldots, n\}).$$

To give logical definitions of the individual integers is of course not sufficient for deriving interesting arithmetical theorems in logic. In order to reproduce within logic the theory of addition and multiplication, one must also, for example, logically define the sum $a + b$ and the product $a \times b$ of two integers a and b. Frege never got that far in his definitions. His system of definitions is thus very fragmentary, but, as Whitehead and Russell showed, completion of the system offers no difficulty.

All the concepts used in the definitions (D1)–(D8) must be accepted as "logical" if the definitions are to suit Frege's purposes. In particular, the notion 'the set of all objects which . . .' must be accepted as a logical concept. The difficulties which Frege encountered in the axiomatization of set theory eventually led him to hesitate on this point.

C. *The derivation of arithmetic from logic*

If we look at how Frege proceeds when he tries to establish the analyticity of arithmetic, we find that it is his ambition to show approximately the following:

(F) There is an L, and S, an R, and a D which together fulfil the following conditions:

(a) L is a formalized language, all the sentences of which are expressed in a purely logical vocabulary;

(b) S is a finite set of logically true sentences in L;

(c) R is a finite set of logically correct formal rules of derivation for L;

(d) D is a definitional system which fulfils Frege's demand for unique translatability;

(e) For every "arithmetical" truth P, one can by means of R, derive from S a sentence P' within L, which can be translated into P with the help of D.

Was Frege successful in showing (F) on the basis of his analysis of the number concept?

Frege's three most important works, *Concept Language*, *The Foundations of Arithmetic*, and the *Fundamental Laws of Arithmetic*, all contain contributions to the derivation of arithmetic from logic. He never got very far (as stated above, he did not even define addition and multiplication) but it is not difficult to see how, from his fundamental view of the concept of number, one could extend his definitions and derivations. At the very moment when Frege finished printing the second volume of the *Fundamental Laws* in 1903, he received a letter from the young Bertrand Russell, showing that his axioms led to a paradox, the so-called Russell paradox. The value of Frege's derivations was thereby put in question. Alternative axiom systems which, so far as we know, do not lead to paradoxes, were soon developed. In 1908 Russell sketched his so-called logical theory of types, and in the same year Zermelo published his set-theoretical axiom system. Since then a long series of alternative axiomatizations have been proposed.

The assertion that arithmetic is derivable from logic and set theory must be qualified. First, the concept 'arithmetical truth' is obviously vague. Given a formalized language like the one with which Frege operated, one can never express more than a denumerable number of properties, for instance $E_0, E_1, E_2, \ldots$, defined for the non-negative integers, 0, 1, 2, $\ldots$. But we can always introduce a new such property E through a simple application of Cantor's so-called diagonal method:

n has E if and only if n does not have E_n.

The new property E cannot be expressed in the given formalized language, so truths about E are not derivable therein. Thus within a given formalized language, only a limited part of the total arithmetical truth is derivable. In 1931, in his epoch-making paper *Über formal unentscheidbare Sätze in Principia Mathematica und verwandten Systemen*, Kurt Gödel published a proof that one such part, consisting of an elementary theory for the addition and multiplication of integers, is in principle incapable of complete axiomatization. That is to say: whatever consistent axiom system one chooses, there will always be propositions in the language which can neither be proved nor disproved on the basis of that system. Hence, the question of the derivability of arithmetic from logic and set theory must be discussed in a much more relativistic spirit than that in which it was approached by Frege. Given a certain formalized part of arithmetic, *A*, and a certain axiomatization of logic and set theory, *L*, we can ask whether the true propositions of *A* can be proved in *L*. While the answer will be affirmative for some choice of *A* and *L*, it will be negative for other choices.

13. SOME CRITICAL REMARKS

Frege's thesis that arithmetic is analytic also calls for reservations but from a totally different angle. That a statement is analytic, means, it will be recalled, that it can be derived from general laws of logic with the help of definitions. We have acquainted ourselves with the formal demand that Frege makes of a legitimate definitional system. But does he not also make certain demands of fidelity of his definitions?

For instance, when he defines:

(D6) $0 = \mathrm{df}\ E\ (\Lambda)$,

which can be translated into:

(D6′) $0 = \mathrm{df}$ the set of all sets which are equinumerous with the set of all objects which are not identical with themselves,

he apparently thinks that this definition expresses, in one way or another, what mathematicians and others mean by 0 (zero). There exists, he seems to imply, a generally accepted usage, such that definition (D6′) is, in some sense or other, faithful to the manner in which 0 (or zero) is understood according to that usage.

One could imagine a series of kinds of faithfulness in a definition, and it is impossible to attempt to survey them all here. Let us limit ourselves to a few kinds which are discernible from Frege's own philosophical standpoint. In the next section we shall describe Frege's distinction between sense and reference. (The reader is asked to look up pp. 113–15 and become acquainted with the distinction.) We can say that a definition is sense-faithful relative to usage *U*, if the *definiens* (in the definer's usage) has the same sense as the *definiendum* has in usage *U*. We can say that a definition is reference-faithful if there is identity of reference. From Frege's point of view a definition can obviously be reference-faithful without being sense-faithful, but not vice versa.

The general impression one receives from reading Frege is that he vacillates between different attitudes. In general, he seems to have the ambition of giving sense-faithful definitions; but in the particular case, he chooses, without any qualms about sense-fidelity, from among different, supposedly reference-faithful definitions, the one which will make possible the desired proof.[13] His doing so is obvious when he defines his sets K_n. They can, as is done by Frege and Russell, be characterized in purely logical terms. But they can also be characterized by reference to empirical facts. When Frege defines 0, he does so with reference to the empty set which he characterizes as the set of all objects which are not identical with themselves. But the empty set might just as well be described as the set of all ruminant canaries. This is likewise the empty set, but only zoology, not logic, can inform us of its emptiness. If one were to choose this method of definition, arithmetic would become in part an empirical science, a branch of zoology.

If, let us suppose, it is correct that the numerals $0, 1, 2, \ldots$ in mathematical usage indicate the sets $K_0, K_1, K_2, \ldots$; who would decide which characterization of these sets mathematicians have in mind? Perhaps the characterization changes from mathematician to mathematician and also in the same mathematician from grammar school to university chair. An analysis of "sense" could hardly lead to a uniform result.

Thus Frege's definition can at most claim to be reference-faithful with regard to mathematical usage. But do they have even *this* kind of faithfulness? As Frege interprets the non-negative integers, we have seen that they can be described by the following equations:

$$0 = E\,(\Lambda)$$
$$1 = E\,(\{0\})$$
$$\text{(i)} \quad 2 = E\,(\{0, 1\})$$
$$\ldots$$
$$n + 1 = E\,(\{0, \ldots, n\})$$

[13] When Frege wrote the *Foundations*, he had not yet come upon the distinction between sense and reference. Thus it would be pointless to ask the author of the *Foundations* which sort of faithfulness the definitions are intended to have. But the distinction belongs to the philosophical background for the *Fundamental Laws*, and its author ought to have a well-reasoned view on this question. However, even there, Frege does not articulate any standpoint.

A much simpler set-theoretical construction was presented in 1928 by von Neumann who proposed the following construction:

$$0 = \Lambda$$
$$1 = \{0\}$$
(ii) $$2 = \{0, 1\}$$
$$\ldots$$
$$n + 1 = \{0, 1, \ldots, n\}$$

From the point of view of the abstract mathematics, Frege's equations (i) have nothing to recommend them over von Neumann's equations (ii). Naturally, Frege could argue against (ii) that they are not in accord with the Platonic insight that a number is an "Idea", of which exactly all sets with that number of elements partake, that is to say, a set having these sets as its elements. But there is no necessity of adopting this Platonic point of view. The statement:

(iii)   I have five fingers on my left hand,

need not be regarded as synonymous with:

(iv)   The set of fingers on my left hand is an element in 5.

Rather, (iii) can be interpreted as synonymous with:

(v)   The set of fingers on my left hand is equinumerous with 5.

If we choose the interpretation (v), we must reject Frege's (i), but could very well accept von Neumann's (ii). One could say with some justification that while Frege's definitions give us Plato's ideal numbers in a modern set-theoretical form, von Neumann's definitions give us Plato's mathematical numbers in such a form.

Von Neumann's series (ii) is far from being the only competitor of Frege's series (i) for the honorific title of constituting the series of non-negative integers. Whichever interpretation of the numbers 0, 1, 2, 3, . . . we choose, it still holds that, for example (iii) is equivalent to:

(vi)   The set of fingers on my left hand is equinumerous with the set $\{1, 2, 3, 4, 5\}$, and it is just by establishing (vi), i.e. by counting, that I usually verify (iii). Besides the Platonic ideal and mathematical numbers, which both have their place in the purely intelligible world, Aristotle refers in the *Metaphysics* to "sensible numbers", by which he seems to mean sets of sensible objects. If one could identify any infinite series of such objects: $a_1, a_2, a_3, \ldots$, then that series, or the series of its initial segments, could function as our number series. Thus there is really no reason to think that Frege's definitions are reference-faithful relative to a generally accepted mathematical or everyday usage.

One can introduce an even weaker concept of faithfulness, which might be called truth-faithfulness. We can say that Frege's system of definitions would be truth-faithful to the mathematicians' usage if the following rule held generally: (r) When the arithmetical statement P can be translated by means of Frege's definitions into the logico-set-theoretical statement P', then P is true if and only if P' is true.

Do Frege's definitions have this truth-faithfulness? The question cannot be answered by a simple yes or no—if for no other reason than that we do not possess a generally accepted criterion of the truth of set-theoretical statements.

14. SENSE AND REFERENCE OF NAMES

A. *Sense, reference, and name*

The view that several kinds of meaning must be distinguished has deep roots in the history of philosophy. Most recently we have met it in Bolzano, who distinguished between the idea-in-itself which a phrase expresses, and the object or objects which it represents. The view was taken up by Frege, who gave it a new twist and elaborated it more thoroughly than any of his predecessors.

If it is correct that:

(i) $2 + 1 = 3$,

must not (i) be the same as:

(ii) $3 = 3$?

If $2 + 1$ is the same thing as 3, is not the assertion of identity

(i) the same as the assertion of identity (ii)? Or, to take a non-mathematical example, if it is correct that:

(iii) The morning star is the same as the evening star,

must not (iii) be the same as:

(iv) The morning star is the same as the morning star?

In order to clarify this and other puzzles one must, Frege holds, make the following distinction. The expressions "2 + 1" and "3" have the same reference (*Bedeutung*), i.e. they both designate the same number, but they do not have the same sense (*Sinn*). Therefore neither do (i) and (ii) have the same sense. Similarly, "the morning star" and "the evening star" have the same reference, they both indicate the planet Venus, but they do not have the same sense; and hence also (iii) and (iv) differ in sense.

In order to grasp the sense of an expression, one needs, according to Frege, only to have command of the language to which the expression belongs. But to perceive the reference of the expression may require difficult investigations. All readers clearly understand the *sense* of the expression "the final sentence in Frege's *Fundamental Laws of Arithmetic*". But how many are acquainted with the reference of the expression? How many know that the expression refers to the following sentence: "*Wenn dies Problem auch noch nicht so weit gelöst ist, als ich bei der Abfassung dieses Bandes dachte, so zweifle ich doch nicht, dass der Weg zur Lösung gefunden ist*"? The reference of an expression is often an object in the outer world. The sense is not. But just as two persons can denote the same thing by a given expression, they can also express the same sense. The sense is therefore "objective", like the reference. Frege is anxious to point out that the sense is not to be confused with the subjective and quickly changing ideas which different persons attach to an expression.

"Name" has a much wider significance for Frege than it has in ordinary usage. Every expression which indicates or purports to indicate any kind of entity Frege calls a name.[14]

---

[14] Occasionally, Frege reserves "name" for those words which actually are names *of something*. Occasionally he distinguishes between names that are correctly

Not only are "Julius Caesar", "Stockholm", and "the sun" names, according to Frege's terminology, but also "2 + 1", "the heavenly body most remote from the earth", "the man who invented gunpowder", and "the extension of the concept 'equinumerous with the concept: distinct from itself' ". To the category of "names" he even refers entire indicative sentences. The distinction 'sense—reference' is, according to Frege, applicable to all names, but it primarily applies to those expressions which are not sentences. When he considers the costumary uses of such expressions, he finds that the following states of affairs regularly occur.

B. *Some semantical principles*

(F1) Every (apparent or genuine) name has one— and only one—sense.

A name has a sense if it can be employed at all in intelligible language, and if it is unambiguous, it has only one sense. (F1) expresses in part a fact, and in part an ideal. Obviously it is difficult to indicate precisely the range of applicability of this principle.

(F2) Every name has at most one referent.

Some purported names lack reference, hence are not genuine names. "The heavenly body most remote from the earth", for example, lacks a referent provided that the universe is infinite. Other names do have a referent, for example "the morning star" which refers to the planet Venus. According to Frege, no name has more than one referent, if we assume its sense to be fixed. If a person objects that, for example "horse" refers to each particular horse, Frege would probably answer that the critic is using "refer" in a sense different from the one intended by him. Frege himself would probably maintain that "horse" ought to be understood as the name either of the concept 'to be a horse' (a function-name) or of the extension of the concept, i.e. the set of all horses.

formed, and names that are not so—meaning by a correctly formed name one which is actually the name of something. I intend to adhere here to the more liberal usage of the word. Both "Zeus" and "Napoleon" will be taken to be names —the former an apparent name and the latter a genuine name.

(F3) If two names have the same sense and one of them has a referent, then they have the same referent.

According to Frege, the reference is uniquely determined through the sense. An apparent counterexample is "the king of Sweden", which appears to have a constant sense, but the reference of which changes each time a new king accedes to the throne. However, the impression of constant sense is here an illusion. "The king of Sweden" has the sense "the present king of Sweden" or "the king of Sweden at time t", where t is that moment at which the expression is uttered. The sense therefore varies with t, just as the referent does.

(F4) Two names can have the same reference without having the same sense.

The sense is not uniquely determined by the reference. This point is illustrated by "the morning star" and "the evening star", which have different senses but the same referent.

Let us suppose that we have the following definitions: $2 = $ df $(1 + 1)$; $3 = $ df $(2 + 1)$; $4 = $ df $(3 + 1)$; $5 = $ df $(4 + 1)$, . . . , and that through them the *definienda* obtain the same senses as their *definientia*. Then diagram (D) illustrates semantical principles (F1)–(F4).

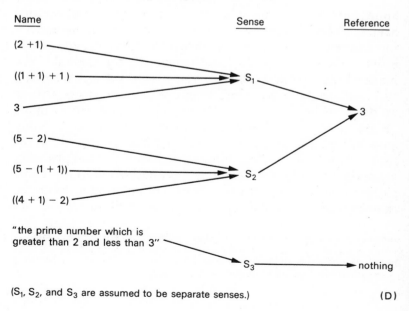

| Name | Sense | Reference |

(2 +1)

((1 + 1) + 1)   → S_1

3   3

(5 − 2)

(5 − (1 + 1))   → S_2

((4 + 1) − 2)

"the prime number which is
greater than 2 and less than 3"

S_3 ——————→ nothing

$(S_1, S_2,$ and S_3 are assumed to be separate senses.)   (D)

(F5) That which constitutes (in a given context) the sense of a name is always distinct from that which (in the same context) constitutes its referent.

The sense which, according to linguistic usage, belongs to "the evening star" is, for example, distinct from the planet which rushes onward in its orbit around the sun.

(F6) There is a class of entities which can play the role of referents but never that of senses.

Every sense is capable of occurring as a referent, but the converse is not the case. Physical objects, for instance, cannot be the senses of names. Similarly, sets (value-ranges) cannot be senses, although they can be referents. The same is also true of Frege's truth values: the True and the False. Etc.

(F7) If a name is part of another name, then the latter has a referent only if the former has a referent.

"The son of God" (taken literally) designates a certain person only if "God" indicates a certain "being"; i^2 designates a certain number (the square of the imaginary number i) only if i does.

If a part of an expression is replaced with another part, which has the same sense as the first, we say that a sense-faithful substitution is made. If the parts have the same referent, we say that the substitution is reference-faithful. With the help of this terminology we can formulate the following theses:

(F8) A sense-faithful substitution does not alter the sense of an expression.

(F9) A reference-faithful substitution does not alter the reference of an expression.

If we suppose that "God" has the same sense as "the perfect being", the "the son of God" has the same sense as "the son of the perfect being". "The capital of Sweden" indicates a certain city. "Sweden" has the same reference as "the eastern country on the Scandinavian peninsula". Thus, "the capital of Sweden" and "the capital of the eastern country on the Scandinavian peninsula" have the same referent.

(F10) 'A is identical with *B*' is true if and only if '*A*' and '*B*' have the same referent.

Since, according to Frege, it is correct that "the number of days in the week is identical with 5 + 2", the "the number of days in the week" and "5 + 2" have the same referent, although they do not have the same sense.

(F11) If a name is a part of another name, then the sense of the former is a part of the sense of the latter.

The sense of "Sweden" is, for example, a part of the sense of "the capital of Sweden".

Frege did not explicitly formulate all these principles in the present manner. But his mode of arguing shows that he· actually made these assumptions, as well as those which I will codify in the remainder of this chapter.

The theory formulated in (F1)–(F11) is far from unproblematic. One can, as Frege himself did, point to a number of apparent exceptions to the rules. In Frege's view the exceptions are either apparent only, or can be eliminated by means of minor and rather unimportant changes in linguistic usage. Even if the theory is problematic at several points, it does not appear "absurd". The doctrine of Frege's which will be presented in the next section must, however, at first glance, provide a theoretical shock.

15. SENSE AND REFERENCE OF INDICATIVE SENTENCES

A. *The semantics of independent indicative sentences*

(F12) The independent indicative sentence is a name, and thus (F1)–(F11) apply to it.

It is difficult to explain in a few words why Frege made this assumption. The best short explanation may be that by means of (F12) a systematic unity is obtained in his semantics, a unity which he saw no possibility of obtaining in any other way.

What then is the sense of a sentence, and what is the referent? The sentence "The sun is shining" expresses the "thought" that the sun is shining. Frege's "thoughts" are akin to Bolzano's "propositions-in-themselves". The thought that the sun is shining is objective, like the proposition-in-itself, and can be apprehended by several persons. When the sentence is true, it has, Frege says, "the truth-value the True"; when it is false it has "the truth-value the False". The referent of the proposition is its truth-value. All true propositions thus have a common referent, the True; and all false propositions also have a common referent, the False.

(F13) The sense of an independent sentence is the thought which it expresses, and its referent is the truth-value which it has.

(E)

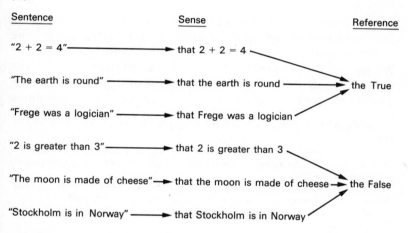

Sentence	Sense	Reference

"2 + 2 = 4" → that 2 + 2 = 4

"The earth is round" → that the earth is round → the True

"Frege was a logician" → that Frege was a logician

"2 is greater than 3" → that 2 is greater than 3

"The moon is made of cheese" → that the moon is made of cheese → the False

"Stockholm is in Norway" → that Stockholm is in Norway

Even if one accepts (F12), one need not accept (F13). Why did Frege propose (F13)? If we interpret sentences as names, subject to the theory of the sense and reference of names, then we must find entities connected with sentences, and behaving as sense and referent should behave. The answer to the above question is probably this: Frege thinks that the thought which is expressed by the sentence, and the truth-value of the sentence, do behave as sense and referent should behave according to (F1)–(F11), and he cannot discover anything else which does so.[15]

---

[15] Kurt Gödel presents, in "Russell's Mathematical Logic", an interesting argument, establishing the conclusion that sentences with the same truth-value have the same referent. The argument rests on Frege's theory as outlined above in (F1)–(F12) (especially in (F9), (F10), and (F12)), and also on certain other ·

Another question prompted by Frege's theory is what sort of objects truth-values are. Frege provides only a very incomplete answer. Sometimes he says that they are the sentential properties of being true and being false. Since Frege identifies properties with what he calls concepts, and concepts in his sense are functions, then truth-values would seem to be functions. But Frege does not adopt this view. In the *Fundamental Laws* he proposes that a truth-value should be identified with the set whose only member is that truth-value. No matter how one interprets this proposal it cannot explain what truth-values are to those who do not already know what they are.

(It could perhaps be argued that Frege uses the phrase "the truth-value the True" merely as a shorthand for "the common referent of all true sentences" and, similarly, the phrase "the truth-value the False" as shorthand for "the common referent of all false sentences". His use of the phrases in question, then, would not imply that he considers

suppositions which appear correct from Frege's point of view. The extra suppositions are:

(S1) Every statement contains some name, and if a statement A contains a name a, A can be considered as a statement $f(a)$ which says that a falls under a concept function f.

(S2) Every statement $f(a)$ has the same truth value and referent as the statement: "a = that object x which fulfils the condition: $f(x)$ and $x = a$."

(S3) Two true statements A and B can always be joined into a true conjunction: A & B.

(S4) A false proposition has the same referent as the negation of some true proposition.

The following lemma may first be proved:

Lemma 1. Every true statement in which a name a occurs has the same referent as the statement, $a = a$.

A true statement in which a occurs can, according to (S1), be looked upon as $f(a)$; and according to (S2), $f(a)$ has the same referent as the true statement "a = that object x which fulfils the condition: $f(x)$ and $x = a$." Since this statement is true, we can, according to (F10), conclude that a has the same referent as "that object x which . . .". According to (F9) and (F12) our statement thus has the same referent as $a = a$.

Next we may prove:

Lemma 2. If A and B are true sentences, then A has the same referent as A & B.

According to (S1), A contains some name, for example a. This name also occurs in A & B. According to lemma 1, A as well as A & B therefore has the same referent as $a = a$.

himself able to give independent characterizations of these referents.)

If sentences are names, then the following proposition constitutes a corollary to (F7).

(F7′) If a name is part of a sentence, then the sentence has a truth-value only if the name has a referent.

If Greek mythology is only a fantasy, then the name "Zeus" has no referent (although naturally it has a sense); hence the sentence "Zeus was the king of the gods" lacks truth-value.

The doctrine expounded above implies certain demands which Frege places on a correct scientific language. What one is striving for in science is truth. Therefore, a minimum requirement is:

(R1) In a correct scientific language every sentence shall have a truth-value.

(The ideal is, of course, that every sentence asserted in

Footnote 15 (*cont.*)

From lemma 2 directly follows:

Lemma 3. Any true sentences have the same referent.

For if A and B are true, then they both have the same referent as A & B.

Further, it follows:

Lemma 4. Any false sentences have the same referent.

For if A and B are false, then according to (S4) they have the same referent as "not-A′" and "not-B′" in which A′ and B′ are two true sentences. According to lemma 3, A′ and B′ have the same referent, and according to (F7) the same holds for "not-A′", "not-B′", and also for A and B. This train of thought can be considered to be a partial "proof" for (F13).

As Bertrand Russell indicates (*Principia Mathematica*, 2nd edn. vol. 1, p. 659) the supposition:

(1) Sentences with the same truth-value have the same referent, is synonymous in Frege's semantics with the supposition:

(2) The truth-value of a sentence A is not changed if one replaces in A the occurrence of a component sentence B with an occurrence of a sentence with the same truth-value as B.

From (1), (2) obviously follows in the light of (F13) and the earlier suppositions to which (F13) points. But from (2), (1) also follows. Let A and B be two arbitrarily chosen sentences with the same truth-value. Since A is a name (F13), it holds according to (F10):

(i) $A = A$.

By virtue of (2) we then get:

(ii) $A = B$.

In view of (F10) we now see that A and B have the same referent.

science shall have the truth-value the True.) If we combine the first demand with (F7′), the further requirement ensues:

(R2)   In a correct scientific language every name shall have not only sense but also reference.

B. *The semantics of subordinate clauses*
Frege maintains:

(F14) In many cases subordinate clauses have the same semantical status as independent sentences have (according to (F12) and (F13)).

But (F14) is a rule with many exceptions. Frege did not attempt to give a systematic survey of them all, but he discussed some common types of exception. (It is probable, but not completely certain, that Frege thought that a correct scientific language ought to be constructed so as to make (F14) hold without exceptions.) Let us consider the proposition:

(i)   Homer said that Zeus was the king of the gods.

If Zeus, as I am inclined to believe, was a creation of the imagination, then "Zeus" is a name which does not designate any object and thus lacks a referent. According to (F7), the subordinate clause:

(ii)   Zeus was the king of the gods,

also lacks a referent (truth-value), and consequently, according to (F7′), the same holds for (i). But isn't (i) true? (i) seems to constitute a counterexample to (F7′) and thus also to (F14).

Through his distinction between the "customary" and the "indirect" sense, and the "customary" and the "indirect" reference, of a name, Frege tries to solve the problem which (i) creates. The following definitions (which are not found in the same explicit form in Frege) formulate the distinction.

(D1) x is the customary sense (referent) of a name $a =$ df x is the sense (referent) which a has when a is a term in an independent statement of identity (a statement of the form "A is identical with B").

(D2) *x* is the indirect referent of a name *a* = df *x* is the customary sense of *a*.

(D3) *x* is the indirect sense of a name *a* = df *x* is the sense which *a* has when *a* has its customary sense for its referent.

Frege now asserts:

(F15) In certain contexts, especially in various forms of indirect discourse, names (including sentences) have indirect reference.

According to Frege, (F15) holds for all contexts of the type: '*X* doubts that *p*', '*X* says that *p*', '*X* concludes that *p*', '*X* commands that *p*', and '*X* asks whether *p*'. When one places a sentence *A* in the place occupied by *p* in these contexts, then *A* and all the names in *A* acquire an indirect reference.

If we consider the sentences:

(iii) Frege thought that 1 is a number,
(iv) Frege thought that Gagarin was the first man in outer space,

then another problem for Frege's semantics appears. Their subordinate clauses:

(v) 1 is a number,
(vi) Gagarin was the first man in outer space,

are both true, and thus have the same referent, the True. (iv) thus comes from (iii) through a reference-faithful substitution. According to (F9), (iii) and (iv) should therefore themselves have the same referent or truth-value. But while (iii) is a true proposition, (iv) is certainly false.

Frege's solution of this problem has already been given. (v) has indirect reference as a component of (iii), and (vi) also has indirect reference as a component in (iv). The indirect referent of (v) is the thought that 1 is a number, and the indirect referent of (vi) is the thought that Gagarin was the first man in outer space. These thoughts are not identical, and therefore the substitution which leads from (iii) to (iv) is not reference-faithful. Thus we have not discovered a genuine counterexample to (F9).

C. *What sort of theory is Frege's semantics?*

Frege's theory of sense and reference contains unclear points which in our time Rudolf Carnap, Alonzo Church, and others have attempted to remove. The scientific status of the theory itself is also a problem. The assertions of the theory might be interpreted as expressing putative empirical discoveries about human language. One might think that Frege had discovered the relations among linguistic expressions, their senses and their referents, in approximately the same manner that a sociologist finds certain social relations within a group of persons. But the assertions of Frege's theory might also be interpreted as definitions or corollaries of definitions. Finally, they could also be understood as recommendations to scientists, logicians, mathematicians, and philosophers, to construct and use their language in accordance with the rules of the theory. Frege's own account and motivation for the different points in the theory sometimes lead our thoughts in one direction and sometimes in another. To ask oneself whether or not Frege's semantics is "correct" would be naïve. It is a scheme of thought rather than a description of reality, and the straightforward question of correctness is inapplicable.

IV
Logic and Empiricism:
Bertrand Russell

16. RUSSELL'S PHILOSOPHICAL MOTIVES

If one were to describe the philosophical outlook of Bertrand Russell (1872–1970) in a short formula, one might say that he represents a synthesis of the mathematical philosophy of Gottlob Frege and the empiricism of David Hume. But, like any such formula, this would be unjust, and misleading. Certain fundamental logico-mathematical and empirical convictions which he has in common with Frege and with Hume certainly constitute something of a fixed point in Russell's long development, which otherwise is rich in radical changes of opinion. But simultaneously he has been open to influences from many directions, and in almost every question which has engaged his attention he has experimented with different positions.

One fundamental motive in Russell's thought is the search for certainty. This motive, of course, is not original to Russell; a very strong need for certainty is often met with in philosophers. As Descartes once did, Russell searched for a truth that was so certain that nobody in his right mind could doubt it. Those who seek absolute certainty easily become over-sceptical about what does not satisfy their utopian demand. But, once they believe that they have found such certainty, they are apt to cling to it with dogmatic conviction. Russell exhibits this combination of scepticism and dogmatism, which can appear rather confusing to people of a different temperament.

Like Plato, Leibniz, and Frege, Russell maintained that the fundamental assumptions of arithmetic must be justified on the basis of principles that lie "deeper" and are more "certain". Like Frege, Russell found these principles in logic. In *Principles of Mathematics* (1903) he outlined, independently of Frege, a logico-mathematical derivation of arithmetic which in its essentials agrees with Frege's. Largely because of the logical paradoxes he discovered at the turn of the century, Russell felt compelled to undertake in this context a thorough revision of Frege's logic. The revision included the adoption of the so-called theory of types. In *Principia Mathematica* (1910–13), written in collaboration with A. N. Whitehead, Russell developed a logicistic interpretation of arithmetic dominated by the theory of types. Many mathematicians and philosophers today think that no reduction of arithmetic is called for, and that logic is not the rock of certainty which Russell sought. Although Russell, the logician, was well aware of the many options and uncertainties of logic, he remained convinced all his life of the correctness of the logicistic interpretation of arithmetic.

On the issue of "our knowledge of the external world", Russell tried a series of different philosophical theories, from *The Problems of Philosophy* (1912) to *Human Knowledge* (1948). With Berkeley and Hume, Russell was not satisfied with the evidence which in everyday life we think sufficient for such assertions as: "There is a table before me"; "There are elephants in Africa"; or "The sun will rise tomorrow". As arithmetic must be proved on the basis of principles which themselves lie outside of arithmetic, so this kind of assertion must be supported by evidence drawn from a sphere other than that of the description of the external world provided by common sense and science. In agreement with the classical British empiricists, Russell held that this deeper and more certain evidence is found in what we "immediately experience", above all, what we immediately experience in sense perception, the so-called "sense-data".

The two basic motives in Russell's epistemology thus reveal a parallelism which diagram (F) illustrates.

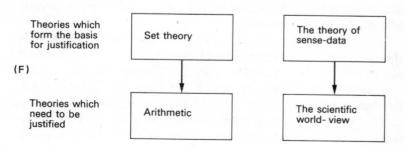

Actually the connection between Russell's theory of arithmetic and his theory of what can be roughly called the scientific view of the world is even closer than this diagram indicates. When Russell tries to justify common sense and science on the basis of sense-data, he makes extensive use of set-theoretical considerations. The "invasion" of philosophy by set theory, commenced in Frege's interpretation of arithmetic, is continued in Russell with its application to the issue of our knowledge of the external world.

If one looks for very certain knowledge, as Russell does, then one ought, it might seem, to be resigned to leaving many questions unanswered, and especially such large philosophical questions as that of "the scope and limits of knowlege", or that of "mind and matter". But besides his sceptical-dogmatic desire for certainty, Russell also had a passionate wish to see, as it were, the nature of things, to solve the riddles of existence, and to arrive at a world-view. In this respect he is an intellectual contemporary of the system-builders of the seventeenth century. The picture, or pictures, of the world which he sketched in *Our Knowledge of the External World* (1914), *The Analysis of Mind* (1921), and *The Analysis of Matter* (1927), were in part motivated by logical and epistemological considerations. His position has similarities to Berkeley's "immaterialism" as well as to Leibniz's monadology, and it is far from unambiguous. The view expounded in the 1927 book was also influenced by modern physics, especially Einstein's theory of relativity.

Russell was one of the most prolific philosophical authors of our time. He presented his philosophical problems and convictions in book after book for almost seventy years. His position underwent many changes during these years, but the changes are not accounted for merely by his longevity. Even within the same book, he often plays off mutually incompatible ideas against each other. This contributes to making many of his works so stimulating and enriching, but also makes it difficult to describe his ideas in a brief and accurate manner. Russell's writings are justly praised for their brilliance, but most of them are scarcely systematic, and their renowned "clarity" is often only on the literary surface. It is interesting to compare Russell's writings from this perspective with, for example, Bolzano's or Frege's or—why not?—the writings of a subtle scholastic like William of Ockham. While Russell often stimulates, not to say exhilarates, the reader, these other authors require tenacity from him. But it is often much easier to see clearly what the latter have to say, than to see clearly what Russell is saying.

Today it is not difficult to see what is problematic in Russell's philosophical positions. However, this ought not to overshadow the indubitable fact that Russell is one of the pioneers in the development of modern philosophy. He is one of the great logicians, taking a place alongside such masters as Aristotle, Leibniz, Boole, Frege, and Hilbert. His combination of a logico-mathematical interest with an interest in more conventional philosophical questions, has effectively contributed to raising the logical level of philosophy. Russell is the philosopher who gave logic its enormous prestige among modern philosophers—and he lived long enough to warn against the advent of a new scholasticism. Not least, his lively, ironic rationalism has helped to disperse many mists of pretentious profundity.

Together with his colleague in Cambridge, George Edward Moore (1873–1958), Russell inspired the so-called Cambridge School of Analysis, which flourished during the first two or three decades of the twentieth century. Among the members of the school were Charlie Dunbar Broad (1887–1971), Frank Plumpton Ramsey (1903–30), Lizzie Susan Stebbing (1885–1943), John Wisdom (1904), and Max Black (1909); the last two have in later years abandoned the logico-analytical programme which was formulated by Russell and Moore. The logician W. E. Johnson (1858–1931), the philosopher of science Norman Campbell (1880), and the economist John Maynard Keynes (1883–1946—in his book *A Treatise on Probability,* 1921) stood close to the Cambridge school, as did the young Wittgenstein, the author of *Tractatus Logico-Philosophicus.* Also the co-author of *Principia Mathematica*, the mathematician and philosopher Alfred North Whitehead (1861–1947), shared in an early phase of his career some of the views and ambitions of the Cambridge school.

In what follows only some glimpses of Russell's philosophical thought can be presented. In section 17 I shall present some of his fundamental ontological and semantical ideas, which have left their imprint on his logicistic interpretation of arithmetic as well as on his general world view. A line of thought from the theory of types will be sketched here. A complete presentation of Russell's logicistic interpretation of arithmetic is superfluous, since the reader has already become acquainted with Frege's interpretation, to which Russell's is very similar. In section 18, I will be concerned with some features of Russell's interpretation which depend on the difference between his logic and Frege's. In sections 19 and 20, I shall present some of Russell's ideas concerning a "logically perfect" language. Section 19 deals with Russell's position on the semantical questions which were brought to the fore through Frege's doctrine of "sense" and "reference", a position which lies at the basis of Russell's ideas about a logically perfect language. These ideas themselves are discussed in section 20. Section 21 tries to present that problem concerning the "external world" which Russell wished to solve, and then section 22 sketches his solution or solutions.

17. INDIVIDUALS AND SETS

The categories which play the most prominent role in Russell's repeated attempts to make an inventory of the universe are: (a) individuals, or particulars; (b) propositional functions; (c) sets and other "extensions"; (d) propositions; (e) facts.

What an *individual* in Russell's sense is I will presently discuss more fully. The word *proposition* is used by Russell in a rather ambiguous way. Often he means by it a sentence. But often the term as used by Russell invites an interpretation which makes it more or less synonymous with Bolzano's "proposition-in-itself" and Frege's "thought". To the proposition "Socrates is mortal" there corresponds the *propositional function* 'x is mortal'. To the proposition "Plato was a pupil of Socrates" corresponds the propositional function 'x was a student of y', and so on. Russell's propositional functions share the ambiguous nature of his propositions. If the proposition "Socrates is mortal" is identified with the sentence, i.e. the series of words: "Socrates", "is", and "mortal", then the propositional function 'x is mortal', derived from it by substituting x for Socrates, must reasonably be identified with the sentence schema, made up of the expressions "x", "is", and "mortal". If, on the other hand, the Russellian proposition is taken to be something like Bolzano's proposition-in-itself, then the propositional function may be thought of as a genuine function, taking propositions as its values.

Sentences and sentence schemata are clearly not kinds of entities that deserve to be made into fundamental ontological categories. To the extent that propositions and propositional functions represent such categories in Russell's thought, the non-linguistic interpretation of them appears to be the most reasonable. To the propositional function 'x is mortal' corresponds the *set* or *class* of all those entities which satisfy the function, that is the set of all mortal beings. To the propositional function 'x was a pupil of y' corresponds analogously in Russell's system the extensional relation between an x and a y which consists in x and y satisfying that function. Just as two sets with the same elements are identical, so two extensional relations which obtain between exactly the same objects are identical. Since 'Socrates is mortal' is true, there is the corresponding *fact* that Socrates is mortal.

Russell's view of these categories is complicated and underwent many changes. Sometimes one, sometimes another of these categories is taken to be the more solidly established, the more fundamental. In the first edition of *Principia Mathematica* (1910–13), (b) is taken to be more basic than (c): sets are treated there as convenient mathematical fictions. In the second edition of the same work (1925), Russell is prepared to be satisfied with (c), and to eliminate (b), considered as a category distinct from (c). In an argument which belongs to the motivation for the theory of types, Russell considers (b) to be derived from (d), while also holding that propositions are fictions in the same way that sets are. Sometimes Russell appears to hesitate about the existence of (a). In short, Russell has tried nearly all conceivable possibilities of economizing on categories. In practice Russell presupposes the existence of individuals and sets (as well as other "extensions") both in his logicistic derivation of arithmetic and in his metaphysics. I shall here sketch a simplified version of the hierarchical structure in which Russell's individuals and sets have their places.

A. *Individuals*

At the bottom of the hierarchy are situated what Russell calls individuals. They have much in common with Aristotle's primary substances. An individual, like an Aristotelian primary substance, cannot be predicated of anything. That is to say, the name of an individual cannot occur as a predicate in a meaningful sentence. An individual also resembles an Aristotelian primary substances in being "naturally conceived as a *this* or something intrinsically analogous to a *this*", whatever that can mean.[1] Just like the Aristotelian primary substances, individuals are "completely self-subsistent":

> . . . each particular that there is in the world does not in any way logically depend upon any other particular. Each one might happen to be the whole universe; it is merely an empirical fact that this is not the case. There is no reason why you should not have a universe consisting of one particular and nothing else.[2]

In terms of temporal duration, however, there is a great difference between Aristotle's concept of a substance and Russell's concept of an individual. A substance, according to Aristotle, is a more or less permanent object, which can change its properties from one moment to the next. Russell's individuals are of an opposite nature. When common sense assumes that an identical object persists through the change of its properties, Russell is inclined to say that the change involves a succession of distinct individuals. In any case he thinks of the individuals as very short-lived entities. Objects as complicated as a horse or a tree are examples of Aristotelian primary substances, but would not pass as individuals in Russell's ontology. Russell often ascribes to individuals the elusive property of "absolute simplicity".

[1] Russell, B., *Logic and Knowledge* (London: George Allen & Unwin, 1956), p. 109.
[2] Ibid., p. 202.

What are the entities which, in Russell's opinion, answer to his notion of individuals? A tentative answer to the question is found in his theory of the external world, which we shall study in sections 21 and 22.

B. *Russell's paradox*

There are sets, the members of which are individuals, or—as we could say with a convenient anthropomorphism—we can "form" sets of individuals. We can also form sets of sets of individuals, and so on. Frege assumed that this construction of sets is not subject to any restrictions. Given any condition whatsoever, he assumed that one could form the set whose elements were exactly the entities which satisfy that condition. This assumption, which is implied by a famous axiom in *Grundgesetze der Arithmetik*, was shown to lead to contradictions.

The simplest and most well known of these contradictions is the so-called Russell paradox. One condition which we can formulate is:

(i) The set x is not an element of x.

This is a condition which most familiar sets seem to satisfy. (The set of all men is not an element of itself, for it is not a man, and so on.) According to Frege's assumption, we can now form:

(ii) The set of all sets x such that x satisfies (i).

Let us momentarily call the supposed set R. Assuming that R exists, it obviously holds that:

(iii) A set x is an element of R if and only if x is not an element of x.

If we apply this to the case $x = R$, the result is the contradiction:

(iv) R is an element of R if and only if R is not an element of R.

(iv) is a contradiction, for either R is an element in R, or R is not an element in R, and according to (iv) either alternative implies its opposite.

It might be supposed that the simplest and best reaction in the face of Russell's paradox would be to say: "Obviously I ought to avoid speaking about the set of all sets which are not elements of themselves." We could adopt the general maxim that every time we fall into a contradiction, we must simply avoid that sort of reasoning. But it is obvious that such a tactic, whatever one may otherwise think about it is incompatible with the ideal of a logical calculus which Russell pursues. What he, like Frege, wishes to create is a formalized system of valid logical laws. If a contradiction can be proved within a formalized system, it shows that the system must contain some invalid principles and that therefore the system is not what is sought. The principles of the system must therefore be revised. Russell's revision was the so-called theory of types, which we shall now discuss.

Ideas which could be described as type-theoretical, in a wide sense, are encountered early in the history of philosophy. Plato's dichotomy: perceptual objects/intelligible ideas; as well as Aristotle's related dichotomy: (primary) substance/universals; can be regarded as an embryo of a theory of types. Russell's closest precursor was Frege. While Frege did not make distinctions of type among his "objects" (and he considered all his sets to be "objects"), he in fact made a division into types of his "functions", a division which, as far as it went, had essentially the same structure as Russell's so-called simple theory of types for propositional functions. As a simplification one could say that what is new in Russell's theory of types is that he extends Frege's division of functions into types to a similar division of sets (and other extensions).

C. *A version of the theory of types*

Russell's paradox forces us to the conclusion that there is no set of all sets which are not elements of themselves. The greatly simplified version of Russell's theory of types which I shall now present, implies primarily a very restrictive theory about what sets there are.

Let $\{x, y, z, \ldots\}$ denote the set with the elements x, y, $z, \ldots$. The order in which the elements are named is irrelevant: $\{x, y, z\}$ is, for instance, the same set as $\{y, z, x\}$. The set

$\{x\}$, which has x as its only member, here is taken to be distinct from x. Individuals form the bottom layer in the hierarchy of types. Let us call this "type 0", and suppose that the individuals are: $a, b, c, \ldots$. The next type on the hierarchy, designated "type 1", is constituted by sets of individuals. Examples of such sets are: $\{a\}$, $\{a, b\}$, and $\{a, b, c\}$. Whatever individuals we select, we can combine them into a set of type 1. A special case of this rule is when we select zero individuals. The result then is an empty set $\{\ \}$ or Λ. To show that we have selected zero *individuals*, we can suitably write $\{\ \}_1$ or Λ_1. The third level of the hierarchy is constituted by sets of sets of individuals, which we can designate "type 2". Examples of such sets are: $\{\Lambda_1\}$, $\{\{a\}\}$, $\{\Lambda_1, \{a\}\}$, $\{\{a\}, \{b\}\}$, $\ldots$. Here too we have the rule: whatever sets of type 1 we select, we can combine them into a set of type 2. If we select zero sets of individuals, we get a new empty set Λ_2. While Λ_1 is the result of our "choosing zero *individuals*", Λ_2 is the result of our "choosing zero *sets of individuals*". According to Russell's theory of types Λ_1 and Λ_2 are two distinct empty sets. The fourth level is constituted by sets of sets of sets of individuals, the fifth by sets of sets of sets of sets of individuals, and so on *ad infinitum*.

The theory of types, in the impoverished version here considered, contains the following:

Ontological principle. There are exactly those sets which belong to the hierarchy indicated above.

The radical implications of this principle are best seen through some examples of what the principle denies. From a naïve standpoint, it would seem that we can combine any given entities into a set. From this naïve point of view the following set exists: $\{a, \{b\}\}$, $\{a, \{a, b\}, \{\{e, d\}\}\}$, and so on. But the ontological principle rules out such constructions. Since a belongs to type 0 and $\{b\}$ to type 1, they cannot be combined to form a set. Also, since a belongs to type 0, $\{a, b\}$ to type 1, and $\{\{c, d\}\}$ to type 2, there is no set which has them as its elements.

From another point of view, the present theory of types appears too liberal. What shall we think of the infinite series of empty sets: $\Lambda_1, \Lambda_2, \ldots$ which the theory acknowledges?

Already the supposition of *one* empty set smacks of fiction. The supposition of infinitely many has an air of Hindu mythology.

In addition to its ontological aspect, the theory of types also has a semantical aspect. Corresponding to the hierarchy of individuals and sets there is a parallel hierarchy of symbols, designating these entities. A name of an entity that belongs to type n in the above ontological hierarchy can be assigned to type n in the parallel hierarchy of symbols. Russell thinks that not only names but also variables can be assigned to a given type: a variable can never range over all entities whatsoever, only over all entities of a given type. Besides the ontological principle, the theory of types thus contains the following:

Semantical principle. The sentences, 'A is an element of B', 'A is not an element of B', are meaningful (true or false) if and only if the symbol A is of type n and the symbol B is of type $n + 1$.

The semantical principle is of course a new assumption that is added to the ontological principle. One could adopt the ontological principle without accepting the semantical, but Russell's theory of types contains them both.

The semantical principle, too, has a paradoxical character. Consider, for instance, the set $\{a, b\}$, the elements of which are the individuals a and b. Considering things naïvely, it appears obvious that "what does not occur" in the set is *not* an element thereof. According to this naïve view the statements: $\{a\}$ is not an element of $\{a, b\}$, $\{\{\{c\}\}\}$ is not an element of $\{a, b\}$, are both true and hence meaningful. But since '$\{a\}$' and '$\{a, b\}$' are of type 1 and '$\{\{\{c\}\}\}$' of type 3, the above statements are ruled out as meaningless and illegitimate by the theory of types.

It is clear that Russell's theory of types eliminates paradoxes like Russell's. The ontological principle of the theory of types already implies—independently of the semantical principle—a solution of the paradox. If we dismiss for the moment the semantical principle, we find that every set in the type-theoretical hierarchy satisfies condition (i) (in B). If there were a set like that described in (ii), it would be the set of *all* sets whatsoever. But the ontological principle forbids the formation of such an all-inclusive set. Also, according to the semantical principle, a statement of the form 'A is (is not) an element of A' is always meaningless. All the expressions (i)–(iv) which occur in the derivation of the paradox, are thus meaningless according to the semantical principle.

D. *More about the theory of types*

The theory which I have indicated is only a fragment of the so-called simple theory of types for "extensions" (there are other extensions than sets in Russell's ontology). This simple theory of types is embedded in the much more complicated, so-called ramified, theory of types. Finally, the theory of types for "extensions" is, in the first edition of *Principia Mathematica*, only a corollary of the more fundamental theory of types for propositional functions. In all justice it should be pointed out that this more fundamental theory is perhaps more plausible than the theory of types for sets, which we encountered above. An attempted justification of the fundamental theory of types is put forth by Russell in the so-called *vicious circle principle*, which he formulated in the words: "Whatever involves *all* of a collection must not be one of the collection"; or, conversely: "If, provided a certain collection had a total, it would have members only definable in terms of that total, then the said collection has no total."[3]

Two other principles which he invokes in order to justify the theory, are the principle that "every propositional function presupposes the totality of its values", and the so-called *homogeneity principle* which says that two propositional functions $f(x)$ and $g(x)$ are either defined for exactly the same arguments x or not defined for any common argument x. This arsenal of logico-philosophical principles is in itself rather controversial and besides, hardly constitutes a sufficient basis for the theory of types.

The simple as well as the ramified theory of types has a constructivistic tendency. The entities which belong to the hierarchy of types are generated in stages in both theories

[3] Russell, B. and Whitehead, A. N., *Principia Mathematica* (Cambridge, 1950), vol. I, p. 37.

using logical processes. Whereas in the simple theory a higher type is generated from lower types, in the ramified theory even each distinct type is generated step by step: each type is divided into orders, and the orders are generated from each other. While the simple theory is sufficient to solve logico-set-theoretical paradoxes like Russell's paradox, the ramified theory is needed to solve the so-called semantical paradoxes (paradoxes in which such semantical concepts as "truth" and "designation" play a role). At the same time, the ramified theory leads to great difficulties in the accomplishment of Russell's logistic project of deriving arithmetic. The simple theory, as we shall see, forces Russell to adopt the logically doubtful axiom of infinity. In order to derive arithmetic on the basis of the ramified theory of types, Russell is compelled to introduce yet another artificial axiom, the so-called axiom of reducibility.

Although Russell's theory of types is problematic in many ways, it is also one of the most interesting and fruitful ideas in the philosophy of logic and set theory this century. Important simplifications of the originally very complicated theory have been proposed by Norbert Wiener (1914), Leon Chwistek (1921), and Frank Plumpton Ramsey (1925). One of those who have studied the possibilities of the theory of types with special energy and imagination is the Harvard logician, Willard Van Orman Quine.

18. THE FOUNDATIONS OF ARITHMETIC

Like Frege, Russell wants to show how the non-negative integers, 0, 1, 2, . . . , can be defined in logical terms, and how the theorems of arithmetic are derivable from the laws of logic.[4] It sometimes happens in the history of science that the same ideas are, at about the same time, proposed by several thinkers working independently of each other. The explanation of this lies in the very nature of the development of science. Scientists are participants in a common, constantly growing tradition, which becomes ripe at certain moments for the promugulation of new ideas. An example is the

---

[4] On the basis of the non-negative numbers he can later construct the other kinds of finite numbers. Cantor's transfinite numbers are also covered by Russell's logicism.

similarity in the ideas of Frege and Russell about the foundations of arithmetic. Frege has a strong priority. His *Grundlagen
der Arithmetik* was published in 1884, while Russell stated
his ideas for the first time in *Principles of Mathematics* in
1903. But Russell learned about his precursor only after
having rediscovered logicism. For those who are already
acquainted with Frege's logicistic derivation of arithmetic,
Russell's theory offers little that is really new.

Like Frege, Russell identifies the number n ($n = 0, 1, 2,$
...), with the set K_n of all sets with n elements, and like Frege,
he succeeds in defining the sets K_n in logico-set-theoretical
terms. The most important difference between Russell's
and Frege's definitions depends on the fact that Russell had,
and Frege lacked, a theory of types for sets. This fact created
difficulties for Russell of which Frege was unaware.

Every set, according to the theory of types, has a determined type. Let us suppose that we consider entities of type
t. From them we can form sets of type $t + 1$. The set K_n of
all sets of type $t + 1$ which have exactly n elements thus will
be of type $t + 2$. According to the usual arithmetic the series
of integers $0, 1, 2, \ldots$ is infinite. In order for the identification $n = K_n$ to succeed, the series of sets $K_0, K_1, K_2, \ldots$
must likewise be infinite. Suppose now that there is only a
finite number of individuals, say N. A simple combinatorial
calculation shows that the number of sets of individuals is
2^N, the number of sets of sets of individuals 2^{2^N} and so on.
That the number of individuals is finite, hence implies that
the number of entities of each type is finite. If there were
only a finite number of individuals, then the series of sets
$K_0, K_1, K_2, \ldots$ of our type $t + 2$ would therefore also be
finite. Thus in order for the identification $n = K_n$ to succeed,
it must be postulated that the number of individuals is infinite.
In fact Russell introduced, if only hypothetically, an *axiom
of infinity* to this effect.

One could try to escape the need for the axiom of infinity
by assigning the successive integers to successively higher
types. Even if there were only one individual, there would
be 2 sets of type 1 (sets of individuals), 2^2 sets of type
2, 2^{2^2} sets of type 3, and so on. The total hierarchy of types
thus includes an infinite number of sets. However, the

semantical principle of the theory of types forbids this escape by making it necessary to find room for all the integers within the same type.

With the introduction of the axiom of infinity, Russell seems to have abandoned the hope of deriving arithmetic from purely logical laws. The number of individuals which there are, is according to Russell's own view, an empirical accident. If a truth at all, the axiom of infinity is not a logical truth. The axiom can be formulated in the terminology of *Principia Mathematica*, and if that terminology is taken to be "logical", then the axiom is a proposition of a logical form. But its truth is, in any event, not logical truth—a truth characterized by logical necessity. (Recall at this point the discussion on p. 97 about true propositions of a logical form and such propositions that are logically true.)

The theory of types carries with it yet another oddity in the logicistic interpretation of arithmetic. We may choose any type t as the starting-point for the construction of the sets K_n of type $t + 2$. In this way we get not *one* but an *infinite number* of distinct systems of integers, systems which are all more alike than identical twins. Only their type-indices distinguish them. So Russell, who wanted to find *one* logical analysis of arithmetic, had infinitely many alternative analyses on his hands.

19. SENSE AND REFERENCE

A. *Russell and Frege*

Expressions which purport to name or designate something, are, it seems, of four different varieties which can be illustrated by the following four expressions:

(I)   The eldest son of the English Queen,
(II) The eldest son of the Dutch Queen,
(III) Peter,
(IV) Apollo.

Expression (I) designates Prince Charles of England, and simultaneously characterizes him from a certain point of view. Expression (II) also contains a characterization, but one which does not apply to anything, since Queen Juliana has no son. Expressions (I) and (II) are composed in a certain way of parts which have an independent meaning. It is through their mode of composition that (I) and (II) characterize or describe. The name (III), used of a definite person, designates the person in question, but at least *prima facie* does not characterize him in any way. The mythological name (IV) seems *prima facie* neither to characterize, nor, since Apollo does not exist, to designate. In contradistinction to expressions like (I) and (II), expressions like (III) and (IV) are not composed of parts with an independent meaning.

In his theory of sense and reference, Frege adopted a definite view concerning these four categories. He took expressions of sorts (III) and (IV) to have the same semantical nature as expressions of sorts (I) and (II). "Peter" presumably has the same meaning as "Brown's eldest son" or perhaps simply "the one who is called Peter". "Apollo" can be taken to have the same meaning as "the god who was worshipped in Delphi" or something similar. As we have seen, however, Frege did not admit expressions of sorts (II) and (IV) into a correct scientific language. All correct designations have, according to Frege, a double semantical function. They have a *sense* whereby they somehow characterize what they designate, and they have a *reference* in so far as the characterization actually applies to something.

Russell's semantical ideas move in a completely different direction. Expressions of the (IV) variety, according to Russell, are mostly but not always abbreviations of expressions of sort (I). For Frege, all expressions that designate an object were "proper names". Russell applies this term (sometimes "genuine proper name", "logically proper name", "proper name from a logical point of view"), only to those expressions of kind (III) which are not abbreviations for expressions of variety (I). In Russell's terminology, a proper name is an expression which actually designates some object, but which does not contain any parts with an independent meaning, and which is not synonymous with (or an abbreviation of) an expression which has such parts. Some although not most expressions of type (III) are thus proper names in this special sense, according to Russell.

Russell's ideas differ most sharply from Frege's concerning

varieties (I) and (II). I shall try to codify these ideas in some brief theses:

(A) Every indicative sentence in which a designation of sort (I) or (II) occurs, is synonymous with an indicative sentence which does not contain any such designation.

(B) In a logically perfect language no indicative sentence which contains a designation of variety (I) or (II) occurs other than as an abbreviation for an indicative sentence which does not contain any such designation.

In keeping with Russell's use of the term "proper name", (B) gives rise to the corollary:

(C) In a logically perfect language, every designation of an object is either a logically proper name or an element in a system of abbreviations.

In contrast to Frege, Russell never endeavoured to develop a consistent philosophical vocabulary. If one took the liberty of using Frege's vocabulary to express Russell's view, one could say:

(D) In a logically perfect language, all designations which are not elements of a system of abbreviations have a "reference" without having any "sense".

Russell often writes that logically proper names "directly refer" to that which they designate, and here "directly" can be construed as indicating that Frege's "sense", the factor intermediate between the sign and the signified, is missing.

B. *The motivation for thesis (A)*

Theses (B)–(D) are associated with the notion of a logically perfect language, which we shall study more closely in section 20. To support them, Russell sometimes employs the so-called principle of acquaintance, one of his postulated principles which has its roots in classical British empiricism. We shall not go into Russell's arguments for the very vague and speculative theses (B)–(D), but we shall see how Russell justifies (A).

In order to give a systematic proof of (A), one would have to make a survey of all the expressions of types (I) and (II) which may occur in language, and of all the types of indicative sentences in which they can occur. Such a survey would be very difficult if the concern were with a natural language like English or Swedish. Russell has not attempted to achieve it. He has limited himself to trying to establish (A) for certain important types of expressions of the kinds (I) and (II). Best known is his theory of so-called definite descriptions.

A *definite description* is an expression of the form:

(i) That which has the property (or satisfies the condition) F.

An indicative sentence in which (i) occurs can often be put into the following form:

(ii) That which has property F has property G.

A sentence like (ii) is true, according to Russell, if and only if the following sentence is true:

(iii) There is some x which fulfils the three conditions: (1) x has property F, (2) nothing but x has property F, (3) x has property G.

He claims that (ii) and (iii) are synonymous.[5]

The validity for natural languages or Russell's analysis has been questioned in recent years by several writers. They have stressed that in many cases we take (iii) to be false

---

[5] Besides sentence of type (ii), Russell also considers sentences of type:

(1)   That which has F exists,

or:

(1') There is such a thing as that which has F.

He takes them to be synonymous with:

(2)   There is some x which fulfils conditions (1) and (2) of (iii) above.

Russell's treatement of definite descriptions gives rise to a well-known problem of "scope". In translating a sentence of the form:

(3)   ... ((ii)) ... ,

we are, according to Russell's recipe, at a loss, without further instructions, to know whether (3) goes into

(4)   ... ((iii)) ...

or into:

(5)   There is some x which fulfils the conditions: (a) x has F, (b) nothing but x has F, (c) ... (x has property G). ...

Russell's solution amounts to the decision that (3) must be made to contain the necessary instruction.

without thereby accepting the negation of (ii) as true. We know, for instance, that the following special case of (iii) is incorrect:

(iv) There is some *x* which fulfils the condition: (1) *x* is presently a king of France, (2) nothing but *x* is a king of France, (3) *x* is bald.

But few of us would therefore agree to accept as a historical truth:

(v) The present king of France is not bald.

We would perhaps rather say, with Frege, that (v) has a sense in which we can understand, but that it lacks truth-value, i.e. that it is neither true nor false.[6]

In the course of this discussion Russell employs two technical expressions which have become widely used. If (ii) and (iii) are stated as above, the definition: (ii) = df (iii); which he recommends, is called a *contextual definition* of (i) since the *definiendum* is not (i) alone but an entire context (an entire sentence) in which (i) occurs as a proper part. (i) he calls an *incomplete symbol*, since the definition in question provides a sense, not for (i) itself, but for an entire context in which (i) occurs. That certain symbols in our language are "incomplete" in this sense and therefore require "contextual definitions", Russell considered to be one of his most important philosophical discoveries .

20. THE IDEA OF A LOGICALLY PERFECT LANGUAGE AND
THE PHILOSOPHY OF LOGICAL ATOMISM

Although the symbolic language of *Principia Mathematica* was primarily created for the needs of mathematics, it also claims a kind of universality. It was Russell's intention that every meaningful statement and every meaningful theory should be expressible in that language, provided that it was enriched with those special symbols which the statement

[6] In addition to so-called definite descriptions, Russell has paid special attention to *class* (set) *descriptions* like:

(vii) The set of all objects which have the property *F*.

It would lead too far here to discuss the manner in which Russell tries to validate (A) with regard to (vi).

or theory might call for. The claim of *Principia Mathematica* to universality, is intimately related to, but not identical with, the metaphysical position which Russell developed during the 1910s and 1920s, and which he called the philosophy of logical atomism. Russell varied the ideas which constitute this philosophy in many ways in the course of the years. No short account can do justice to the diversity of his thought. However, one pattern of thought is the following.

A. *The idea of a logically perfect language*

To every assertion there corresponds a fact, which either verifies or falsifies the assertion. "Gangtuk lies in Sikkim" is verified by the fact that Gantuk lies in Sikkim. "Jagganath Puri lies in Bengal" is falsified by the fact that Jagganath Puri does not lie in Bengal. A fact is always something complex, it always has certain constituents or parts. A fact like, for example, "*a* has the property *F*" has, we may suppose, *a* and *F* as parts. From the structure of the sentence one cannot always directly read off the constituents of the corresponding fact. The sentence:

(i)   Nothing frightens me,

might give the impression that "nothing" is a constituent of the corresponding fact; compare the speculation of German and French existentialists about "*das Nichts*", "*le néant*". But (i) expresses the same as:

(ii)   There is not anything which frightens me,

and from (ii) one sees that the first impression is wrong.

According to Russell, philosophy as logical analysis ought to distinguish the constituents which enter into facts, and to classify the sorts of facts into which given constituents can enter. Such an analysis can be more or less complete. His ideal was to arrive at the absolutely simple constituents, the "logical atoms" of which facts are ultimately composed. Russell believed that the analytical task can best be fulfilled by developing a language in which the composition of the sentence mirrors the composition of the corresponding facts. A language of this sort would be a "logically perfect language" (an ideal language). If we ignore the abbreviations which one might, for reasons of convenience, wish to introduce into the logically perfect language, one of the demands which Russell makes of this language can be formulated as follows:

I. In the logically perfect language a name (sentence) A is composed of names $B, C, \ldots$, if and only if what is named (expressed) by A is composed of what is named by $B, C, \ldots$.

A special case of I is:

I'. In the logically perfect language a name is simple (a "logically proper name") if and only if what is named is a simple entity.

Russell's interest in logical analysis in this sense has several different motives. One is the Socratic desire to eliminate, by means of analysis, linguistically motivated mistakes like the puzzle concerning "nothing" mentioned above. Another reason is metaphysical: by means of analysis, Russell wants to gain an insight into the ultimate structure of reality. Russell's position here has an obvious similarity to that of Leibniz.

B. *The logical atom*

On page 131, I referred to Russell's assumption:

II. All individuals are simple.

Russell has never intelligibly clarified how he arrived at this opinion. One remembers that Aristotle had already called the primary substances, the ancestors of Russell's individuals, "atoms". But in that expression, Aristotle did not include the simplicity which Russell postulates. II is in fact a consequence of Russell's ideas about a logically perfect language, and it could be that Russell arrived at II by this route. A constituent is simple if the symbol which indicated it in the logically perfect language is simple. According to thesis (C) in section 19—if we ignore abbreviations—every symbol in the logically perfect language that designates, is a simple proper name. Thus every constituent of the facts that can be expressed in that language must be simple, and hence every individual is simple if, as Russell usually thinks, individuals are constituents.

One might object to this hypothetical reconstruction of Russell's argument that the assumed inference leads to a much stronger conclusion than I, namely:

III.   Every entity in the type-theoretical hierarchy is simple.

However, III is, in fact, an assertion which Russell, the logical atomist, made. Is there then nothing complex? During his period of logical atomism Russell often affirmed:

IV.   Facts, and only facts, are complex.

Assertions II–IV are, to say the least, paradoxical. My typewriter, for instance, is obviously composed of many parts. But the typewriter is not a fact in Russell's sense, i.e. something which is expressible by means of an indicative sentence. Thus it must belong to the type hierarchy, and according to III it must be simple. In *The Philosophy of Logical Atomism* (1918), Russell says that he does not believe that there are complex objects (such as my typewriter seems to be). Another claim is that the complex always belongs to another and higher type than the parts of which it is composed. How should this be interpreted? I suppose that during the time when he was a logical atomist, Russell might have explained his position as follows (I am putting words into Russell's mouth).

'Simple' and 'complex' are ambiguous. They have both a strict and a figurative meaning. In the former sense, which is of primary interest to the logical atomist, only simple entities exist—with the exception of facts. In the figurative sense, the typewriter can be said to be complex. But the following explanation is more accurate. Suppose that what, from one point of view, are the parts of the typewriter, belong to type n. Then the typewriter ought to be taken to be the set of these parts, and its type will be $n + 1$. This is just as in geometry. In ordinary language we say that a line is "composed" of the points which lie on it. But in geometry we consider the line to be rather the set of those points. If a point is of type *m*, then the line is of type $m + 1$. In the strict meaning, the set 'the typewriter' is just as simple as its elements.

The picture of the universe provided by logical atomism is almost as strange as Parmenides' doctrine of Being. For Russell, as for Parmenides, a kind of logical analysis is that razor's edge which leads us past illusions into the secrets of existence. The mystical pull in logical atomism is hardly less pronounced than in Parmenides' philosophy. The beginnings of logical atomism are present in Russell's writings from the first decade of the century. It crystallized during his association with Wittgenstein in the second decade. In *Tractatus Logico-Philosophicus* (1921), Wittgenstein stated his own version of logical atomism, and accentuated its mystical aspect through his mode of presentation. Certain ideas of logical atomism reappear also in Carnap's *Der logische Aufbau der Welt* (1928).

C. *The principle of acquaintance*

If we wish to find that logically perfect formulation which is a translation of a given sentence of our ordinary language, we must of course find the constituents of the fact expressed by the sentence. How should we go about finding them? Russell proposes a psychological-semantical principle which he calls *the principle of acquaintance* and which limits the area which we have to search. One of his formulations of the principle reads: "Every proposition which we can understand must be composed wholly of constituents with which we are acquainted."[7] I believe that the principle can be restated as follows without distortion of Russell's meaning:

V. If we understand the meaning of a sentence, then we must have direct acquaintance with all the constituents of the fact which correspond to the sentence.

In Russell's view, which at this point is close to that of classical British empiricism, there is very little with which we are directly acquainted. In dreams, fantasies, and hallucinations we are aware of various "images". In sense-perception we are aware of sense-data ("sensations", "percepts"). During his earlier, more Platonistic period, Russell also maintained

[7] Russell, B., *The Problems of Philosophy* (Oxford, 1948), p. 58.

that in conceptual thought we are immediately aware of universals. But we do *not* have direct awareness of material objects, or generally of anything that belongs to the world of natural science. We do *not* have direct awareness of other men, either of their bodies or of their minds. There are some memories, which make us directly aware of a fragment of the past, but these fragments are vanishingly small compared to the great bulk of the past of which we are not aware. According to Russell, that of which we are directly aware largely coincides with the world of "perceptions", which, according to Hume, constitutes the whole range of our consciousness.

Together with Russell's assumptions about what we are and are not directly aware of, the principle of acquaintance acquires very far-reaching consequences. Consider the sentence "London is in England." Neither London nor England is a constituent of the fact which corresponds to the sentence. Or, consider "Brutus murdered Caesar." Neither Brutus nor Caesar belongs to those entities of which we are directly aware, and thus neither of them is a constituent of the fact corresponding to the sentence. And so on. Whatever we seemingly talk about, the constituents of the facts that we affirm and deny, are never anything beyond what occurs in our restricted world of private experience. If we choose to say that the constituents of the facts which correspond to our sentences are what we actually "talk about", then we must also say that we are always talking about things entirely distinct from those we believe we are talking about. To know what we are actually talking about becomes an enormously difficult problem, which only specialists in logic, metaphysics, and epistemology have a chance to solve.

Does ordinary language at all contain words or expressions which designate constituents in the facts which we affirm or deny? Russell is doubtful about the possibility of finding such expressions. The best chance of representing an individual constituent belongs to the pronouns "this" and "that", when employed to indicate elements of which we have a direct present experience. Names of perceived qualities like "red", "green", and so on, are also considered by Russell to represent constituents of the facts.

Every name in a sentence of the logically perfect language

ought to indicate a (simple) constituent of the fact which corresponds to the sentence. On the strength of the principle of acquaintance, the following must hold:

VI. Every name in the logically perfect language designates an entity with which the user of the language is directly acquainted.

The principle of acquaintance V and its corollary VI would have catastrophic consequences if Russell had not limited their application to those symbols in the logically perfect language which are proper names of entities. In a logically perfect language, Russell allows variables which range over all entities of a certain kind, even if we are not directly acquainted with each one of these entities. Thus, the variables become the linguistic tools with whose help we can speak about entities beyond our private world of experience. For instance, I can meaningfully say:

(iii) There is an x such that x does not belong to my private experience,

In which x is a variable representing individuals. In more ordinary language, (iii) becomes:

(iv) There is an individual which does not belong to my private experience.

(iii) is not only meaningful, but, Russell would say, probably true. If I let a or "this" be the name for a given individual, then I can also meaningfully say:

(v) I do not directly experience a (this).

But, according to the principle of acquaintance, (v) can never be true. The individual a is a constituent of the fact which corresponds to (v) assuming that (v) is a logically perfect sentence, and according to the principle of acquaintance I then have direct acquaintance with a. In contrast to (iii), an assertion like (v) is always false. In Russell's semantics, it is only by means of variables that, in the logically perfect language, we can talk about the "transcendent".[8]

[8] Russell stressed especially that sentences involving definite descriptions can be known by us to be true although we are not acquainted with the entities

21. THE PROBLEM OF THE EXTERNAL WORLD

In *The Problems of Philosophy* (1912), Russell asks questions such as: Is there an external world, and if so what is it like? Does matter exist, and if so what is its nature? From *Our Knowledge of the External World* (1914) on, his question is gradually recast in the direction of the following problem.

Like his precursor Berkeley, Russell accepts science and common sense as providing a correct picture of the external world. When common sense maintains for instance, "There is a table in the room", this is something which philosophy should not question. When science says: "The speed of light is about 300,000 km/second", that is also something which philosophers ought to take for granted. The radically sceptical arguments which Russell so often puts forth, do not have the aim of making us doubt the essential correctness of the world picture of science, but rather of making us realize how difficult it is to interpret that picture philosophically. I think it can be said that Russell, like Berkeley, accepts the correctness, in principle, of those sentences (called "*m*-sentences" in Vol. I, Ch. VI, § 27) which common sense and science hold to be true. His problem is: How can one give a philosophically adequate analysis of these sentences?

In order to give this question a clear sense, one must clarify those conditions which a philosophically adequate analysis should fulfil. In this section we shall study what Russell, explicitly or implicitly, thought on this matter. One could say that Russell's solution to the problem of the external world consists of sketching, admittedly very vaguely, a certain language which could be called the language of analysis, and of supplying it with a series of definitions of the form:

$$A = \mathrm{df}\ B,$$

where the *definiendum* A is an expression occurring in the *m*-sentences, and the *definiens* B is an expression from the language of analysis. From one point of view, these definitions are merely rules of abbreviation which make it possible to

---

described. They are knowable just because, upon analysis, variables are seen to play a vital role in them. "Knowledge by description", as Russell says, extends further than "knowledge by acquaintance".

express assertions in the language of analysis in a more concise manner. But, from another point of view, they are rules for the philosophical translation of *m*-sentences into the language of analysis. Looking at Russell's project in this way, we can say that he would have completely presented this solution only if he had first explained the language of analysis, and second provided all the translation rules (definitions) required to translate the *m*-sentences into this language.

Now we can also see which demands could be placed *a priori* on a solution of Russell's problem. First, one could obviously put demands upon the language of analysis itself, and obviously Russell himself did so. The clarity which Russell sought, he would not consider himself to have achieved by means of a translation into any language whatsoever. The language of analysis must in itself have certain philosophically valuable characteristics. Second, one can place demands upon the method of translation. Translations can have many different types and degrees of faithfulness. Obviously, Russell expects some specific kind of fidelity from his translations.

At the same time that Russell (in the 1910s) first conceived of his theory of the external world, he also developed his ideas about a logically perfect language (cf. section 20). Occasionally he entertains the thought that the language of analysis should be a logically perfect language. But he hardly ever seriously maintained that he succeeded in realizing that goal. Occasionally Russell seems to think that a formulation can be said to be "logically more perfect" than another, without being "logically perfect" in the absolute sense. (The analysis of a complex can be more or less complete. Those parts of the complex which are distinguished at a given stage of analysis, can themselves be complex and analysable. The logically more perfect formulation would correspond to a more complete analysis.) A demand which Russell puts on the language of analysis should thus be:

I. The language of analysis shall be as logically perfect as possible.

By a "minimum vocabulary" for a given theory Russell means a vocabulary, a conceptual apparatus, which is as meagre as possible (contains as few terms, concepts, as possible), but which is nevertheless sufficient to express all that one wishes to say in the theory. When Russell and Whitehead chose the undefined terms for *Principia Mathematica*, they strove for this kind of minimum vocabulary for logic—even though the words "minimum vocabulary" first occur much later in Russell's writings. A corresponding demand is placed on the language of analysis:

II. The language of analysis shall contain a minimum of undefined terms (shall be based on a "minimum vocabulary").

When, in the 1910s, Russell turned his interest to the problems of traditional epistemology, he had just completed *Principia Mathematica*. The conceptual scheme and formal apparatus of *Principia Mathematica* are the patterns which constantly shine through his epistemological considerations. Although Russell never says so in so many words, it seems that he felt that a formalization of the language of analysis could be obtained if one completed the language of *Principia Mathematica* in a suitable manner.

Russell often points to Ockham's razor as the principle which guided him in his study of the epistemological problem of the external world. He usually quotes Ockham's razor in the following formulation (not necessarily an authentic one): *"Entia non sunt praeter necessitatem multiplicanda"* (one ought not multiply entities beyond what is necessary). The entities which Ockham himself was especially interested in shaving off were Platonic–Aristotelian universals. Russell customarily uses the razor in an almost opposite way. In practice, Ockham's maxim means for Russell that one ought to give the status of "individual" to as few entities as possible, while assigning as many kinds of entities as possible to higher levels in the type-theoretical hierarchy.

Suppose that a certain number of individuals (in the sense of the theory of types) are given to us: say $a, b, c, \ldots$. The more extra individuals which we suppose to exist, the greater risk we run, according to Russell's view, of making a mistake. On the other hand, Russell seems to think that the existence of the given individuals, $a, b, c, \ldots$ automatically guarantees the existence of all sets of individuals, all sets of sets of individuals, and so on indefinitely, that are postulated in the theory of types. By the very fact that a certain domain of individuals is given to us, the entire type-theoretical hierarchy which rests on it is thus considered given in an unproblematic way.[9] If one wishes to economize within the theory of types, there is for Russell only one point at which one can economize, and that is at the point of individuals. The choice of a domain of individuals determines the choice of an entire hierarchy. As used by Russell, Ockham's razor thus implies:

III. The domain of individuals (in the sense of the theory of types) of the language of analysis ought to be as small as possible.

Russell formulated a maxim which he sometimes seems to consider equivalent to Ockham's razor, and which we can call the *principle of logical construction*: "Wherever possible, substitute constructions out of known entities for inference to unknown entities."[10] Russell considered himself to have used this principle already in *Principia Mathematica*, when he interpreted arithmetic as a theory about certain sets of sets. If logicism is taken to be an application of the principle of logical construction, the existence of these sets is regarded as better known than the existence of the integers in themselves. In the light of this and similar uses of the principle, I believe that it can be reformulated as follows.

Suppose that there are two theories (or systems of presumably true sentences) T and T'. Suppose that T' appears to be a certain (or at least more certain) theory which concerns only "known entities". Suppose that T deals with entities which are "unknown" (or at least less certainly known), and that T appears prima facie as an (uncertain, thus not demonstrative) "inference" from T'. In this case, one ought, if possible, to deduce T from T' by means of definitions ("constructions"). In *Principia Mathematica* Russell is inclined to

[9] This is a simplification of Russell's complicated point of view. The sets (and other extensions) are sometimes treated by Russell as fictions which make it possible for us to state, in a short form, complicated assertions about so-called propositional functions. Further, on the question of propositional functions, Russell at different times tried all conceivable standpoints: Platonism, constructivism, and nominalism. But the abbreviated discussions in the text seem to me to present the attitude which Russell exhibits when he employs the theory of types in his epistemological arguments.

[10] Russell, B., *Logic and Knowledge*, p. 326.

think that arithmetic (*T*) and the theory of sets (*T'*) are such a pair of theories.

In keeping with the tradition of British empiricism, Russell considers material objects to be "unknown entities", and our beliefs about them to be (uncertain, non-demonstrative) "inferences" from what we directly experience in perception, i.e. sense-data. Thus the theory *T* is here the picture of the physical world accepted by common sense and science, while *T'* is a theory or a system of assertions about sense-data and other entities epistemologically on a par with them. For the problem of the external world, the principle of logical construction thus implies the methodological demand that *this* theory *T* ought to be reduced, through a system of definitions ("constructions") to *this* theory *T'*. Summing up, we can say:

IV. The realm of individuals of the language of analysis ought to include only sense-data and possibly some other entities epistemologically on a par with sense-data.

The principle of logical construction has a further aspect. Material objects are in themselves "unknown entities", which we infer in a problematic way. By logically "constructing" them from "known entities" their problematic character is eliminated. Russell thus seems to think:

V. The uncertainty which adheres to the translation *S'*, in the language of analysis, of an *m*-sentence *S*, ought, if possible, to be less than the uncertainty which attaches to *S* in itself.

Until now we have almost exclusively studied the demands which Russell puts (explicitly or implicitly) on the language of analysis. Another matter is the demands he places on his method of translation. On this point Russell says so little that he also forces the historian of philosophy into silence. I sometimes have the impression that he thought the translation and the translated should express the "same fact" or have the "same meaning". But just as often it seems as though he had some unspecified, very much weaker demand in mind.

22. NEUTRAL MONISM

A. *Material objects as sets of 'aspects'*

Russell's logicistic interpretation of arithmetic is guided by the idea that the natural number n can be identified with the set of all sets with exactly n elements. Russell's neutral monism is inspired by an analogous idea. Let us suppose that a number of persons stand looking at a statue. Each one experiences something which Russell calls an "aspect" of the statue. If the persons are grouped about the statue at various distances from it, all these aspects are distinct from each other. The relation between the immediately experienced aspect and the statue itself offers all those problems which have been discussed in epistemology since antiquity. Berkeley held that one could solve these problems only by identifying the statue with the set of its aspects. This identification is the basic idea also in Russell's neutral monism.

On the basis of the epistemological presuppositions which Russell makes, this basic idea can, or rather must, be further specified. According to Russell, we get to know about the experiences of other persons only through physical symptoms: the sounds, expressions, and gestures they make, what they say or write, and so on. Knowledge of other minds thus is based on observation of phenomena of a material character. What aspects of the statue other observers may experience, is, according to Russell's epistemology, as problematic as the nature of the statue itself. To identify the statue with the set of all the aspects which observers experience cannot, therefore be the final solution to the problem of the external world. The ideal for Russell becomes to identify the statue with the set of those aspects of the statue which Russell himself observes.[11] But this ideal meets great, if not insurmountable, difficulties. Russell's neutral monism in its different forms is a compromise: he retains the ideal as long as possible without getting obviously stuck in the difficulties.

---

[11] Russell considers the statue, as a continuant, to be a set of successive momentary objects. He identifies a momentary object with the set of its aspects. The statue hence becomes a set of sets of aspects. This, and other similar refinements of the argument, which I ignore, can be supplied by the reader in the following discussion.

B. *Russell facing Berkeley's problem*

In order that the basic idea of Russell's theory should be workable, obviously certain conditions must be fulfilled. *One* of them is this:

If m and m' are two distinct material objects:

$$m \neq m'$$

and if K_m is the set of the aspects of m, and $K_{m'}$ the set of the aspects of m', then we can make the identifications:

$$m = K_m, m' = K_{m'},$$

only if K_m and $K_{m'}$ are two distinct sets, i.e.:

$$K_m \neq K_{m'}.$$

If K_m contains only those aspects which were experienced by Russell, then this condition is fulfilled only in a few exceptional cases. Those material objects which Russell ever had an opportunity to observe were a vanishingly small minority of all the material objects there are in the universe. Thus, for the majority of material objects m, it follows that K_m is an empty set. But there is only one empty set (of a given type, according to the theory of types). If only the aspects experienced by Russell are taken into account, it follows that in most cases $K_m = K_{m'} =$ the empty set, although $m \neq m'$.

To avoid this difficulty, Russell deserts his ideal. He includes in K_m all the aspects of m which are experienced by any person or sentient being, including, I should think, animals and residents of Mars (if such exist). *As far as we know*, even this drastic step is not sufficient. Many material objects are not observed, *to the best of our knowledge*, by any sentient being whatsoever. The difficulty to be overcome is still there.

Berkeley could avoid the difficulty in a very convenient manner by supposing that God always perceives everything, and by letting K_m also contain those aspects of m which only God perceives. This way out is closed to the atheist Russell. However, in *Our Knowledge of the External World* (1914) he resorts to a thought which is equally bold. While Berkeley, in order to maintain the equation

(i) $m = K_m$,

makes use of aspects which are perceived, not by residents of the Earth or Mars, but by God, Russell, for the same purpose, resorts in 1914 to aspects which are experienced—by no one! Even if no one looks at the statue, it is a fact that *if* someone *were* to place himself in a certain position *vis-à-vis* the statue, then he *would* experience certain aspects of the statue. Russell expresses this as follows: even when no one is looking at the statue, it is the source of certain "merely possible" aspects. He supposes, at least hypothetically, that these merely possible aspects do exist in addition to the "actual aspects", i.e. the aspects which are actually experienced by someone. Russell then interprets K_m to be the set of all the aspects of m, merely possible as well as actual.

Independently of what view we take of the hypothesis about the existence of merely possible aspects, we find that Russell misses the point here in precisely the same way that Berkeley did. Equation (i) ought to clarify how I can know about m although I cannot know anything but the aspects of m which I myself experience. If K_m is made to contain other elements than the aspects of m which I experience, then (i) obviously fails in its purpose.

C. *Material objects as sets of events*

The postulate of the existence of merely possible aspects, presented in 1914, is replaced by another postulate in *The Analysis of Matter* (1927). Even if no one looks at the statue, it is the source of an enormously complicated system of events in its environment. For instance, light rays are emitted by the statue. The passage of a light ray through a point in the environment is an event, or at least a part of an event. Russell now supposes, at least hypothetically, that all these events have a "real" existence. The aspects of the statue which sentient beings perceive are only a special kind of such events, according to his new terminology. (What character-izes an "event " in Russell's ontology, is that it is momentary and occupies a small portion of space.) In 1927 Russell includes in the set K_m, with which he identifies the material object m, all those events which have their source in m; this is the same sense in which the statue is the source of those aspects which Russell experiences, or is the source of any emitted light ray's passage through a point in its environment. Russell's position in 1927 is an attempt to bring neutral monism closer to the modern physicist's picture of the universe as a system of point-events in four-dimensional space–time. If the epistemological presuppositions which Russell embraced in 1914 are retained, the 1927 position appears just as strange as the 1914 position.

The difficulty with which Russell wrestled, and which eventually led him even further away from his original epistemological ideal, has a counterpart in the logicistic interpretation of arithmetic in *Principia Mathematica*. The postulate about the actual existence of the "merely possible" aspects, or of non-experienced events, fulfils the same function in the construction of material objects as the axiom of infinity fulfils in *Principia Mathematica*'s construction of the integers. In an over-confident moment Russell said that postulating certain objects (e.g. numbers, physical objects) has the same advantage over constructing them as theft over honest toil. In the same language one could, *with* the 1914 Russell, raise the objection *against* the 1927 Russell that honest work with stolen goods (the axiom of infinity, the postulates about the existence of the merely possible aspects, or of non-experienced events) is not entirely respectable.

At the same time that Russell's method for the construction of the external world was gradually changing, his epistemological presuppositions underwent a corresponding shift. The epistemologist Russell of 1914 occasionally gives the impression of not condoning the use of uncertain, non-demonstrative inductive inferences. In *Human Knowledge, its Scope and Limits* (1948), on the other hand, the study of induction stands at the centre of Russell's interest. He presents a number of inductive principles which are thought to justify inferences to unknown events from known events. For the epistemologist Russell of 1948 the supposition of non-experienced events is no longer illegitimate. It appears that for the Russell of 1948, the principle of logical construction is not the forceful imperative that it was for the Russell of 1914.

D. *Matter and consciousness*

Up to *The Analysis of Mind* (1921), Russell believed that there was a fundamental difference between mind and matter. The name "neutral monism", which Russell applied to his theory after 1921, indicates the abandoning of that belief. Just as one ought to identify the material object with the set of its aspects, so one ought, according to Russell's neutral monism, to identify a mind (a mind's history) with the set of those contents of consciousness which belong to that mind.

When I look at the statue *m*, I am aware of a certain aspect *a* of *m*. *a* is at once an element in the set K_m which is the statue *m*, and an element in that set which is my mind. With some simplification one can say that for Russell the assertion:

I see the aspect *a* of thing *T*,

is synonymous with the assertion:

a is an element of *I* (or *I*-now), and *a* is an element of *T* (or *T*-now),

where *I* (*I*-now) and *T* (*T*-now) are taken to be sets.[12]

Exactly the same building blocks can occur both in a material object and in a mind. With regard to the distinction between mind and matter, these building blocks are therefore "neutral". Russell thinks of 'aspects' (1914–21) or 'events' (1927), as "neutral stuff" out of which the universe is made. In this way he provided one of the most precise formulations of that concept of mind which has been developed within what I called (Chapter 1, section 2, E) the Hume–Mach tradition in philosophical psychology.

E. *Russell's definitions*

To say, in accordance with Russell's basic idea of 1917, that the material object *m* is identical with the set of all the aspects

[12] A mind, in the sense of a mental "biography", is, for Russell, a set of successive momentary mental states. Each momentary mental state is taken to be the set of its constituents. Strictly speaking, a mental biography is thus, according to Russell, a set of sets of contents of consciousness, or neutral elements. Such technicalities are bypassed here.

of *m*, is of course not to give a definition. It is only a thought, which points the way to be followed in defining the concepts which occur in the *m*-sentences. Russell never achieved a carefully developed system of definitions. But, in several books and articles he did intimate, in principle, how he thought a system of definitions ought to look. Those who are interested are referred especially to C. A. Fritz, jun., *Bertrand Russell's Construction of the External World* (London, 1952).

Although Russell did not formalize his ideas in this field, it is obvious that he constantly had the conceptual apparatus of *Principia Mathematica* in mind. In order to move from the abstract conceptual schema of *Principia Mathematica* to the world-picture of neutral monism, one must give a concrete content to the theory of types. For the formalization of Russell's 1914 position, one can suppose the domain of individuals to contain all the aspects of material objects (the "merely possible" as well as the "actual"). With regard to the 1927 position, one can analogously consider the domain of individuals to include all events. Besides those individuals which are especially relevant for the construction of material objects, Russell acknowledges certain other individuals, for example the "images" which we experience in imagination, dreams, or hallucinations.[13]

While in 1927 Russell includes events of a physical kind in the domain of individuals, he consistently denies that "material objects" in the ordinary sense (atoms, stars, chairs, and houses), can be classified as individuals. In formalizing neutral monism, the vocabulary of *Principia Mathematica* must also be enriched with certain empirical concepts. As primitive concepts of this kind Russell seems inclined to use concepts which describe the inner structure of aspects or events and concepts which express what he calls "direct" temporal and spatial relations between aspects or events.

[13] On the question of how large are the pieces from the world of our experience which ought to be counted as individuals, Russell held various positions. While he sometimes seems to include rather big pieces among the individuals (for example entire aspects of material objects), he occasionally seems to include among the individuals only the lesser constituents of a total perceptual content, which psychologists once used to call "sensations". Occasionally he goes one step further by holding that the contents of perception are composed of "qualities", which constitute the genuine individuals (*Inquiry into Meaning and Truth*, 1940).

V
Tractato Logico-Philosophicus

23. LUDWIG WITTGENSTEIN AND THE *TRACTATUS*

The ideas which the Viennese Ludwig Wittgenstein (1889–1951) presented in the work of his youth, *Tractatus Logico-Philosophicus* (1921), had their roots in German as well as English traditions. German epistemological idealism (Kant, Schopenhauer), the philosophy of science of the physicist Heinrich Hertz, and the logic of Gottlob Frege (and perhaps also Fritz Mauthner's critique of language) were some of Wittgenstein's most important German sources of inspiration. In England, where Wittgenstein lived during 1908–14 and from 1929 until his death in 1951, he came in contact with the Cambridge philosophers Bertrand Russell and George Edward Moore. Russell's logic and his philosophy of logical atomism strongly caught Wittgenstein's interest, and Russell's influence can be traced in many of the basic views of the *Tractatus*. It is difficult to believe that Moore did not influence Wittgenstein, but in the *Tractatus* there is almost no trace of such influence. During his later period (1929–51) however, Wittgenstein was to develop ideas which had essential points in common with Moore's philosophical method.

The *Tractatus* must be largely unintelligible to anyone not acquainted with its historical background. A great part of it consists of comments, criticisms, suggestions, and dogmatic declarations, in a rather esoteric metaphysical, logical, and semantical discussion, with Frege and Russell as the two other main participants. At the same time the book puts forward an original and intensely personal philosophical vision. It is splintered, kaleidoscopic, and ambiguous at almost every point. Perhaps in a literary fashion, though not intellectually, Wittgenstein succeeded in bringing together the antithetical ideas which struggled with each other in his mind: a belief in the "mystical", inside and outside the world, alongside an extreme scientism, according to which only the natural sciences are capable of making meaningful statements; the idealism and even solipsism of classical German philosophy alongside a realistic and even mechanistic picture of the world; the conviction that ordinary language is "completely in order" alongside the dream of a logically perfect symbolic language, a "concept language" *à la* Frege and Russell; the belief in philosophy as a logico-metaphysical insight *above* natural science alongside the condemnation of all philosophy as nonsense; and so on.

The claim stated in the preface of the *Tractatus* that the book offers the final solutions to the problems discussed, stands in marked and almost tragic contrast to the unfinished character of the aphoristically presented ideas. The obscurity of the *Tractatus* makes the question whether its ideas are "correct" seem, in most cases, inappropriate. What Wittgenstein did was to enrich the philosophical debate with new material, to open up new possibilities of thought. That such is the case can hardly be disputed by anyone who is acquainted with the recent history of philosophy.

The *Tractatus* immediately became influential in Cambridge in England as well as in Wittgenstein's home town of Vienna. In 1925 Russell provided the second edition of *Principia Mathematica* with a new introduction in which he revised several basic conceptions in keeping with ideas which he claimed to have found in the *Tractatus*. F. P. Ramsey was also strongly influenced by Wittgenstein. It was especially the more technical logical thoughts in the *Tractatus* which caught the interest of Russell and Ramsey. The so-called Vienna Circle, from which logical empiricism was to develop, was formed in Vienna in 1925. Wittgenstein, who was never a member of the circle, was one of the thinkers to whom its members constantly referred with respect, whether in agreement or in criticism. What they especially took from the *Tractatus* were: the condemnation of metaphysics; the distinction between "tautological" sentences which are *a priori* and without content, and "non-tautological" sentences which have content and must be empirically verified; and the view that the classical problems of philosophy are meaningless and that philosophy ought to be pursued as the "logical syntax" of language. Wittgenstein's notion that all the sentences of the language are "truth-functions of atomic sentences", also met with a positive response. The *Tractatus* was thus one of the factors which contributed to the formation of the general outlook of logical empiricism. When Carnap, at the end of the 1930s, abandoned his first, exclusively "syntactical" approach to language, and made himself a spokesman for a "semantical" study of language, he re-established contact with the thoughts in the *Tractatus*.

On almost all questions the *Tractatus* can be interpreted in several different ways. Passages supporting one interpretation can be set against passages supporting another. For those who wish to have clear-cut statements, the book will be a disappointment. But the ambiguity of the *Tractatus* is also a kind of richness, in that the formulations suggest many interesting interpretations. In this connection, Wittgenstein's friend G. H. von Wright has called the *Tractatus* "many-dimensional", and suggested that this characteristic is found in many of the great classical philosophies. Because of considerations of space I must limit myself here to essentially *one* interpretation. It makes no claim to being the only one possible. Other interpretations may be found for which the evidence is just as good, and which are equally, or more, interesting.

Whoever wishes to understand the *Tractatus* can now receive some help from Wittgenstein's *Notebooks 1914–16*, which were published posthumously (1961), and in which one gets glimpses of how the *Tractatus* came into being. Throughout his life Wittgenstein was in the habit of writing down his thoughts daily in notebooks, which became a kind of philosophical diary. (Most of these books were destroyed during his lifetime on his orders.) The *Tractatus* is essentially an arrangement of reflections which were initially written in such diaries, and many of its aphorisms can be found more or less verbatim, in the *Notebooks*. These are more candid than the *Tractatus*, both about Wittgenstein's struggle to arrive at a view of life and about his attitude to his own thoughts. The brooding doubt which permeates the *Notebooks* gives place in the *Tractatus* to the preacher's certainty. The *Tractatus* also conceals some of the paradoxical consequences to which its doctrines lead—consequences which disturb the author in the *Notebooks*. To what extent does this fact depend on a change of mind in Wittgenstein during 1916-18[1] and to what extent is it a romantic literary attitude? The question can be asked, but the answer is unknown.

The aphorisms in the *Tractatus* cover a very large field. It contains reflections on questions in logic, the philosophy of mathematics, the philosophy of physics, ethics, and so on. In the following sections I shall discuss only some of the basic ideas about the world (section 24), about language (sections 25-7), and about philosophy (section 28).

24. THE WORLD

A. *Things and facts*

Things (*Gegenstände, Dinge*) and *situations* (*Sachlagen*) are the two fundamental ontological categories in the *Tractatus*. Many of Wittgenstein's opinions seem to presuppose that everything which one can speak about, or think of, is either a thing or a situation. Let us look first at his doctrine of situations.

Every meaningful sentence represents (or expresses) a (conceivable, possible) situation. That situation which is expressed by a sentence is said to constitute the sense (*Sinn*) of the sentence. The sentence is true if the situation does not obtain (or does not exist). "The earth is round", for example, represents the situation that the earth is round, and the truth of the sentence is due to the existence of that situation.

A situation can be composed of other situations. If, for example, *p* and *q* are two situations, then *p and q* is a situation which is composed of them. According to Wittgenstein, all situations which are composed of other situations must ultimately be composed of situations which are not composed of other situations. Such non-complex situations he calls states of affairs (*Sachverhalte*).[2]

[1] When Wittgenstein became a prisoner of war on the Italian front in 1918, he is said to have had the complete manuscript of the *Tractatus* with him in his knapsack.

[2] Wittgenstein's terminology is far from consistent, and exceptions to the above explanation are easily found in the *Tractatus*. In a letter to Bertrand Russell, printed in *Notebooks 1914-16*, he explains his terms in a manner that is entirely irreconcilable with our interpretation. In this letter, "state of affairs" (*Sachverhalt*)

The relation which, according to the above analysis, obtains between the concepts 'state of affairs', 'situation', and 'fact', is illustrated by diagram (G).

Wittgenstein's notion of a situation is similar to Bolzano's notion of a proposition-in-itself and to Frege's notion of a thought. To the extent that Russell's propositons are of a non-linguistic nature, situations in Wittgenstein's philosophy play a role similar to that of propositions in Russell's philosophy. Wittgenstein's states of affairs are also, on many scores, comparable to Russell's atomic propositions. These, according to Russell, have one of the forms:

The property F belongs to a,
The relation R obtains between $a, b, \ldots$,

and Wittgenstein takes the same view of his states of affairs. Those situations of Wittgenstein's which are not states of affairs correspond, roughly speaking, to Russell's "molecular" and "generalized" propositions. If p and q are atomic propositions, then, according to Russell's terminology, the following are molecular propositions:

not-p, p and q, p or q, if p then q, and so on.

Propositions which are or contain propositions of the forms:

It is the case for all x that $\ldots x \ldots$,
It is the case for some x that $\ldots x \ldots$,

are generalized.

Although a state of affairs cannot be analysed into situations

is explained as signifying what "existing state of affairs" (*bestehender Sachverhalt*) signifies in our explanation. The word "fact" (*Tatsache*) is said to signify an existing situation which is a conjunction "p and q and ...", of states of affairs, $p, q, \ldots$. This explanation hardly agrees with the actual usage prevailing in the *Tractatus*.

—it has no situations as genuine constituents—it is nevertheless complex in another sense. A state of affairs consists of things. Wittgenstein says that a state of affairs is like a chain whose links are things. All things are (in some sense) absolutely simple. On this point the *Tractatus* and Russell's logical atomism completely agree, and both are equally paradoxical. If all things are simple, and if everything can be exhaustively divided into things and situations, then complexes occur only among situations. In the *Notebooks* Wittgenstein wrestles with this problem: he finds it difficult to surrender the belief in complex things and also doubts that there are any (in an absolute sense) simple things. In the *Tractatus*, on the other hand, the doctrine of the simplicity of things is stated without reservations, and the consequent paradoxes are never mentioned. No examples of simple things are given in the *Tractatus*. Wittgenstein seems to think that their existence can be proved *a priori*: the analysis of complexes into their constituents must ultimately come to an end at simple constituents which cannot be further analysed. What the simple things are like is considered an empirical question without philosophical relevance. (For the author of the *Tractatus* there was an iron curtain between philosophy and experience.) When trying to visualize simple things, he thought of points in the visual field, as he says in the *Notebooks*, and, in particular, of the pointlike impressions made by light from the fixed stars. He also asked himself whether the particles of atomic physics could be the simple things for which he was looking.

Wittgenstein's doctrine of simple things is close to Russell's doctrine of simple individuals, and Wittgenstein actually compares the two theories in the *Tractatus*, as well as in his later work, *Philosophical Investigations*. For Russell, there is, besides propositions (when these are understood in a non-linguistic sense), an entire hierarchy of entities in which the individuals constitute only the bottom layer. Wittgenstein expresses himself in several places as though, besides situations, there is nothing but simple things. A comparison of Russell and Wittgenstein seems to reveal three alternative possibilities of interpretation.

(1) It is conceivable that Wittgenstein obtained his ontology

in the *Tractatus* by eliminating from Russell's ontology everything which is not a proposition (= situation) or an individual (= thing). If so, his position would have a strong nominalistic flavour. There are various arguments in the *Tractatus* which seem to support this interpretation. It probably indicates one aspect of Wittgenstein's (here as always) ambivalent thought.

(2) Conceivably, under the concept of "simple thing" Wittgenstein intended to include not only Russell's individuals but also everything else which Wittgenstein was prepared to accept from Russell's ontology, excluding only the "propositions" which in Wittgenstein appear in the guise of "situations". In the *Notebooks* he writes, for example, "Relations and properties, etc. are *objects* too."[3]

(3) Finally, it is possible that Wittgenstein had in mind a more complex ontological classification than the simple dichotomy: situation/thing. Perhaps he was prepared to acknowledge, for example, properties of things, and relations among things, as additional ontological categories. He undeniably sometimes speaks of the properties and relations of things as if they were a realm of entities existing besides the things themselves. It is hardly likely that Wittgenstein had a well-considered, consistent view on this issue when he wrote the *Tractatus*.

It is not merely the simplicity of the things which reminds one of the ancient concept of the atom. Wittgenstein also asserts about his things, just as the ancient atomist had about their atoms, that exactly the same things occur at all moments.[4] (In this context Wittgenstein can hardly have

---

[3] Wittgenstein, L., *Notebooks 1914–1916* (Oxford: Basil Blackwell, 1969), p.61.

[4] Cf. *Tractatus*, 2.0271. Since the doctrine of the world in the *Tractatus* is supposed to be free from contingent, empirical elements, this assertion about the existence of things at all moments is curious. Possibly, Wittgenstein held that every atomic fact has the temporal form:

a has the property F at time t,

or:

The relation R obtains between $a, b, \ldots$ at time t.

According to one form of the law of excluded middle it is then the case that:

Either a has F at t, or a does not have F at t.

He might have thought that if a has or does not have F at t, then a occurs at t, and thus that a occurs at every moment. However, it would be pure guesswork to ascribe this line of thought to Wittgenstein.

included properties and relations among things. Things here are what have properties and relations).

Let us designate the set of simple things by T. Wittgenstein occasionally argues as though he meant that there is a given set of operations Σ with which states of affairs are built from things, and that each such operation has a determined finite number of "places". If f is an n-place operation in Σ and $t_1, \ldots, t_n$ are things from T on which the operation f can be performed, then $f(t_1, \ldots, t_n)$ is a state of affairs.[5] The set of states of affairs, which we can designate by S, could, on this analysis, be described as the set of everything which is obtainable by applying the operation in Σ to the things in T. Wittgenstein further holds that there is a set of operations Λ, with the aid of which one can form, from the elements of S, a more extensive set of situations. This set of situations, which we can designate L, is thus the set which results from the (iterated) use of the operations Λ on the states of affairs S. These five entities, T, Σ, S, Λ, and L, constitute the inescapable "What", that according to Wittgenstein, comes before every "How", every question about "how things are", about what reality is like, about what the facts are. That the ontological system, whose corner-stone is T, Σ, S, Λ, and L, should be other than it is, is "inconceivable". The system belongs, as we shall see, to the "unsayable".

Wittgenstein distinguishes between two types of properties of, and relations among, things: external ("proper" or "material"), and internal ("structural" or "formal"). As with most of Wittgenstein's terms, these have several meanings. One of their meanings can be explained roughly as follows. A property F is an external property of a thing a if and only if a state of affairs of the form, a has F, exists. Similarly, the relation R is an external relation between $a, b, \ldots$ if and only if the state of affairs, R obtains between $a, b, \ldots$, exists.

---

[5] Wittgenstein's dicta are too meagre to enable us to reconstruct his ideas here with certainty. However, it is unlikely that he thought that every n-place operation f in Σ can be performed on any arbitrarily selected sequence $t_1, t_2', \ldots, t_n$ from T. By the "form" of a thing Wittgenstein means (2.0141) the thing's possibility of occurring in states of affairs. If every operation in Σ could be performed without restrictions on things from T, then according to this definition all things would have the same "form", something which Wittgenstein scarcely assumes.

According to the Principle of Independence (W2), which Wittgenstein adopts and which we shall soon examine (p. 171), it is always conceivable (possible) that a state of affairs, which *de facto* happens to exist, might not exist. If a property belongs externally to a thing (or a relation externally obtains among several things), it is thus always conceivable (possible) that such would not be the case. In order to establish the presence of an external property or relation, one must study how the states of affairs are in fact divided into existing and non-existing. On the other hand, a property F is an internal property of a thing a if we can find that a has F just by inspecting the ontological system T, Σ, S, Λ, and L, without considering how the states of affairs happen to be divided into existing and non-existing. Since the system T, Σ, S, Λ, and L, is something inescapably given, it is inconceivable that a should not have F if F is an internal property of a. In accordance with the view of language which Wittgenstein embraces in the *Tractatus*, he can legitimately claim that internal properties and relations belong to what cannot be said.

Not only do things have internal properties and relations, but so also do situations. To be a thing is an internal property. That a thing occurs as an element in a state of affairs is an internal relation between the thing and the state of affairs. To be a state of affairs, or a situation, is an internal property. That one situation is a constituent in another is an internal relation between them. And so on. All assertions to this effect are, therefore, nonsense, on Wittgenstein's view of language. The totality of internal properties of something (a thing, a state of affairs, a situation, the world, a name, a sentence, or the language) is sometimes called its "logical form".

Wittgenstein's interpretation of the concept "difference" is of special interest in connection with his doctrine of possible worlds. According to him, there are not any states of affairs (situations) of the forms: $a = b$, $a \neq b$. Identity and difference are thus not external relations among things, and the assertions $a = b$ and $a \neq b$ are nonsense—like all assertions which attribute non-external concepts to something. One might have expected that Wittgenstein would consider identity and difference as internal relations, but he does not. Yet the difference between the different simple things has the same fundamental status as internal properties and relations do in the ontological scheme of the *Tractatus*. The distinction among things is something given before, and independently of, what possible world happens to be realized.

Before leaving Wittgenstein's concept of thing, let me point out that Wittgenstein often seems to look upon the external properties of a thing as being literally something external to the thing, a sort of clothing which the thing wears in the world. Only the "internal" properties are (as it were) actually constitutive of the nature of the thing. "In order to know an object, I must know not its external but all its internal qualities" (*Tractatus*, 2.01231). "Two objects of the same logical form are—apart from their external properties—differentiated from one another only in that they are different" (2.0233). At this point Wittgenstein's concept of a thing resembles the Scholastics' concept of substance, against which Hume directed his famous criticism: substance as an "unknown something" to which the properties are fastened, an anonymous peg, as it were, on which they are hung.

B. *Conceivable worlds*

Let us suppose that the set of states of affairs is:

$$S = \{p_1, p_2, \ldots\}.$$

Wittgenstein says nothing about how many states of affairs there are; indeed, he expresses a view which implies that it would be nonsense even to try to state the number of elements in S. Let us, however, imagine that the number is some (finite or infinite) number n. Then there are 2^n different ways of dividing S into two subsets, say $E, S - E$; where E is a subset (empty or non-empty, proper or improper) of S, and $S - E$ is the set of all elements in S which do not belong to E. Wittgenstein makes, more or less explicitly, a number of important assumptions about these divisions, assumptions which I shall here formulate in my own manner.

(W1) There is exactly one subset E of S such that all states of affairs in E exist and all in $S - E$ do not exist.

This assumption, which I shall call the Principle of Determinateness, implies that each state of affairs has exactly one of the two attributes: *exists, does not exist*. The principle expresses, in other words, that the laws of excluded middle and of contradiction hold in regard to these attributes. From the point of view of classical logic, (W1) is self-evident.

The remaining assumptions do not have this logical self-evidence. Wittgenstein adopts a Principle of Independence, which can be stated as follows:

(W2) Whatever subset E of S we select, it is possible (or conceivable) that all states of affairs in E exist and all states of affairs in $S - E$ do not exist.

In this sense, states of affairs are completely independent of each other. The knowledge that a given state of affairs exists does not allow any inference as to whether or not any other state of affairs exists. The Principle of Independence probably has a historical relationship to Hume's criticism of the belief in a "necessary connection" between distinct events, and to the entire philosophical tradition which culminated in Hume's critique. But, the Principle of Independence involves a sharpening of Hume's standpoint. Wittgenstein's discussion of states of affairs, and the things which occur in them, is too meagre to allow us to establish with certainty exactly how far-reaching the bearing of the Principle of Independence is. If, for the sake of simplicity, we suppose that the states of affairs are constructed from a set of things, T, and a set of properties of things, F, then it follows by the Principle of Independence that it is possible that all the things in T have all the properties in F, and also that no thing in T has any property in F. If colours belong to F, it would be possible that all things have all colours as well as that no thing has any colour.[6]

---

[6] In the article "Some remarks on logical form" (1929), Wittgenstein is no longer prepared to maintain an unlimited Principle of Independence for states of affairs (and for elementary sentences). He supposes that the sentences:

Red at point p at time t,
Blue at point p at time t,

are examples of "atomic propositions" (= "elementary sentences"), and he acknowledges that they "exclude" each other. Later, Carnap in his study of probability was to consider a very similar problem. Cf. his *Logical Foundations of Probability*, pp. 76–8.

Wittgenstein implicitly assumes something which could be called The Principle of Completeness. In order to express this principle concisely, we need some symbolic abbreviations. If p is a situation, then its negation is also a situation, according to Wittgenstein: let us express the negation of p by *not-p*. If X is a set of situations then *neg* (X) will indicate the set which contains (exactly) all the negations of the situation in X. If X and Y are two sets, then $X + Y$ will designate that set which results when we conjoin them. Wittgenstein's supposition, the Principle of Completeness, can now be formulated as follows:

(W3) Whatever subset E and whatever situation p we select, either p follows from $E + neg$ $(S - E)$, or *not-p* follows therefrom.[7]

The Principle of Completeness says, in other words, that if we affirm each state of affairs in E and deny each state of affairs in $S - E$, for any arbitrarily chosen E, we have in principle (correctly or incorrectly) answered every conceivable question about the nature of the world.

In accordance with (W2) and (W3), Wittgenstein considers any conceivable division $(E, S - E)$ of the states of affairs as determining a possible or conceivable world. A possible world can hence, if we like, be identified with such a division $(E, S - E)$, or with the first term E, since this determines the division. "The world" or "reality", that possible world which happens to exist, can similarly be identified with the set E whose elements are exactly all existing states of affairs. Let E^+ be the set of all situations that follow from $E + neg$ $(S - E)$. By (W2), E^+ will be consistent, and by (W3) it will be complete (contain either p or *not-p*, whatever situation p might be). It is easily seen that there obtains a one-to-one correspondence between the divisions of the states of affairs $(E, S - E)$ and the divisions of the situations $(E^+, L - E^+)$. "The world" itself can therefore also be identified with the division $(E^+, L - E^+)$, where all the situations in E^+ exist and all in $L - E^+$ do not exist; or it can be identified with the first term of this division, E^+. These are the sorts of ideas which lie behind the aphorisms which open the *Tractatus*.

---

[7] In *Notebooks 1914-1916*, p. 98, Wittgenstein seems to attribute this principle to Russell, probably incorrectly.

The *Tractatus* states: "It is obvious that an imagined world must have *something*—a form—in common with it—however different it may be from the real one. This fixed form consists of the objects" (2.022–2.023). One manner in which this utterance can be understood is obviously the following. If, for example, $\phi(a)$, where a is a thing, is a state of affairs, then it holds of every possible world that either $\phi(a)$ or *not-$\phi(a)$* exists in that world. In fact, the following is a direct corollary to (W3):

(W4a) For every E and every thing a there is a situation p of which a is a constituent, and which follows from $E + neg\ (S - E)$.

However, it is conceivable that Wittgenstein wishes to say something more in the passage just quoted. It is natural (although not strictly necessary) to suppose that the following principle holds:

(1)   If $\phi(a)$ or *not-$\phi(a)$*, then a exists.

In the *Notebooks* (p. 98) Wittgenstein says: "No world can be created in which a proposition is true unless the constituents of the proposition are created also."

If Wittgenstein did accept this principle in the *Tractatus*, then he might also have wished to say the following:

(W4b) For every E and every a, it is the case that 'a exists' follows from $E + neg\ (S - E)$.

However, it is also possible that the author of the *Tractatus*, following his mentor Russell, would have rejected (1), and thus (W4b), as nonsense.[8]

---

[8] It is interesting to observe that if one takes Frege's rather than Wittgenstein's semantical–ontological point of view, one obtains another spectrum of "possible worlds" from the spectrum with which the *Tractatus* deals. Let us replace Wittgenstein's "states of affairs" with the "thoughts" which are their analogues in Frege's system. Suppose that there are n "states of affairs", thoughts, n being some finite or infinite number. For each thought p there are three possibilities in Frege's system:

p is true,
p is false,
p has no truth-value.

The third alternative occurs if to some "thing-sense" in p there does not correspond any thing. Instead of Wittgenstein's 2^n possible worlds, we now get 3^n

C. *What is the world? Is the world all that exists?*

The views of Wittgenstein discussed above do not provide us with any intuitive picture of "what the world is like". There are several passages that can be quoted in support of the interpretation that the *Tractatus* inclines toward an extreme "scientific" or even "mechanistic" view of the universe. "The totality of true propositions is the whole of natural science (or the whole corpus of the natural sciences)" (4.11). This aphorism *can* be understood to maintain that everything which can be correctly said about the world must be said by the so-called natural sciences, for example physics, chemistry, and so on. He further says; "Mechanics is an attempt to construct according to a single plan all *true* propositions which we need for the description of the world (6.343).

On the other hand, the *Notebooks* are dominated by a type of self-nullifying solipsism, of which there are also vivid traces in the *Tractatus*. Like Schopenhauer (whom he cites) he holds that the world is his "representation". But the representing self, the I who has the representation which is the world, cannot then itself belong to the world. The I is related to the world as the eye to the visual field. "I know that this world exists. That I stand in it like the eye in the visual field."[9] "There are two divinities: the world and my independent self."[10] "And the subject does not belong to the world, but is a boundary for the world."[11] But, if the I is not in the world, does it exist at all?

Isn't the thinking subject in the last resort mere superstition? Where in the world is a metaphysical subject to be found? You say that the situation here is just as with the eye and the visual field. But you do not actually see the eye. And I believe that there is nothing in the visual field which entitles me to conclude that it is seen by an eye . . . . The I, the I is the deeply mysterious. The I is not an object. I objectively confront every object. But not the I.[12]

such worlds. The possible worlds which Frege's position can thus be construed as countenancing, contrast with Wittgenstein's possible world in that they do not all contain the same things.

[9] Wittgenstein, L., *Notebooks 1914–16*, pp. 72–3.
[10] Ibid., p. 74.   [11] Ibid., p. 79.   [12] Ibid., p. 80.

Both in the *Notebooks* and the *Tractatus* Wittgenstein tells himself in identical words that solipsism, if rigorously pursued, will coincide with "pure realism". "The I of solipsism shrinks to an extensionless point and what remains is the reality co-ordinated with it" (5.64).

The self-nullifying solipsism of Wittgenstein is one of the sources of the fascinating "dimension of depth" in the *Tractatus*, of the feeling of dizziness which the book may sometimes inspire. In the *Notebooks*, solipsism as a conception of life is set forth even more explicitly and in greater detail. Being a part of the represented world, one's own body has no closer connection with the representing self than other bodies in the world. Just as my world comes into existence with me ("Of what concern is history to me? My world is the first and only."[13]), so it passes out of existence with my death. Good and evil have nothing to do with the representing self and the represented world, but only with the willing self. My will, too, does not belong to the world. "The world is given to me, i.e., my will goes forth to the world as to something that is already there."[14] At the same time my will is the world will. And so on.

There is no reason to believe that Wittgenstein decisively broke with this realm of ideas, strongly influenced by Schopenhauer, when finishing the manuscript of the *Tractatus*. But since his solipsism fused with "pure realism", he could unite Schopenhauerian solipsism with a mechanistic materialism.

Is "the world", the "world" dealt with in the *Tractatus*, understood by Wittgenstein to be all that exists? Or, does there exist something outside the world? In one sense, the world is for Wittgenstein all there is. According to his view of language, we inevitably fall into nonsese when we attempt to speak about something outside the world. But even so, according to the *Tractatus*, there are some things which do not belong to the world. The representing and willing self, whose representation the world is, stands as we have just seen, outside the world. Further, neither "God" nor "the mystical" are *in* the world. Aphorism 6.432 states, *"How the world is, is completely indifferent for what is higher.*

[13] Ibid., p. 82.   [14] Ibid., p. 74

God does not reveal himself *in* the world." And 6.522, "There is indeed the inexpressible. This *shows* itself; it is the mystical." The *Tractatus* both opens and shuts the window to something "higher", something "mystical", something which lies beyond the limits of the world.

25. LANGUAGE

A. *Names and sentences*

Wittgenstein's view of language is, in certain respects, parallel to his view of the world. According to the *Tractatus*, language is a "picture" of reality. The simple names in the language correspond to the simple things in the world, the elementary sentences in the language correspond to the states of affairs, and the total stock of sentences in the language corresponds to the total stock of situations. When Wittgenstein writes about "*the* world", he hardly breaks with our linguistic customs, since we (or many of us) are rather used to thinking that there is exactly one world. When Wittgenstein writes about "*the* language", the reader cannot help being puzzled since there are so many languages. In section 26 I shall return to the difficult problem of interpretation encountered here. When Wittgenstein writes about language in the *Tractatus*, he thinks of a language containing exclusively indicative sentences and designed solely for an objective (scientific) description of reality. A language can, of course, be used for many other purposes, but other functions of language are not considered in the *Tractatus*.

Simple names correspond to simple things. Wittgenstein usually says that the name signifies (*bedeutet*) or designates (*bezeichnet*) that object of which it is the name. He seems to maintain that there is a many–one relation between names and objects signified. In other words, he seems to assume that every name designates exactly one object, and that every object is (at least potentially) designated by at least one name. In agreement with Russell but in opposition to Frege, Wittgenstein assumes that genuine names lack semantical structure, i.e. that a genuine name does not contain any independent parts which themselves signify. Again with Russell but against Frege, he maintains that names do not have a "sense" (in the meaning in which this word is used by Frege) distinct from what they signify or designate.

Further, Wittgenstein apparently assumes a many-one relation between sentences and situations. He seems to assume that each sentence represents (*darstellt*) or describes (*beschreibt*) exactly one situation, while every situation (at least potentially) is represented by at least one sentence. The sentences which represent states of affairs are called elementary sentences. An elementary sentence as conceived by Wittgenstein is always simple in the sense that it does not have parts which are sentences.

We already know that a sentence is true if the represented situation obtains (exists, or is a fact), and that otherwise it is false. Diagram (H) is entirely parallel with the ontological diagram on p. 165.

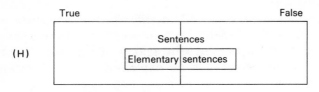

(H)

B. *Possible descriptions of the world. The ranges of sentences*

Let us now give a new meaning to the symbols E and S, used in section 24. S will now be the set of all possible elementary sentences (without unnecessary duplication by synonymous sentences!), and E will be some (empty or non-empty, proper or improper) subset of S. To the previous postulates (W1)–(W3) correspond the following postulates in Wittgenstein's theory of language.

LI   There is exactly one subset E of S such that every sentence in E is true, while every sentences in $S - E$ is false.

This principle, which we shall call the Principle of Determinateness for Elementary Sentences, is obviously equivalent to (W1). The following Principle of Independence for Elementary Sentences is equivalent to (W2):

LII   Whatever subset E of S we select, it is possible that every sentence in E is true, while every sentence in $S - E$ is false.

Similarly, the following Principle of Completeness for Elementary Sentences is equivalent to (W3):

LIII. Whatever subset E and whatever sentence p we select, either p follows from $E + neg$ $(S - E)$, or *not-p* follows therefrom.

(Of course, *not-p* here stands for the negation of p and *neg* $(S - E)$ for the set of negations of sentences in $S - E$.)

According to LII and LIII, a complete specification of a possible world is given by stating for every elementary sentence whether it is to be considered true or false. Accordingly aphorism 4.26 states: "The specification of all true elementary sentences describes the world completely. The world is completely described by the specification of all elementary sentences plus the specification, which of them are true and which false."

Wittgenstein expresses LIII in the words, "sentences are truth-functions of elementary sentences" (5). Here appears *one* of the many uses which he makes of the word "truth-function", a use which can be explained by the following definition:

(D1) The sentence p is a truth-function of the set X of sentences = df Whatever subset Y of X we select, either p follows from $Y + neg$ $(X - Y)$, or *not-p* follows therefrom.

We shall meet other uses of the word "truth-function" in part C of this section.

With regard to LII, Wittgenstein labels every division of elementary sentences $(E, S - E)$ a truth-possibility. According to LIII, every truth-possibility assigns a truth value to every sentence in the language. If a truth-possibility implies that a given sentence is true, then the possibility is a truth-ground for the sentence. The set of all the truth-grounds of a sentence constitutes the logical range of that sentence. With the help of the concept of logical range Wittgenstein defines a series of other concepts. If all truth-possibilities belong to the logical range of a sentence, then that sentence is a tautology. If the logical range of a sentence is empty (does not contain any truth-possibilities) the sentence is a contradiction. Sentences which are neither tautologies nor contradictions are called proper sentences. If the logical range of sentence A is part of the logical range of sentence B, then B is a logical consequence of, or derivable from, A. If the number of truth-possibilities which belong simultaneously to the logical range of A and to that of B is m, and the number of truth possibilities in the logical range of A is n, then, according to Wittgenstein, B has the probability m/n in relation to A. (This definition obviously only works if m and n are finite numbers and $n > 0$.)

Wittgenstein indicates his epistemological position in connection with this notion of logical range. The tautological sentences, which he identifies with the "theorems of logic", constitute the entire field of *a priori* knowledge. An "*a priori* true thought [sentence]", is considered to be one "whose truth can be read off from the thought [sentence] itself (without an object of comparison)" (3.05). More specifically, Wittgenstein seems to think that there is an algorithm through which one can, given a tautological sentence, always decide that it is a tautology. "Whether a proposition belongs to logic can be calculated by calculating the logical properties of the *symbol*" (6.126). "Every tautology itself shows that it is a tautology" (6.127). Tautologies are without content: they tell us nothing about the nature of reality, since they allow all truth-possibilities. The truth-value of a proper sentence, i.e. one which is neither a tautology nor a contradiction, can be determined only by comparing it with a fact, a reality, outside the sentence. Proper sentences come within the jurisdiction of empirical natural science: "the totality of true sentences is the total natural science" (4.11). Thus, according to the *Tractatus*, every truth must be either a logical truth (a tautology) or a factual truth of "natural science".

C. *Truth-functions*

The term "truth-function" plays a dominant role in Wittgenstein's theory of language. The doctrine of truth-functions has, as we have already seen, very deep roots in the history of philosophy. Wittgenstein's mentors Frege and Russell both based their logical systems on truth-functions. About the time when the *Tractatus* was published, the concept of truth-function was dealt with systematically both by the Pole Jan Lukasiewicz and by the American E. L. Post. Although Wittgenstein's work thus has points of contact with a highly developed tradition, it is, paradoxically enough, far from obvious what the term "truth-function" signifies in his various statements. With (D1) (p. 178) we have already tried to grasp one sense of the term. But it has other senses as well. Let us consider some conceivable uses of the term and compare them with Wittgenstein's usage.

(1) *Truth-functions in Frege's sense.* Frege introduces into his logic functions which correlate truth-values with combinations of truth-values (the True $= t$, and the False $= f$). Negation, which we can write $n(x)$, is, for example the function which satisfies the conditions:

$$n(t) = f; n(f) = t.$$

Implication, which we can write $i(x, y)$, is the function which satisfies the conditions:

$$i(t, t) = i(f, t) = i(f, f) = t; i(t, f) = f.$$

Truth-functions, in Frege's sense, are thus functions over the set of the two truth-values, t and f. Truth-functions of this kind do not occur in the *Tractatus*.

(2) *Truth-functions over a set X.* To the truth-value t there corresponds within language the set of true sentences, and to f the set of false sentences. On the abstract plane postulated by Bolzano and Frege, there correspond to the truth-values sets of "propositions-in-themselves" (Bolzano) or sets of "thoughts" (Frege). On a psychological plane, one often talks of true or false "judgements", considered as certain acts of thinking. On all these planes, one can employ a further concept of truth-function, which can be explained as follows:

Let X be some set (of sentences, propositions-in-themselves, judgements, or other comparable entities) which can be divided into two subsets, the class of 'truths' T and the class of 'falsehoods' F. Let us say that two elements in X are equivalent if both belong to T or both belong to F. A function f, which takes ordered n-tuples of elements of X to elements of X, and which is thus a function over X, may satisfy the following condition of invariance:

(Inv) $f(x_1, \ldots, x_n)$ is always equivalent to $f(y_1, \ldots, y_n)$, provided that the respective pairs x_1 and $y_1, \ldots, x_n$ and y_n are equivalent.

A function f over X which satisfies this condition can be called a truth-function over X.[15]

When Russell writes about truth-functions in *Principia Mathematica*, at least sometimes he intends truth-functions over the set of "propositions" in the present sense. What Wittgenstein calls "truth-operations" in the *Tractatus*, are truth-functions over the set of sentences, again in the present sense.[16]

(3) *Sentences as truth-functions.* The truth-functions, which we have taken cognizance of under (1) and (2), are all functions in the mathematical sense, i.e. methods of correlation. But the "truth-functions" of the *Tractatus* are not functions in that sense, they are sentences. One way in which the term "truth-function" is used in the *Tractatus* can be explained in the following manner.

A sentence can be a part (proper or improper) of another sentence. (Every sentence is an improper part of itself.) The sentence:

(i) The sun is round,

is a proper part of:

(ii) The sun is round, and the moon is shining,

---

[15] The connection between this concept and Frege's concept can be stated in the following manner. Let $v(x)$ be the truth-value of x, i.e.:

If x belongs to T, then $v(x) = t$,
If x belongs to F, then $v(x) = f$.

On this basis we can offer this definition:

f is a truth-function over X = df (i) f is a function which takes ordered n-tuples of elements from X into elements of X, and (ii) there is a truth-function in Frege's sense, g, such that $v(f(x_1, \ldots, x_n)) = g(v(x_1), \ldots, v(x_n))$ for all $x_1, \ldots, x_n$ of X.

[16] Concepts of this sort can obviously be varied indefinitely. Thus Wittgenstein talks of a fundamental truth-operation N which takes sets of sentences into sentences and which satisfies the condition that $N(Y)$ is a true sentence if and only if every sentence in the set Y is false. (Cf. 4.42, 5.2522, 5.5, 5.501, 5.502, and 6.)

and also of:

(iii)   Karl believes that the sun is round.

If, in (ii), we replace (i) with any arbitrarily chosen equivalent sentence, the result will be equivalent to (ii). But this is not the case with (iii). For instance, (i) is equivalent to:

(iv)   The square root of 2 is irrational,

but if we replace (i) with (iv) in (iii), the result becomes:

(v)   Karl believes that the square root of 2 is irrational.

Obviously, (iii) and (v) need not be equivalent, although (i) and (iv) are. Wittgenstein says that (i) is a truth-argument in (ii) but not in (iii). If we form the conjunction of (ii) and (iii):

(vi)   The sun is round, and the moon is shining, and Karl believes that the sun is round,

we can say that the first occurrence of (i) in (vi) is a "truth-argument" in (vi), while the second occurrence of (i) in (vi) is not. One could define truth-argument as follows:

(D2)   An occurrence of a sentence B is a truth-argument in a sentence A = df If that occurrence of B is replaced with an occurrence of some sentence equivalent to B, the result will be equivalent to A.

The following definitions do not occur in the *Tractatus*, where the discussion is informal throughout. But I think they may claim to be a good approximation of Wittgenstein's intentions. (They can be varied in many different ways, and it is very likely that some other variant would be a better approximation.) 'Simple sentence' in what follows will mean a sentence which does not contain any sentence as a proper part.

(D3)   Sentence A is *truth-functional* = df Every occurrence of a simple sentence in A is a truth-argument in A.

This concept does not occur in Wittgenstein, but is introduced here in order to facilitate the formulation of the following definitions. (i), (ii), and (iv) above are truth-functional, while (iii), (v), and (vi) are not.

Let us say that a schema results from a given sentence when we replace every occurrence of a simple sentence with a letter (different letters for different occurrences, even if these are occurrences of the same sentence). From (i), (ii), (iii), and (vi) we can obtain the following schemata:

(i*)   *P*
(ii*) *P* and *Q*
(iii*) Karl believes that *P*
(vi*) *P* and *Q*, and Karl believes that *R*.

Now let us state what it is for a schema to be truth-functional:

(D4)   A schema *S* is *truth-functional* = df *S* results from a truth-functional sentence when all the simple sentences in that sentence are replaced with letters.[17]

(i*) and (ii*) are truth-functional, but not (iii*) and (vi*). Truth-functional schemata often occur in the *Tractatus*, but the expression "truth-functional schema" does not.

The following definitions which are designed to capture an idea in the *Tractatus* are now tentatively introduced:

(D5)   The sentence *A* is a *truth-function* (in the *narrower* sense) of the set of sentences *X* = df *A* results from a truth functional schema through the replacement of all the letters (sentential variables) in the schema with sentences from *X*, and every sentence of *X* has at least one occurrence in *A*.

[17] (D4) is possibly too wide. It is conceivable that it must be strengthened in order to make (D5) and (D6), which are based on it, express what Wittgenstein meant. If we suppose that there is an omniscient God, the schema "God knows that *P*" and the schema *not-P* are truth-functional according to (D4). These two schemata are subject to the truth-tables:

P	God knows that *P*	*not-P*
t	t	f
f	f	t

However, the truth-table for "God knows that *P*" may be thought to hold only *de facto*, whereas the truth-table for *not-P* holds on the strength of the meaning of negation. One could place the stronger demand on a truth-functional schema, that it must resemble not-*P* rather than "God knows that *P*" in this respect.

The concept 'truth-functional schema' of (D4) is intimately related to "truth-function" as defined under (2), and thus also to truth-functions in Frege's sense. The operation of replacing the letters in a truth-functional schema with given sentences, amounts to a truth-function over the set of sentences in the sense of (2).

(D6) The sentence A is a *truth-function* (in the *broader* sense) of the set of sentences X = df A is a truth-function (in the narrower sense) of some subset of X.

The distinction between the narrower and the broader sense does not occur in the *Tractatus*, but it seems to me that some of Wittgenstein's statements are best interpreted through (D5) and others through (D6). (ii) above is a truth-function (in the narrower sense) of 'The sun is round' and 'The moon is shining'. (vi) is likewise a truth-function (in the narrower sense) of 'The sun is round', 'The moon is shining', and 'Karl believes that the sun is round'. (iii), however, is not a truth-function of 'The sun is round'. Instead of saying that sentence A is a truth-function of the sentences in X, Wittgenstein often says that A is obtained by applying a truth-operation to X.

We have already quoted (p. 178) the assertion: "sentences are truth-functions of elementary sentences" (5), and have offered a preliminary interpretation in terms of (D1). In the sense of (D1), a given sentence can obviously be a truth-function of elementary sentences without being itself an elementary sentence or containing elementary sentences as parts.[18] However, the assertion can also be interpreted in the light of (D5) and (D6). It then expresses a theory which I believe can be summarized in the following statements:

(A) Every occurrence of a sentence B in a sentence A is a truth-argument in A.

(B) Every simple sentence is an elementary sentence.

From (A) and (B) follow:

(C) Every sentence is a truth-function (in the sense of (D5) of some set of elementary sentences.

That (C), and hence also (D) follow from (A) and (B) is easily seen. Every occurrence of a simple sentence in a given sentence A is, according to (B), an occurrence of an elementary sentence. According to (A), every such occurrence is also

---

[18] This may occur, for example, as follows: if the simple sentence A is synonymous with the complex sentence "B and C", where B and C are elementary sentences, then A, just as much as the complex sentence itself, is a truth function of B, and C, in the sense of (D1).

a truth-argument in *A*. According to (D2)–(D4), *A* is thus a truth-function (in the narrower sense) of those elementary sentences which occur in *A*.

The *Tractatus* provides support for the claim that Wittgenstein embraced the theory which I have summarized by theses (A) and (B) above. But how could he do so? Our ordinary language contains unquestionable counterexamples to these theses. (iii) above shows that (A) does not hold good for ordinary English. The sentence "All men are mortal" is simple, it does not literally contain any other sentence as a part, but Wittgenstein would certainly never dream of recognizing it as an elementary sentence. This sentence is therefore a counterexample from ordinary English to (B). The obvious incongruity between Wittgenstein's theory and the facts about an ordinary language like English raises the question of what his theory is really about. *Is* it a theory about a language like English, or is it a theory about something *else*? This question will be discussed in section 26.

(4) *Sentences as truth-functions.* Wittgenstein discusses (5.541–5.542) the counterexample to his thesis (A) constituted by sentences of the forms:

(vii) *A* believes *p*, *A* thinks *p*, *A* says *p*.

Concerning a sentence of the third form, he seems to think that what it expresses could just as well be expressed by a sentence of the form:

(viii) "*p*" says that *p*,

and that (viii) is not a counterexample to thesis (A). *If* (note *if*) the preceding account is a correct (even if incomplete) interpretation of Wittgenstein, then we are confronted here with a new notion of "truth-argument" and therewith presumably also a new notion of "truth-function". In a sentence of type (viii), say:

(ix) 'The sun is round' says (that) the sun is round,

neither the first nor the second occurrence of 'The sun is round' is a truth-argument in the sense of (D2). Although (ix) is true, both of the following sentences are false:

(x) "$\sqrt{2}$ is irrational" says (that) the sun is round,
(xi) "the sun is round" says (that)$\sqrt{2}$ is irrational,

in spite of the fact that "The sun is round" and "$\sqrt{2}$ is irrational" are equivalent. However, in the following somewhat queer sense one can say that "The sun is round" (not any given occurrence of it) is a truth-argument in (ix).

(D7) Sentence A is a truth-argument in sentence B = df A occurs in B, and if each occurrence of A in B is replaced with an occurrence of one and the same sentence equivalent to A, then the result will be equivalent to B.

D. *Elementary sentences as pictures*

Given a suitable grammar and dictionary we are able to understand the meaning of every one of the infinitely many sentences which can be formulated in a language. That one can understand a sentence without having had the meaning of just *that* sentence explained (cf. 4.021) depends, according to Wittgenstein, on the presence of a similarity between the sentence and the situation which the sentence expresses. Wittgenstein wants to explain this affinity through his famous theory that language is a "picture" of reality, that sentences are "pictures" of the situations they represent, and especially that elementary sentences are "pictures" of the states of affairs they represent.

The most easily accessible part of this picture theory is that which deals with elementary sentences. In what follows I shall limit myself to trying to understand what the theory says about elementary sentences. We can say that the phrase "The table" in the sentence "The table is brown" has the property of standing immediately to the left of the phrase "is brown". We can likewise say that in "The vase is standing on the table", the expressions "The vase" and "the table" have to each other the relation that the former stands on the left and the latter to the right of the phrase "is standing on". When names of objects are brought into elementary sentences, they thus acquire certain properties and relations. Let us call the properties and relations of this kind, which are of interest to the picture theory of language, exhibited properties and relations.

To each exhibited property or relation there corresponds exactly one property or relation among things in the world, which the former shows. Let us use R^* to denote the property or relation among things, which the exhibited property or relation R shows. If R is a property, R^* is also a property. If R is an n-place relation ($n = 2, 3, \ldots$), so is R^*. Let us call the properties and relations which the exhibited properties and relations show, the shown properties and relations.

To every name in language there corresponds, as we have already learned, exactly one thing in the world which the name designates. For the sake of brevity let us use a^* to denote the thing, which the name a designates. Now we can formulate the picture theory for elementary sentences in the following manner:

(P1) If the name a in an elementary sentence A exhibits the property R, then A represents the state of affairs that a^* has R^*. If the names $a, b, \ldots$ in the elementary sentence A exhibit the relation R, then A represents the state of affairs that R^* obtains between $a^*, b^*, \ldots$.

According to the picture theory the following is obviously the case:

(P2) If the names $a, b, \ldots$ in the elementary sentence A exhibit the relation R, then A is true if and only if R^* obtains between $a^*, b^*, \ldots$.

The significance of the picture theory depends on which constituents of a sentence are taken to be "names", and, since names and things are correlated, which entities are taken to be "things". The interdeterminacy which we have already encountered in Wittgenstein's concept of a thing recurs in the picture theory. Aphorism 3.1432 says, "We must not say, 'The complex sign "aRb" says "a stands in relation R to b"'; but we must say, 'That "a" stands in a certain relation to "b" says that aRb.'" It seems, in this remark, that Wittgenstein does not acknowledge any "names" but names of individual things: "a" and "b" are names, but not "R". On the other hand, he says in 5.5261 that 'ϕ' as well as 'x' in 'ϕx', "stand independently in designating relations to the world". The predicate 'ϕ' is here said to designate, and thus to be a name.

Wittgenstein's picture theory also contains the following paradoxical assumption:

(P3)   The exhibited property F *can* belong to a name a in an elementary sentence, if and only if the shown property F^* *can* belong to the designated thing a^*. Analogously, the exhibited relation R, *can* obtain among the names $a, b, \ldots$ in an elementary sentence, if and only if the shown relation R^*, *can* obtain among the designated things $a^*, b^*, \ldots$.

Thus, according to Wittgenstein, we cannot combine names in a simple sentence in such a manner that the sentence expresses what is logically impossible. 3.02–3.031 say: "The thought [read just as well: the sentence] contains the possibility of the state of affairs which it thinks. What is thinkable [sayable] is also possible.—We cannot think [say] anything illogical, or otherwise our thinking [speech] would have to be illogical.—It used to be said that God could create everything, except what was contrary to the laws of logic. The truth is, we could not *say* of an 'illogical' world how it would look." Wittgenstein's reason for maintaining (P3) are obscure.

The picture theory further asserts:

(P4)   The exhibited properties and relations cannot be named in the language.

This thesis is puzzling too. To regard "a" and "b" as the only names in "aRb" seems to be an arbitrary choice of one from among several possibilities. The only consideration that would prevent us from regarding "R" as a name would be that there is no relation R. But Wittgenstein himself supposes that there are properties and relations. Cf. 3.1432 quoted above. It is also plausible to think that what is not named but merely shown in one symbolism could be named in another symbolism. (If I were to use "ab" to express the state of affairs that $a \, R \, b$, I would name a and b, but merely "show", not name, the relation R. When I then rewrite "ab" as "aRb", this might be seen as the introduction of a name "R" for a relation that had previously been merely shown.) But Wittgenstein's conception is a totally different one. For him the distinction between what can be named and what can only be shown is absolute. This aspect of the picture theory is one of the sources of his doctrine that there is something unsayable which language shows through its structure.

Is it possible to formulate the picture theory without attempting to name that which, according to the theory, cannot be named, i.e. the shown properties and relations? Wittgenstein himself seems to have been inclined toward a negative answer. The picture theory is *one* of the reasons why at the end of the *Tractatus* he declares the book to be nonsense.

26. THE PURPOSE OF WITTGENSTEIN'S THEORY OF LANGUAGE

We have already found reasons to ask *what* Wittgenstein's theory of language is a theory about. It may be instructive to regard it initially as an abstract axiomatic system—much like pure mathematicians regard, for example, an axiomatic system of geometry. Except for some concepts of a general logical nature, which must occur in practically every theory, there are three categories of concepts in Wittgenstein's theory of language. First, there are those which we have met in Wittgenstein's view of the world:

(I)   thing, state of affairs, fact, and so on.

Second, there are those concepts with which he describes the syntactical nature of language:

(II)   name (a_1), elementary sentence (a_2), sentence (a_3), and so on.

Third, there is that group with which Wittgenstein describes the connections between the language and the world, for instance:

(III)   the name x *designates* the thing y (b_1), the sentence x *represents* the situation y (b_2), etc.

Let us take for granted that the concepts in category (I) have already been defined within Wittgenstein's doctrine of the world. Then, his view of language can be regarded as a collection of postulates, imposing certain conditions upon the concepts $a_1, a_2, a_3, \ldots, b_1, b_2, \ldots$. As long as we have not given these concepts a fixed meaning, the postulates do not have a truth-value. Only when we interpret the concepts do the postulates acquire a truth-value. Under some interpretations they may turn out to be true, while under other interpretations false. One could now ask: Which interpretation, or which interpretatons, of the concepts involved, did Wittgenstein have in mind in the *Tractatus*? And, what is the truth-value of his theory of language under the interpretation, or interpretations, that he adopted? A definitive answer cannot be given to these questions. Here I will merely sketch some different ways of reading Wittgenstein.

Reading 1. We suppose that the theory is intended to hold for any language whatsoever, and the terms from categories (II) and (III) should be understood in a rather unsophisticated manner—let us naïvely say, in the manner in which "ordinary usage" understands them. However, this reading immediately shows itself to be unworkable. Some of the terms in categories (II) and (III) have no "ordinary use" (for example "elementary sentence"), and other terms (for example "name" and "sentence") are not consistently employed in ordinary usage. On this reading, theses like (A) on p. 184 also completely lose touch with reality.

Reading 2. We suppose that the theory is intended to hold for any language whatsoever, but that the terms of categories (II) and (III) are to be understood in some sophisticated manner, which has little or no connection with customary philosophical or non-philosophical usage. There are many suggestions, both in the *Tractatus* itself and even more in the earlier *Notebooks*, which can be adduced in support of this reading. A sophisticated idea encountered in both books is that a name is what all signs which designate the same thing have in common, or that a name is an entire class of signs with the same designation. In the *Notebooks* this idea is sometimes called the "class theory". Analogously, Wittgenstein seems to have been inclined to identify sentences with the same logical range, or to consider a sentence as an entire class of linguistically distinct expressions with the same logical range. Wittgenstein's enigmatic hints do not suffice to clarify how his theory of language might fare on this reading.

Reading 3. Conceivably Wittgenstein did not wish to describe any current language, but to express the demands which he makes on a "logically perfect" language. One can find much support for this reading, but it is certainly not exhaustive.

Reading 4. The following is a kind of combination of readings *1* and *3*. The rules of the theory of language with which the *Tractatus* deals, do not hold directly for an ordinary language like English, but they hold indirectly in the following sense: In principle, one could construct a language *L* such that every meaningful English sentence *A* would correspond to exactly one sentence *A'* in *L*, which would be the "complete analysis" of *A*. The rules of the theory of language stated in the *Tractatus* hold for a language like *L*.

To support this interpretation one can cite aphorisms like the following: "There is one and only one complete analysis of the sentence" (3.25). "In the sentence the thought can be so expressed that to the objects of the thoughts correspond the elements of the sentential sign" (3.2). "These elements I call 'simple signs' and the sentence 'completely analyzed'" (3.201). "The simple signs employed in the sentence are called names" (3.202). "The postulate of the possibility of the simple signs is the postulate of the determinateness of the sense" (3.23). The talk about a "complete analysis" should be understood in the light of Russell's ideas which were discussed in the preceding chapter.

Reading 5. Possibly, the postulates of Wittgenstein's theory of language are intended not as demands which a "logically perfect" language must fulfil, but as demands which a "logically perfect" conceptual apparatus for the description of any language whatsoever must fulfil, in other words, as demands upon a "logically perfect" description of language. According to this reading, Wittgenstein demands that in the description of any language whatsoever, we define the terms from categories (II) and (III) in such a manner that his postulates become satisfied. Those hints about a sophisticated interpretation of "name" and "sentence" which were mentioned in connection with reading *2*, could be construed as an attempt on Wittgenstein's part to fulfil this demand. The question as to the possibility of satisfying the demands

is, of course, unavoidable, and it remains unanswered in the
Tractatus.

Reading 6. In the *Tractatus* there are actually three parallel
structures: the world, language, and thought. Thought receives
little consideration in comparison with the other two structures, figuring mostly as some sort of shadow of language.
Most of what is said about thought could just as well have
been said about language. An interesting suggestion (presented
by the Dane David Favrholdt) is that the language Wittgenstein
is writing about *is*, in Ockham's terminology, not the arbitrary
signs of a spoken or written language, but the "natural" signs
occurring in thought, the *intentiones animae*. This reading
can, at most, fit a subordinate aspect of the theory of language
in the *Tractatus*, but I do not think it can be completely
ruled out.

Perhaps one achieves the most faithful, if not the clearest,
understanding of the theory of language in the *Tractatus* by
cautiously blending the different readings.

27. NONSENSE AND THE INEXPRESSIBLE

The theory of language is for Wittgenstein a means of drawing
the boundaries of what can be meaningfully said. Meaningful speech consists, he maintains, of elementary sentences
and truth-functions of elementary sentences. A sentence is
an elementary sentence if it represents a state of affairs:
when it does, the names in it designate things in the world,
and the mode of combination of the names in the sentence
corresponds to a possible mode of combination of the things.
A sentence is a truth-function of elementary sentences only
if the truth-value of the sentence can be determined solely
on the basis of the truth-values of elementary sentences.
Expressions which fall outside the boundaries are, according to Wittgenstein, simply nonsense.

An example of a nonsensical assertion is "Socrates is
identical". Its nonsensical character is due to the fact that,
in this context, we have not co-ordinated any property with
the word "identical". We could provide a meaning for
"identical", even in this context, and thereby give the entire
sentence a meaning. But we have not done so. Wittgenstein

says that most of the questions and sentences which are uttered by philosophers are nonsense of this sort.

Wittgenstein himself does not distinguish between different kinds of nonsense. However, I believe that his views will be more clearly set out if we distinguish between a "lower" and a "higher" type of nonsense. In the lower kind I count sentences such as "Socrates is identical", which contain some expression to which we have neglected to give an appropriate meaning in the context in which it occurs. As higher nonsense I consider that sort of assertion which, according to Wittgenstein, is nonsense in that it attempts to say the unsayable, in that we try to give it a meaning which cannot be expressed in a language. Wittgenstein countenances nonsense of this higher kind. The *Tractatus* culminates in the assertion that the sentences of the book are nonsense. One can interpret this as an assertion that the *Tractatus* is nonsense of the higher sort. Wittgenstein does not make his doctrine of nonsense very precise. But it is interesting to consider how, on the basis of the position in the *Tractatus*, a higher type of nonsense can arise, and especially how it will occur in the *Tractatus*.

The boundaries of meaningful language are, as Wittgenstein says, identical with the limits of the world. The meaningfulness of an elementary sentence presupposes that the names which occur in the sentence are correlated with things in the world. On the question of whether the world is literally all that exists, or whether there is something outside the world, Wittgenstein's position, as we have seen, is ambiguous. God, values (goodness, beauty), the mystical—does he or does he not believe in their existence? And what about the epistemological self? If these entities do exist, none the less they are not things *in* the world, and so all talk of them must be nonsense of the higher sort. The world in its entirety is not some thing *in* the world. So when we speak about the world in its entirety, we fall victim to nonsense of the second category.

But there are also other kinds of higher nonsense. According to the picture theory of language, there are properties of, and relations among, things in the world, which cannot be named in language. But the picture theory itself speaks of these properties of, and relations among, things. Thus, the picture theory is itself an attempt to say the unsayable and therefore an instance of higher nonsense.

If a truth is not a tautology, it could always have been false, although it happens to be true. But, when Wittgenstein says, for instance, that things are simple, he considers the opposite inconceivable. The sentence "Things are simple" can hardly be a tautology on Wittgenstein's position. Thus, that sentence does not fulfil a demand which every sentence must fulfil in order to be meaningful. Therefore, this sentence is nonsense, although nonsense of a higher sort. We saw in section 24, part A, that Wittgenstein distinguishes between internal and external properties (relations) of things (and of states of affairs). All internal properties and relations are in the same predicament as the simplicity of things. Any sentence in which we ascribe an internal property (relation) to something is thus nonsense. That a thing *a* is a *thing*, that a relation *R* is a *relation*, that a number *n* is a *number*, that a function *f* is a *function*, and so on—all these sentences affirm internal properties of something and are therefore nonsense.

According to Wittgenstein, logical properties of, and relations among, linguistic expressions are also internal, and therefore any attempt to describe the logic of language must result in nonsense. That one sentence is the negation of another, that a sentence is a tautology (contradiction, proper sentence), that a sentence follows from other sentences, and so on—all these assertions about language are concerned with internal properties and relations, and therefore they are nonsense.[19]

Logic itself, the logic of the world (section 24), and the logic of language (section 25), thus belong to the unsayable.

The *Tractatus* does not set out to describe what is actually the case in the world. The book claims to describe features

---

[19] Although we cannot meaningfully say that something is a thing, our language can *show* that something is a thing in that the name of that thing has a characteristic form. (The same holds for relations, numbers, functions, etc.) Although we cannot meaningfully say that the thing *a* is different from the thing *b*, we can show that they are different by using different names for *a* and *b*. Internal properties and relations of the entity referred to by a linguistic expression are shown, Wittgenstein seems to think (cf. 4.124, 4.125), through the fact that the linguistic expression itself has corresponding internal properties and relations.

which the world and the things in the world could not conceivably lack. Wittgenstein does not say: "This is so", but over and over again he says: "This must be so". This, too, is a reason why the *Tractatus*, according to its own assumptions, will be nonsense. For, according to the assumptions, meaningful language is always truth-functional. But "must-sentences" are not truth-functional in the sense defined in (D4) (p. 183). A frequently used example, which clarifies this is the following: "7 + 2 = 9" and "The number of the major planets is 9" are equivalent; but while "It must be the case that 7 + 2 = 9" is correct, it would be rash to assert "It must be the case that the number of the major planets is 9." Perhaps some day we will discover a tenth! Thus, all the "must-sentences" in the *Tractatus* are nonsense.

28. PHILOSOPHY AND SCIENCE

For Wittgenstein, the nature of philosophy was constantly a problem as urgent as any special philosophical question. We have already become acquainted with two of his claims about philosophy:

(i) Most questions and sentences which have been put forth in philosophy are nonsense of (what I have called) the lower kind.

(ii) There is a philosophical nonsense of (what I have called) a higher kind. The assertions in the *Tractatus* are mostly nonsense of this sort.

Wittgenstein's view of philosophy is based on a sharp distinction between philosophy and empirical science. Their domains are mutually exclusive: if a question or sentence belongs to empirical science, then it does not belong to philosophy, and conversely. Darwin's doctrine of biological evolution, which during the latter half of the nineteenth century so deeply influenced what is usually called philosophy, has no philosophical relevance, according to Wittgenstein. Psychology, too, which during the same period had such an intimate connection with philosophy, is philosophically irrelevant. Wittgenstein's determination to keep philosophy entirely free from empirical elements is a feature which can be traced back to Platonism.

The distinction between philosophy and science becomes, in Wittgenstein, paradoxical. All true sentences about reality belong, according to him, to empirical science, indeed, "natural science". What, then, remains for the philosopher to say? How can we escape the conclusion that the philosopher must either content himself with tautologies (or, even worse, contradictions) or observe a pregnant silence? Occasionally Wittgenstein seems to compromise. The world certainly belongs to natural science, but the logical structure of the language with which we describe the world is a suitable territory for philosophy. At times he expresses the position:

(iii) Philosophy is, or ought to be, the same as the "logical syntax", or "logical grammar" of language.

With special emphasis on the idea that philosophy must uncover errors and imperfections of language, he maintains that:

(iv) Philosophy is, or ought to be, the same as "critique of language".

Also, those truths which can occur in a philosophical investigation of language, must, according to the *Tractatus*, be either tautologies or empirical truths of the natural sciences. Does Wittgenstein wish, with (iii) and (iv), to recommend to philosophers that they limit themselves to the assertion of tautologies about language? If so, one can reasonably ask why tautologies about the linguistic part of reality are more philosophical than tautologies about the non-linguistic part. Or, does he wish to limit philosophy to an empirical study of language? But then, after all, philosophy would become empirical. And why should an empirical investigation of language be more philosophical than any other empirical investigation? Certainly Wittgenstein himself was aware of these complications.

From the *Tractatus* one can also get the impression that Wittgenstein thinks:

(v) Philosophy is, or ought to be, the same as higher nonsense.

But then the *Tractatus* also puts forth the point of view that:

(vi) True philosophy consists in showing that all (other) philosophy is nonsense.

Wittgenstein seems to consider philosophy to be a therapeutic activity which results in the liberation of the patient from nonsensical philosophical problems.

Another thought in the *Tractatus*, a Socratic one, is related to the above but not identical with it:

(vii) The task of philosophy is to make thoughts clearer.

The point of view which Wittgenstein seems finally to embrace is the most radical.

(viii) True philosophy is the observation of silence on all questions which do not belong to the natural sciences.

VI

Experience and Language:
Rudolf Carnap and Logical Empiricism

29. LOGICAL EMPIRICISM

The philosophical movement known as logical empiricism (also logical positivism or neo-positivism) was born in Vienna in the 1920s. Its origin was the "Vienna Circle", which gathered around Moritz Schlick, a professor of philosophy in Vienna from 1922 until his tragic death (by murder) in 1936. Scientists representing many disciplines belonged to the circle: mathematician Hans Hahn, sociologist Otto Neurath, historian Victor Kraft, jurist Felix Kaufman, physicist Philipp Frank, and, as permanent members or occasional visitors, many others. The most systematic philosophical talent of the circle was Rudolf Carnap, who gradually became its indubitable leader.

The Vienna Circle purposefully established contact with similar philosophical groups elsewhere, for example the "Berlin group" (Reichenbach, Dubislav, Grelling, Hempel, and others) and the Polish "Lwow–Warsaw group" (Lukasiewicz, Kotarbinski, Lesniewski, Ajdukiewicz, Tarski, Chwistek, and others). Influential philosophers in other parts of the world, like Eino Kaila in Finland, Arne Naess in Norway, Jörgen Jörgensen in Denmark, A. J. Ayer in England, L. Rougier in France, and Ernest Nagel and W. V. O. Quine in the United States, were deeply influenced by the ideas of the circle. In this way an international movement developed. The intellectual bonds which held it together certainly varied in strength. The strongest tie was a common interest in the methodology of science and an opposition to "traditional", "metaphysical" philosophy. Hitlerism and the Second World War dispersed or exterminated the continental members of the movement. Annihilation struck many of the scientists of Jewish birth who were in sympathy with the movement in Germany and Poland. Some members, including

Carnap, Reichenbach, Frank, von Mises, Feigl, Kaufman and Hempel, found refuge in the United States, which became the new homeland of the movement. Little by little it has met the fate which often befalls philosophical schools: dogmas have been forgotten, positions have been modified, and ideas which first appeared revolutionary have become common property. The generation which once enthusiastically experienced a springtime of ideas is vanishing.

The designation "logical empricism" points to the two sources from which the movement derived its original inspiration: mathematical logic, especially as formulated by Bertrand Russell, and empiricist epistemology. Many empiricists have had an inclination toward a phenomenalistic interpretation of (statements about) the external world. The Vienna Circle of the 1920s also thought along phenomenalistic lines. The phenomenalistic tendencies were soon broken by a materialistic (or physicalistic) trend which was later to become dominant.

The Vienna Circle was in sympathy with many of the ideas expressed by the Viennese Wittgenstein in his *Tractatus*. Metaphysics is nonsense; everything which can be meaningfully said can be said in the language of science; analytic sentences are *a priori* but uninformative while synthetic sentences are to be empirically verified; philosophy must be the analysis and criticism of language—these are some of the positions on which the Vienna Circle and the *Tractatus* were in agreement.

The Vienna Circle shared the respect for science which in the young Wittgenstein took an almost mystic form. The word "science" can be used simply as a collective term designating a rather vaguely delimited and heterogeneous set of men, institutions, activities, methods, observations, experiments, theories, books, etc., in other words, everything that the history of science deals with. When the word is used in this way, science varies in quality. To decide whether or not something is science is in many cases as difficult, not to say as fruitless, as to decide whether or not something is art. When the term is used in this historical sense, it can hardly figure in abstract reasonings with a claim to precision. For the Vienna Circle, however, "science" became a term of approbation surrounded by a nimbus of authority, and also a word which was confidently used in the intellectual game as though it were a well-defined chess-man. Venerable and obscure concepts like "the scientific language", "the fundamental scientific theory", "the basic postulates of science", and so on, are constantly encountered in Carnap. The step from respect for authority to a claim to authority for oneself is seldom long. The Vienna Circle called its own world-view "the scientific world-view". Its physicalism was occasionally referred to as "scientific materialism".

The struggle against metaphysics which was carried on with special intensity during the twenties and thirties was partly motivated by disgust for what was considered to be fruitless and obscure prattle, by a longing for intellectual clarity. But as latter-day enlightenment philosophers, many with socialist leanings, the logical empiricist must also have looked upon certain "metaphysical" ideas as a threat to the human values they cherished. During the years when logical empiricism flourished, the anti-human forces that were to plunge the world into war and, in passing, to sweep logical empiricism off the continent, grew in Germany. The myths in which these forces clothed their ambitions were often "metaphysical" in the word's most derogatory connotation. (It would be interesting to know whether for the logical empiricists, as for, for example, the Swede Axel Hägerström, the struggle against metaphysics also involved a personal liberation. To the best of my knowledge, none of them has made a confession on this point.) If, in their respect for science, they followed one German tradition, the logical empiricists reacted against another German tradition in their condemnation of metaphysics. The intensity of both the respect and the condemnation must be understood against the background of the cultural milieu.

Logical empiricism set out with a number of theses or slogans, the thesis of the meaninglessness of metaphysics, the verification principle, the physicalistic thesis, and so on, which gave expression to a common outlook, which served as unifying bonds among its members, and which were all aimed against "metaphysics" and "traditional philosophy". Much of the philosophical work done within early logical empiricism was devoted to the elaboration of these theses. Along with this work, logical empiricists, and scientists in sympathy and contact with them, made a large number of particular studies in the logic and philosophy of science. Although these investigations were often inspired by the general theses, in substance they are as often as not independent of the latter. In the long run, these particular studies will probably stand out as the most important contribution of logical empiricism. Unfortunately, these studies do not admit of a brief non-technical account. Well aware of the fact that the following presentation does not do full justice to the movement, I shall focus here on the general theses. Carnap was the thinker who made the most vigorous efforts to impart precision to them, and our attention will, therefore, be focused on his ideas.

Rudolf Carnap (1891–1970, successively attached to the universities of Vienna, Prague, Chicago, and Los Angeles) was primarily a logical constructor. To philosophize was for him essentially to attempt through "logical analysis" to give precision to vaguely understood intuitive concepts and thereby to solve philosophical perplexities and conflicts. This can best be accomplished, he thought, through the construction of formalized languages in which the originally vague concepts obtain their well-defined places. Fundamental philosophical differences (for example that between phenomenalism and materialism) are solved, he thought, when the opposing positions are clothed in such languages (in this instance, a phenomenalistic and a materialistic language). What language one chooses to speak is, according to Carnap, essentially a question of expediency. Through formalization the philosophical dispute is transformed into a discussion of the advantages and disadvantages of the respective languages. (Carnap takes for granted that such discussion does not force us to take up again the initial dispute. He also takes for granted that one cannot construct formalized languages within which the dispute can be carried on!)

Carnap's writings, of which the most important are *The Logical Structure of the World* (*Der logische Aufbau der Welt*) (1928), *The Logical Syntax of Language* (*Logische*

Syntax der Sprache) (1934), *Introduction to Semantics* (1942), *Meaning and Necessity* (1947), and *Logical Foundations of Probability* (1950), are all devoted to the task of constructing formalized languages and discussing their properties. In 1934 Carnap formulated his "principle of tolerance": "It is not our business to set up prohibitions, but to arrive at conventions";[1] or, "In logic, there are no morals. Everyone is at liberty to build up his own logic, i.e. his own form of language, as he wishes".[2] Since 1934 he has restated his principle several times, with minor modifications. However, Carnap is not actually a philosophically-neutral framer of languages. His constructive activity is determined by his adherence to the ideas of logical empiricism, and is an attempt to give concrete shape to these ideas. There is, it might seem, a personal contradiction between the dismissal of philosophical arguments in favour of neutral language construction, on the one hand, and the lifelong attachment to a certain philosophical outlook, on the other.

"Empiricism" is the major term in "logical empiricism". Apart from the discussion of epistemological principles, the movement demonstrated its empirical interest primarily through logical analysis of theories of natural science, an analysis which often took the form of axiomatization or even formalization. But logical empiricists have themselves seldom studied empirical questions empirically. This is connected with the Platonistic view taken over from Wittgenstein, that empirical investigations are the concern of "the sciences", not of "philosophy". Here too we meet a personal paradox. At the centre of the logical empiricists' interest stands human knowledge as expressed in human language, the separation of the scientific use of language from other uses, for example the metaphysical use, and the analysis of the languages of science. When reading, for example, Carnap's discussions of such questions, we often find ourselves in an abstract combinatorial sphere far above the confused voices of the human crowd. The contact between the abstract arguments and what they are supposed to illuminate is often obscure.

---

[1] Carnap, R., *The Logical Syntax of Language* (London: Kegan Paul, Trench, Trubner, & Co., 1937), p. 51.

[2] Ibid., p. 52.

The picture of Carnap, the philosopher, also offers another paradox. Within the framework of his general logico-empirical convictions, Carnap has several times altered his views rather radically. In this respect he can most readily be compared with Bertrand Russell. Each of Russell's standpoints bears the mark of being obtained by weighing the arguments for and against it, of his seeing the objections and somehow remaining in doubt. Carnap, on the other hand, states each of his successive views in a manner as if he has now seen, and is telling the reader, how things are. He gives the impression of being a thinker who again and again, finds a new house for his old faith.

30. THE CRITIQUE OF METAPHYSICS

A. *What is "metaphysics"?*

The word "metaphysics" is used in very many different ways. When an author discusses, defends, or condemns "metaphysics", in general terms, one must always ask just what he understands by the word. The types of question and view which logical empiricists pre-eminently regarded as metaphysical were the following:

(1) *Transcendental questions.* To this category we may refer such questions as are obviously concerned with what is far removed from the realm of sense experience. Questions about the existence and nature of God belong here. Further, positions like Parmenides' doctrine of being, Plato's doctrine of heavenly ideas, Spinoza's doctrine of substance, Leibniz's doctrine of monads, Kant's doctrine of the thing-in-itself, Hegel's doctrine of the Absolute, and so on. Transcendental views have traditionally been targets for criticism from empiricists.

(2) *Questions of existence.* To this group we may count questions such as these: Does an external world exist? Does matter exist? Do space and time exist? Do universals exist? Do numbers (natural, rational, real, complex, transfinite, and so on) exist? Do classes (sets) exist? Do things like Bolzano's propositions-in-themselves exist? While logical empiricists were inclined to discard all questions of this sort as pseudo-problems, they also had a tendency to adopt

phenomenalistic (later materialistic, or physicalistic) and nominalistic points of view.

Obviously, logical empiricists did not regard all questions of existence as metaphysical. Questions like: "Did Moses exist?", or "Are there infinitely many prime numbers?", are never ruled out as metaphysical. Exactly how the line between the metaphysical and the non-metaphysical ought to be drawn here is not at all clear. Carnap now and then suggested that questions as to the existence of particular entities within a "system" (or "framework") that we take for granted, are meaningful, but that questions as to the existence of the "system" as a whole are metaphysical nonsense. The question of the existence of Moses, or of an infinity of prime numbers, is, he maintains, of the former kind, whereas questions about the external world or the number system are of the latter.

(3) *Questions about essences.* Under this title I bring together questions such as these: What is the nature of the external world? Is it (as Russell said) a logical construction from sense-data, or does it have an independent reality (as realists of different persuasions assert)? Is the material world really mental (as, for example, according to Leibniz's doctrine of monads), or is it non-mental? What is the nature of time and space? Is Newton's absolutist or Leibniz's relativist interpretation correct? Are universals mere names (as nominalists argue), ideas in the mind (*intentiones animae*), as the medieval conceptualists taught, or do they have an independent reality, as Plato assumed? Are the non-negative integers sets of equinumerous sets, as Frege and Russell argued, or is some other interpretation of their nature the correct one?

(4) *Semantic questions.* What is the meaning of this or that expression (word, sentence)? Does this expression have the same meaning as that? Etc. The attitude of logical empiricists to semantic questions radically changed with time. In the 1930s Carnap thought that questions of meaning, as usually understood, are metaphysical or, at least, that they are a source of metaphysics. But he also maintained that metaphysical questions of meaning can, to a large extent, be translated into legitimate syntactic questions. Under the

influence of Tarski's semantic investigations, Carnap later abandoned this point of view, and came to think that the semantic study of language is as legitimate as the syntactic.

(5) *Questions of values.* Logical empiricism harboured a large number of divergent views as to the nature of value statements and normative statements. In 1928 Carnap thought that value concepts could be defined within science. With several other logical empiricists (Ayer, von Mises, etc.), he later took the position that value statements have approximately the same status as metaphysical assertions and fall victim to essentially the same critique as these. Logical empiricists also sometimes defended an emotive theory similar to that propounded by Hägerström and Stevenson.

B. *The content of the critique*

The critique that logical empiricists levelled against metaphysical sentences (statements) follows approximately the following schema (C):

(i) A sentence is meaningful if and only if it is empirically verifiable.

(ii) S is not empirically verifiable.

(iii) Hence, S is meaningless.

(i) is a very rough formulation of the so-called verification principle (or principle of verifiability), the content of which we shall study in greater detail in sections 31 and 32. Together with (i) the following principle was often assumed:

(iv) A sentence is meaningful if and only if its negation is meaningful.

Hence, if sentence S is meaningless, by virtue of (iv) its negation non-S is meaningless too. According to this version of the logical empiricist critique, the assertions "The external world exists" and "The external world does not exist", are both equally meaningless. If a yes-or-no question is taken to be meaningless when both the affirmative and the negative answer are meaningless, then the very question "Does the external world exist?" is meaningless.

In addition to the so-called verification principle the logical empiricists of the 1920s and 1930s invoked several other semantic principles. Frequently they referred to Russell's theory of types in its semantic version. Sentences whose construction seemingly did not agree with this theory were held to be meaningless, and the claim was advanced that sins against this theory recur especially often in metaphysical discourses.

C. *The plausibility of the critique*

The critical schema (C) is only a sketch of a line of reasoning. It lacks the power to convince as long as (a) the so-called verification principle has not been made more precise and justified by good reasons, and (b) the criticized sentence S has not been shown, by detailed argument, actually to lack empirical verifiability, in the sense of the principle. The meaning of the verification principle was the subject of a long discussion, which never led to generally accepted results. In the following sections we shall get some glimpses of this discussion. It seems that the logical empiricists were never aware of the need for thorough analysis in connection with (b). They were usually satisfied with judging, rather impressionistically, that this or that sentence, which was classified as "metaphysical", also lacked "empirical verifiability".

Obviously, a sentence cannot, in an absolute sense, be said to possess or lack empirical verifiability. Its verifiability depends on the "interpretation" given to it. The very same sentence may be verifiable upon one interpretation and unverifiable upon another. If we have succeeded in specifying an interpretation under which a sentence S is unverifiable, we do not thereby acquire the right to assert that S as it occurs in the writings of philosopher X is unverifiable. In order to establish the latter assertion, we must undertake a presumably very arduous investigation showing that X actually interprets S in the specified manner. (X's interpretation of a given sentence may also change from one time to another, from one page to the next in a given book.) A methodical investigation of metaphysical texts was never presented by any logical empiricist. Thus, whatever one may think of the verification principle, the logical empiricist critique of metaphysics never becomes very convincing.

The mistrust of so-called metaphysical questions, which

logical empiricists felt, cannot be other than sound. The types of questions listed in (1)–(5) above are in one way or another obscure or indefinite. In order to be profitably discussed, they ought to be made more precise, i.e. replaced by other related but clearer questions. It seems, however, an unfortunate policy to rule out categorically questions of this sort with the claim that they are meaningless. How many unclear questions have been the impulse to fruitful research? How many such questions have been capable of interesting clarification? To be cautious in dealing with what is not clear is reasonable, but to shut one's eyes to it may be narrow-minded.

Through the development of his thought on semantic questions, Carnap himself gives food for critical reflection of this kind. During his syntactic period in the 1930s he rejected questions of meaning as metaphysical. Later he became one of the foremost exponents of logical semantics, and during his semantic phase, Carnap made many statements of the sort which he earlier repudiated as metaphysical. In *Meaning and Necessity* (1947) he reintroduced, for instance, a series of distinctions (predicate/attribute/class; individual name/individual concept/individual; and sentence/proposition/truth-value), which he earlier regarded as belonging to a metaphysical Platonism.

An unbiased investigation of language would probably show that there are an almost boundless number of statement properties which may be intellectually desirable, that they generally occur in varying degreees, and that what degree of what property is desirable depends on the context in which the statement occurs. The logical empiricists' division of statements into meaningful and meaningless seems to be an example of oversimplifying black-and-white thinking. A feeling for this state of affairs is noticeable in both Hempel's and Carnap's later publications. Although logical empiricists originally used the dichotomy meaningful as against meaningless largely without qualification, in these later publications the verification principle is said to be concerned with "cognitive", "theoretical", "scientific", or "empirical" meaning, it being recognized that there are also other kinds of meaning. Already in *Testability and*

Meaning in 1936–7, Carnap had maintained that one must distinguish different notions of cognitive meaningfulness. But this budding awareness of nuance never led to a radical reorientation of logical-empiricists thought. In fact, Carnap never abandoned his conviction that one can draw a sharp boundary between the meaningful and the meaningless; as late as 1956 he proposed what he supposed to be such a boundary.

31. VERIFIABILITY AND MEANING

A. *The methodological character of the verification principle*

The verification principle was given a large number of divergent formulations by different authors at different times. Thus, the phrase "the verification principle" is used here only as a common name for logical-empiricist ideas about a connection between meaningfulness and empirical verifiability.

The fundamental intuition is closely related to the Empiricist Theory of Knowledge which we have met in the classical British empiricists and especially in Hume. On Hume's view the only method of acquiring knowledge about "matters of fact" is that which empirical science employs and which Hume attempted to describe. Logical empiricism was in essential agreement with Hume, even if it did not underwrite his description. But logical empiricism sharpened Hume's thoughts. Statements which do not admit empirical verification fall outside the boundaries, not only of knowledge, but also of sense.

Of such statements, Hume said that they were only "sophistry and illusion", and he added rhetorically that books consisting of them ought to be burned. Logical empiricists usually acknowledged that meaningless sentences might have a value in contexts other than the quest for truth, for instance in poetry. But obviously the thesis of verifiability implies a repudiation of non-verifiable sentences which is different from Hume's only in degree. The thesis involves a prohibition against introducing non-verifiable sentences into scientific and philosophical discussions, or at least the proposal that one ought not to do so. During the early *"Sturm-und-Drang"* years of logical empiricism, in the

1920s and 30s, the thesis was often put forward in a manner arrogant enough to justify the characterization of it as a prohibition. In the more cautious formulations to be found in the later writings of Carnap and Hempel, the thesis is better characterized as a proposal, which is also how the later Carnap described it.

The prohibition, or proposal, was often considered to imply a clarification, or (as Carnap preferred to say) an "explication", of a pre-existing "intuitive" concept of meaning. If we consider ordinary language and the "intuitions" which it embodies, we shall no doubt find many concepts of meaning. There are many kinds of rejection of a statement which can be expressed in ordinary language by the claim that it is "meaningless". If the verification principle is advanced as an explication of some intuitive concept of meaning, one ought in some way to specify that concept. Several intuitive notions of meaning can, in fact, be distinguished in the logical-empiricist discussions of the thesis.

(1) *A meaningful sentence is a sentence which is true or false*. This concept of meaningful sentence plays a central role in Russell's theory of types, and was borrowed therefrom by logical empiricism. We may call it *Russell's concept of meaning*.

(2) *A meaningful sentence is an intelligible sentence, one which expresses a "thought" in Frege's sense*. This can be called *Frege's concept of meaning*. As we have seen, Frege distinguished between the "sense" of a sentence, i.e. the "thought" which it expresses or evokes in those who understand it, and its "reference", which he takes to be its truth-value. In a natural language a sentence can be meaningful without having a truth-value, although this situation is regarded as an anomaly by Frege. From his point of view, his and Russell's concepts of meaning do not coincide.

(3) *A meaningful sentence expresses something which could possibly be the case*. This notion is found, for example, in Schlick, and if we wish to have a name for it, we could call it *Schlick's concept of meaning*. A sentence which is meaningless in this sense can presumably be meaningful in the sense of Frege as well as in that of Russell.

(4) *A meaningful sentence is one which is correctly formulated in either a natural or a formalized language*; i.e. is a "sentence" or "well-formed formula", according to the grammar of the language. This concept of meaning occasionally appears in the early writings of Carnap. It is, however, easily seen to be philosophically completely uninteresting: for every conceivable combination of symbols we can construct a formalized language in which that combination of symbols is labelled a correctly constituted sentence or formula.

(5) *A meaningful sentence is one which serves a genuine function (to be stated more precisely) in empirical science.* This could be called the *empirico-functional concept of meaning*. *A priori*, it appears plausible that a sentence could be meaningful in all the preceding senses although, in the present state of science, it lacks this kind of meaning.

At its inception logical empiricism seems to have been primarily interested in (1). Little by little, especially in the writings of Carnap and Hempel, (5) has become predominant. This shift in emphasis corresponds to another change in the verification principle. It was initially presented as though it expressed a fixed boundary for the languages of science and philosophy. In the later publications of Carnap and Hempel, the boundary has become variable. It is made dependent on the content of scientific theory and will shift as this content changes. A sentence which does now serve the function implied by the empirico-functional concept of meaning may come to lose it. The difference between the earlier and later interpretations can be somewhat drastically expressed as follows. According to the earlier one, a meaningless sentence is like a cog-wheel which is useless because of a flaw in its manufacture. According to the later one, it is like a cogwheel which in itself is without fault but which is not at present put to work in the machinery. The thesis of verification has also undergone a change in another respect. At an earlier stage it was often presented as a criterion with the help of which one can rather effectively decide whether or not a given linguistic expression is a meaningful sentence. In the later discussion, on the other hand, an essentially theoretical interest is attributed to the thesis. In 1950, Hempel called the thesis a "criterion", but he expected above all that it should, together with the explication of certain other concepts, "provide the framework for a general theoretical account of the structure and the foundations of scientific knowledge".[3]

B. *Atomistic formulations of the verification principle*

The attempts to make the verification principle precise, can, roughly speaking, be divided into what I shall call the atomistic and the holistic ones. In the holistic attempts a certain (formalized) language L is indicated, and meaningful sentences are then identified with those sentences which either themselves belong to L, or can be translated into sentences that do. The atomistic attempts do not have this character: they explain meaningfulness as a property which belongs to a sentence independently of its inclusion in, or translatability into, a more comprehensive language. The early attempts at precise formulation were on the whole atomistic, while the later were generally holistic. In this section we shall take a brief glance at some early atomistic formulations. In sections 31, part C, and 32, some holistic attempts will be reviewed.

At the basis of all the attempts lay certain rather vague ideas of the following sort. To know what a sentence means, is to know what would be the case if it were true. To know what the sentence means, it was also said, is to know what difference to the world it would make if it were true rather than false. But to us the world is the world of our experience. To know what the sentence means is, hence, to know what difference to our experience it would make if it were true rather than false. If it is true, one experiential fact, or set of facts, will obtain; if it is false, another. Hence, a meaningful sentence is one that can be verified in experience, if it is true—or falsified, if it is false. This was the way the argument would often run. The upshot was roughly this:

VP 1. Sentence A is meaningful, if and only if A is verifiable or falsifiable through experience.

[3] Hempel, C., "Problems and Changes in the Empiricist Criterion of Meaning", *Revue International de Philosophie*, vol. 11 (1950), p. 60, (reprinted many times in other contexts).

The early formulations of the verification principle were mostly very informal and open to different interpretations. *VP 1* would better agree with some early formulations if "verifiable or falsifiable" were replaced by "verifiable", with others if it were replaced by "falsifiable". The following formulations *VP 2* and *VP 3* should be read with this observation in mind.

Logically true, or analytic, sentences are true by virtue of their very meaning, and genuine experiential testing of them was usually thought to be impossible. The same was assumed to be the case with the logically false, or contradictory, sentences. Therefore, it seemed reasonable to restrict the verification principle to sentences which are neither logically true (analytic) nor logically false (contradictory). Also, in some sense, human experience never comprises more than a finite number of observations. When these considerations are taken into account, it may seem reasonable to rewrite the preliminary *VP 1* as:

VP 2. If the sentence A is neither logically true (analytic) nor logically false (contradictory), then A is meaningful if and only if A can be verified or falsified through a finite number of observations.

All of the more careful attempts to make the verification principle precise were based on the idea of what were called "observation" or "protocol" sentences. Such a sentence was one that could be verified conclusively by a single observation, or one that described the content of a single conceivable observation. Observation sentences were thought of as the linguistic counterparts of conceivable observations. In terms of this idea, *VP 2* becomes:

VP 2^x. If A is neither logically true (analytic) nor logically false (contradictory), then A is meaningful if and only if A or the negation of A follows from a finite, consistent set of observation sentences.

Opinions have differed as to what sentences should be considered as genuine observation sentences. Schematically, there were at least the following three positions on the question:

(a) Observation sentences describe what a person is

directly experiencing or could directly experience at a given moment of time, for example: "blue here now", "red there", "red circle now", etc. (This is the verbless baby-talk that logical empiricists in the 1930s often preferred in this context, for unknown reasons.)

(b) Observation sentences say that a person at a given moment of time directly experiences something, for example, "*P* now sees a red circle".

(c) Observation sentences describe directly observable physical phenomena, for example "A red cube is lying on the table". (A picturesque synthesis of these ideas was proposed by Otto Neurath, the chief proponent of physicalism. On his view, an observation sentence ought to read like this: "Otto's protocol at 3.17 p.m.; At 3.16 p.m. Otto told himself; (At 3.15 p.m. there was in the room a table that was observed by Otto.)")[4]

The same hesitation as in Hume between a subjectivist and an objectivist interpretation of epistemologically basic sentences is thus apparent in logical empiricism. Obviously, just as in Hume, the choice between the various interpretations will have far-reaching consequences. Choosing (a), the verification principle will turn out to admit one set of sentences as meaningful. Choosing (b), the principle will most probably turn out to admit another. Etc. The difficult choice has to be made.

The notion of "following" is another critical point in $VP\ 2^x$. In the early days of logical empiricism, no problem was perceived here. However, if the field of this relation coincides with the set of meaningful sentences, $VP\ 2^x$ appears quite unnecessarily complex: a meaningful sentence is then the same as a sentence belonging to that field, and it could be defined as such. If, on the other hand, the relation is explained so as to make its field comprise also sentences without meaning, unreasonable results may ensue, as Hempel has pointed out. A sensible syntactical relation of "following" must, Hempel thinks, satisfy the condition that if A follows from B, then "A or C" follows from B, even if C is a non-sense sentence. Assume now that B is an observation sentence, and that A is found to follow from B and hence is

[4] Neurath, O., "Protokollsätze", *Erkenntnis*, vol. 3 (1932–33), p. 207.

established as meaningful. Then, "*A* or *C*" will also follow from *B* and be meaningful even when *C* is meaningless. But this, Hempel observes, goes against the principle generally accepted by logical empiricists that a compound sentence (for example "*A* or *C*") is meaningful if and only if all its component sentences (here *A*, *C*) are meaningful.

Further, *VP 2*^{x} seems to limit the scope of sense to an absurd degree. The purpose of the verification principle is to save scientific discourse from intrusions by metaphysical discourse. The principle should certify sound science as meaningful while ruling out metaphysics as meaningless. But *VP 2*^{x} apparently cuts away most of science. Neither Newton's mechanical laws, nor Maxwell's electrodynamical equations, nor Einstein's theory of relativity satisfy the demand of *VP 2*^{x} upon meaningful sentences. No theory of this kind, nor its negation, strictly follows from any finite consistent set of observation sentences. When Newton was thought to be refuted by the Michelson–Morley experiment, a wealth of scientific theory was taken for granted in the interpretation of the experiment.

It was sometimes suggested that the verification principle should be stated roughly as follows:

VP 3. If a sentence *A* is neither logically true (analytic) nor logically false (contradictory), then *A* is meaningful if and only if *A* or the negation of *A* follows from a finite consistent set of observation sentences together with established scientific theory.

This formulation, too, is open to a number of serious objections. What is "established" scientific theory? Does it have to be meaningful? If it does, by what criterion shall this meaningfulness be judged? Does the negation of Newton really *follow* from the Michelson–Morley experiment, in the light of other accepted theory? Isn't the negation at most rendered more or less probable? Should we then replace "follows from" in *VP 3* by "is rendered probable by", or something of the sort? But here "probability" cannot be the probability of statistical theory. What "probability" is it then?

In this way, one can continue to introduce more and more items and provisos into the atomistic formulations of the principle, but new objections are seen constantly to arise. As a matter of fact, the number of atomistic formulations that occur in the early writings of logical empiricists is very large and they are, as a whole, extremely confusing. Reverting to *VP 2*, we find a new fundamental objection to the whole atomistic approach. If A is without meaning, what about "*A* or not *A*"? Should it be labelled logically true (an instance of the law of the excluded middle) and hence meaningful? But this contradicts the principle we have already invoked against *VP 2*^{x}, viz. that a compound sentence is meaningful if and only if its components are meaningful. Or should "*A* or not *A*" be labelled as meaningless in this case? If so, by what criterion? The more one studies the atomistic approach to the problem of meaning, the stronger grows one's conviction that it was stillborn.

Beside the epistemological notions of observation and observation sentence, the atomistic attempts to elucidate the verifiability thesis made use of such logical notions as:

Sentence A follows from the set of sentences S,
The set of sentences S is consistent,
Sentence A is analytic,
Sentence A is contradictory.

As the entire modern logico-philosophical discussion shows, these concepts are far from unproblematic. According to a view which Carnap forcefully asserted and which is now widely held by analytical philosophers, these concepts must be explicated with reference to some definite, preferably formalized language. This view is one reason why logical empiricists moved from atomistic to holistic formulations of the verifiability thesis.

Gradually logical empiricists came to agree that the set of meaningful sentences should be considered closed under a number of logical operations. It was, for example, as we have seen, commonly assumed that a sentential compound (not A, A and B, A or B, etc.) is meaningful if and only if each one of its components (A, B, etc.) is meaningful. The assumption of such closure properties was yet another reason why the principle of verifiability came to be formulated as a characteristic, not of isolated sentences, but of an entire language.

The holistic approach to meaning merged with the attempt to frame a "universal language", a language capable of expressing everything that can be meaningfully said in the sciences. Thus, a sentence came to be thought of as meaningful if it either itself belongs to the assumed universal language or can be translated into a sentence which does. In this way, the verification principle fused with the ideas of a "universal language" and of "the unity of science".

32. THE UNITY OF SCIENCE AND THE IDEA OF A UNIVERSAL LANGUAGE

A. *The unity of science*

One of the banners under which logical empricists rallied in the 1930s was "the unity of science". The slogan denounced the arbitrary and often artificial boundaries which linguistic usage and academic organizations have created between scientific disciplines, and it called for interdisciplinary as well as international scientific co-operation. It called especially for close contact between philosophy and the various sciences. The programme was put into action through interdisciplinary congresses and publications. The theoretical ideas for which the slogan also stood were sometimes expressed through the assertion that all objects with which science deals, or can ever deal, are of "the same kind", and also that all concepts with which science describes its objects are of "the same kind". If presented without amplification, such assertions say nothing, since what is counted as "the same kind" is entirely conventional. What logical empiricists had in mind when arguing for the unity of science, is perhaps best understood by taking a look at some of the suppositions which, on their view, run counter to the unity, for example:

"Pure mathematics and logic are concerned with a world of ideal objects, different in kind from physical reality."
"The psychical is in principle distinct from the physical."
"The sphere of values and the sphere of facts are distinct."
"Man as studied by the humanistic disciplines (*Geisteswissenschaften*) is distinct from man as studied in biology."

The idea of the unity of science is intimately related to attempts like Bertrand Russell's to "construct" reality on a unified basis and to Wittgenstein's view of "the world" in the *Tractatus*. The logical empiricists tried to give precision to the idea by constructing a formalized universal language. Within logical empiricism it has often been pointed out that the unity of the sciences may be either a unity in regard to objects and concepts or a unity with respect to laws. A unity in regard to laws would be achieved if one succeeded, for example, in systematizing the laws of physics and deriving from them those laws which are assumed in the rest of empirical science. The thesis of the unity of science affirms a unity with regard to objects and concepts. It was acknowledged that unity regarding laws exists at present only to a very small extent, and the logical empiricists were cautious when it came to prophesying in this respect. The unity of science was thus thought to prevail in the sense that all scientific sentences can be formulated within a common universal language. Within this language the sets of sentences accepted within the different sciences (physics, chemistry, biology, psychology, sociology, history of literature, etc.) might be logically more or less isolated continents.

In accordance with their empiricist convictions the logical empiricists demanded that the universal language of science should have empirical content. The successive proposals for the formulation of a universal language, especially those presented by Carnap, constitute attempts to meet both the requirement of universality and that of empirical content. These two demands showed themselves to be more difficult to reconcile than had at first been believed. For Carnap the problem is further complicated by his desire that the universal empirical language should be, at least to some extent, a formalized language.

B. *The Logical Structure of the World* (*Der logische Aufbau der Welt*)

Using *Principia Mathematica* as the logical foundation, Carnap sketched, in his 1928 volume *The Logical Structure of the World*, a supposedly universal empirical language. For the sake of simplicity I shall call this language L_{28}. The signs in L_{28} are divided into types according to Russell's theory of types, and the construction of sentences from the type-determined signs follows the rules of this theory. L_{28} is a formalized language in so far as the construction of sentences is formalized. Carnap does not, however, formally define any concept of theorem in L_{28}. At the bottom of the type hierarchy in L_{28}, just as in *Principia Mathematica*, there is a domain of individuals, or, as Carnap said in 1928, basic elements. *Principia Mathematica* assumed (at least in hypothetical form) that there are infinitely many individuals, but left their nature undetermined. In L_{28} Carnap adopts a "methodological solipsism" implying that the individuals are his own so-called "elementary experiences". An elementary experience in Carnap's sense is a momentary cross-section of the mental stream. According to Carnap, the elementary experiences of a person are finite in number. Hence the axiom of infinity of *Principia Mathematica* fails to hold in L_{28}. (On this point there is a serious lack of clarity in *The Logical Structure of the World*. The axiom of infinity is brought into *Principia Mathematica* to make the construction of numbers (natural, whole, rational, real, and so on) possible. In *The Logical Structure of the World* it is supposed that the individuals are a finite number of elementary experiences, but at the same time physical space–time is constructed as a continuum of quadruples of real numbers. Where do these real numbers come from?)

In *Principia Mathematica* there are only logical signs. In order to make L_{28} capable of expressing assertions about empirical states of affairs, it is necessary also to introduce signs with an empirical meaning. Carnap maintains that a single such sign is sufficient (one expressing a dyadic relation between elementary experiences). The universality which Carnap expected L_{28} to have can be roughly explained as follows. Two predicates have the same extension if the corresponding attributes (properties, relations) have the same extension. A sentence S' is an extensional translation of a sentence S, if S' is obtained from S by substituting for certain predicates others with identical extensions. In this terminology, the universality which Carnap claims for L_{28} signifies that every meaningful sentence of science can be extensionally translated into L_{28}. In *The Logical Structure of the World*, Carnap adheres to the thesis of extensionality, which says that the truth-value of a sentence remains unaltered when a predicate is replaced by another with the same extension. By virtue of this thesis, the universality of L_{28} implies that if S' in L_{28} is an extensional translation of S, then S' and S have the same truth-values.

The same claim of universality for L_{28} could be expressed in a slightly different way. Let us say that a definition introduced into L_{28} of the form:

(a) $A = \mathrm{df}\ B$,

is extensionally adequate (relative to a given usage of the expression A), if A (in that usage) has the same extension as B. Let us say that a sentence (with a given usage) can be extensionally adequately formulated in L_{28} if the sentence can be introduced into L_{28} via definitions which are extensionally adequate (with regard to that usage). The claim of universality can now be expressed by saying that every meaningful sentence can be extensionally adequately formulated in L_{28}. In fact, L_{28} is connected with a definite policy of definition. Carnap sketches the beginning of a chain of definitions which are all presumed to be extensionally adequate, a chain which, on the strength of the claim to universality, could be extended to include every meaningful concept. (Like Carnap I ignore the obvious difficulty that the expressions and sentences of scientific language do not have a formally determined meaning (cf. Chapter VII, 37, G).)

Is L_{28} a universal language in this sense? The answer depends on what we are *a priori* inclined to regard as meaningful scientific expressions and sentences. If the realm of individuals of L_{28} is finite, and we accept classical mathematics and the physics formulated with its help as meaningful, then we can assert with great certainty that L_{28} is not universal. If, on the other hand, we accept as meaningful nothing but what can be expressed in L_{28}, then with the same certainty we can affirm that L_{28} is universal. (Our opinion on the universality of L_{28} will also depend on how we regard the theory of types, incorporated into L_{28}. The theory of types forbids certain combinations of signs in L_{28}. If we do not accept the corresponding type-theoretical prohibitions for our scientific language, we cannot, of course acknowledge L_{28} as universal.)

The question as to the universality of L_{28} also has another aspect. From one point of view, as we have seen, the presumed universality implies that every concept A can be introduced into L_{28} through an extensionally adequate definition of form (a). The extensional adequacy of (a) implies in turn that *definiendum* A and *definiens* B have the same extension. The supposition that the A and the B of (a) have the same extension must obviously very often be a kind of empirical hypothesis. Thus, to suppose that L_{28} is universal is to suppose that it is possible, in principle, to establish a very great number of correct empirical hypotheses about extensional identity. In *The Logical Structure of the World*, Carnap, in fact, assumes several empirical hypotheses of this sort, hypotheses whose correctness is far from obvious. The supposition that L_{28} is a universal language is thus seen to be itself an empirical hypothesis of a higher speculative order.

However, let us for a moment suppose that we, with Carnap in 1928, accept L_{28} as universal in the present sense. If a language is universal in this sense, that is naturally in itself an interesting fact about our world. But in 1928 Carnap was not satisfied merely with demanding a theoretical interest for L_{28}. "The first aim [of science] , not in a temporal, but in a logical, sense", is, he says, to define ("construct") its concepts through a chain of definitions in a language like L_{28}.[5] Thus in 1928 he apparently wanted science to develop in such a manner that more and more of its concepts be defined through extensionally adequate definitions in L_{28} or some similar language. He seems to think that this wish is in harmony with empiricism. However, if what was said above is correct, then his desire would seem to militate against what is usually understood by empiricism. If on the basis of the empirical hypothesis:

(b) A has the same extension as B,

one defines A by definition (a), then one deprives oneself of the possibility of stating (b) as an empirical hypothesis in

[5] Carnap, R., *The Logical Structure of the World* (Berkeley: University of California Press, 1967), p. 288.

L_{28}. Then (b) becomes merely a trivial corollary to definition (a). When switching to the universal language L_{28}, one is not, as we have seen, forced to alter former modes of expression. The presumed universality of L_{28} guarantees that every meaningful sentence of science can itself be formulated in L_{28} with the aid of extensionally adequate definitions. What the shift to L_{28} primarily implies is that what were previously empirical hypotheses have now been transformed into (corollaries to) definitions. One who chooses to speak L_{28} thereby places himself in the following awkward position: *either* he must openly acknowledge himself deprived of the possibility of expressing many interesting scientific hypotheses, *or* he must disguise them as definitions.

This criticism, which applies to the use of L_{28} as a universal language, is, in its essentials, applicable also to the universal languages which were proposed later by Carnap.[6]

C. *Physicalism and logical behaviourism*

The solipsism of *The Logical Structure of the World* was meant to be only "methodological". When Carnap let the individuals of L_{28} be his own elementary experiences, he consciously chose from among several alternatives that he presumed to be equally legitimate. A permissible alternative choice would have been all the elementary experiences that belong to any person (any member of the species *homo sapiens*) whatsoever. The individuals of the universal language could also have been chosen from among the entities of physics. The elementary particles of atomic physics, the points of physical space–time, or the points on the world-lines, in Minkowski's presentation of the theory of relativity, could all have served as individuals. It was for epistemological

---

[6] Dr Thorild Dahlquist, of Uppsala University, has communicated to me an interesting objection to my criticism. The objection, as stated by him, rests on the assumption that, in the pre-Carnapian stage of science, it will usually be the case that A is a defined term. Let us assume that we are confronted with such a case, and that a pre-Carnapian definition equates A with C. Thus, at this stage the empirical hypothesis (b) says the same as:

(c) C has the same extension as B.

This statement remains unaffected by our redefining A as B, only it can no more be abbreviated into (b). I concede the point, but what about the terms that are undefined in pre-Carnapian science?

reasons that he chose to take his own elementary experience as individuals; he considered these experiences to be what is primarily given.

Through the influence of the ideas of Otto Neurath, which in their turn were inspired by Marxism, Carnap began in the early 1930s to regard methodological solipsism with a certain disapproval. He did not consider it wrong, but unsuitable, partly because L_{28} is a private language which strictly speaking can be understood only by Carnap himself, the owner of those elementary experiences with which L_{28} deals, and partly because L_{28} might be misunderstood as a seriously meant philosophical idealism. Carnap now adopts the physicalistic thesis, first proposed by Neurath, which says that "the language of physics" is universal. In papers from the beginning of the 1930s Carnap occasionally wrote (with a Marxist accent) of physicalism as an expression of "scientific materialism", and saw in it the crown of a development in which the names of Copernicus, Darwin, Marx, Nietzsche, and Freud marked earlier milestones. Physicalism was, in other words, presented as the completion of an intellectual development through which man was transformed into an element of the natural chain of things and events, and the supernatural was eliminated. Strictly speaking, however, Carnap's physicalism is not a form of naturalism, is not even a world-picture at all. Carnap never surrendered the thought that if we want, we could choose a non-physicalistic, for example phenomenalistic, universal language *à la* L_{28}. If physicalism could claim to place man in his subordinate place in nature, then the choice of language in *The Logical Structure of the World* could, therefore, with equal right, claim to place the human mind (more precisely, Carnap's mind) at the centre of reality. Carnap sharply rejected the latter claim. But, as far as I know, he never asserted with equal force the neutrality of physicalism in the debate between world-views.

A universal physicalistic language of the sort which Carnap and other logical empiricists had in mind, ought to have the following characteristics: (i) the formation of its sentences is formalized; (ii) all its terms and sentences have a physical content; (iii) all its terms and sentences are *empirical* ("empirically meaningful"); (iv) it is *universal*. The significance of the key words in (ii)–(iv) is itself problematic, and Carnap's definitions of them have varied from time to time. At this point I shall briefly consider only the term "physical". Some light on what logical empiricists had in mind when using this term is shed by the debate on so-called logical behaviourism. An obvious corollary to physicalism is that all meaningful statements about the conscious states of men and animals must be capable of translation into the language of physics. More precisely, a meaningful statement about somebody's state of consciousness must always be translatable into a statement about his "behaviour". For this thesis the term *logical behaviourism* was coined at the beginning of the 1930s.

In defence of logical behaviourism, the logical empiricists of the 1930s often argued roughly as follows. In the spirit of the verification principle, they asserted:

(a)   A statement is meaningful for a person P if and only if it can be empirically verified by P.

(b)   Two sentences, which are to be verified empirically by the person P in exactly the same manner, have the same meaning for P.

In addition, the following was thought to be an obvious fact:

(c)   A person P can empirically verify a statement about the conscious state of another person (or animal) Q only by verifying a statement about Q's behaviour,

where the intended behaviour was the macro-behaviour, for example sounds, movements, facial expressions and colour, and so on. From (a), (b), and (c) it was thought that the following conclusion could be drawn:

(d)   A statement meaningful for P about the conscious state of another person (or animal) Q has the same meaning for P as a statement about Q's behaviour.

Occasionally logical empiricists would halt at (d). Thus they treated statements about the conscious states of others differently from statements about their own conscious states. By further lines of reasoning logical behaviourism was often stretched to cover also the philosopher's own conscious states, and thus consistent physicalism was thought to be saved.

Another line of argument cited the hypothesis of psycho-physical isomorphism. This hypothesis can be characterized as a belief that in the future it will be possible to establish a sufficient amount of theory asserting appropriate isomorph-isms. The significance of such a theory can be schematically represented as follows. Let M be a set of phenomena apper-taining to a person P's mental life, and let N be a set of neuro-physiological phenomena in P. If $A_1, \ldots, A_n$ are concepts applicable to elements in M; if $B_1, \ldots, B_n$ are concepts applicable in N; and if R is a one-to-one correlation between the elements in M and those in N, then such a theory can look as follows:

(1)   The concept A_i ($i = 1, \ldots$, n) is applicable to certain elements in M if and only if the concept B_i is applicable to the elements in N correlated with these elements in M through R.

The hypothesis of isomorphism amounts to the belief that one can establish theories of this sort powerful enough to cover all phenomena of consciousness. On the assumption of theory (1), and provided that the elements $b_1, \ldots, b_p$ of N are correlated by R with elements $a_1, \ldots, a_p$ of M, one can, logical empiricists sometimes assumed, "translate" the psychological statement:

(2) A_i is applicable to $a_1, \ldots, a_p$ in M,

into the neurophysiological statement:

(3) B_i is applicable to $b_1, \ldots, b_p$ in N.[7]

It may be left to the reader to ponder on the value of these two arguments in favour of logical behaviourism.

D. *The universal physicalistic language*

In *The Logical Syntax of Language* (1934) Carnap sketched a language, we can call it L_{34}, which he thinks could serve as

---

[7] Unless $a_1 \rightleftharpoons b_1, \ldots, a_p = b_p$, a "translation" of this kind is clearly not extensional in the sense of p. 218 above. Thus we here encounter a type of translation different from that which Carnap had in mind in *The Logical Structure of the World*. In *The Logical Syntax of Language* Carnap introduced the notion of an "equipollent translation" which was perhaps intended to fit into the present context. Cf. p. 225 below.

a universal physicalistic language. L_{34}, like L_{28}, is constructed according to approximately the same type-theoretical pattern as *Principia Mathematica*. However, the individuals in L_{34} are the natural numbers, 0, 1, 2, ... On their basis the real numbers are constructed. The four-dimensional space-time of physics is identified with the set of all space–time points, which, in the spirit of analytical geometry, is again identified with the set of all ordered quadruples (x, y, z, t) where the space coordinates x, y, z, and the time coordinate t, are real numbers.

If observations called for it, Carnap was prepared to allow an *n*-dimensional physical world with $n > 4$. The kind of observations which Carnap had in mind were those which parapsychology and spiritualism claim occur at seances. If physical objects were demonstrably to come into being and to disappear again within a perfectly closed room, then according to Carnap this observation might motivate the construction of, say a 5-dimensional universe.

The scientific description of the world was thought to be produced with the aid of functions and predicates defined for points or regions in space–time. The assertion: *temp* $(x, y, z, t) = q$, where *temp* is a function, could express the statement that the temperature at point (x, y, z, t) is q degrees. The assertion: $R (x, y, z, t)$, where R is a predicate, could express the statement that the same point is red.

If we add a sufficient number of such functions and predicates, we can, Carnap thought in 1934, create a universal language. The universality should be here understood in the following sense. Let V be "the total scientific language", of which all separate scientific languages are parts. Let us suppose that L_{34} is a part of V. Assume that certain sentences P in V have the status of "postulates" or "principles". It is now possible, Carnap maintains, to produce a lexicon, with the help of which every sentence A in V can be translated into a sentence A' in L_{34}, in such a way that the postulates P entail the equivalence of A and A'. Carnap calls a translation of this sort an "equipollent translation". Thus he maintains that L_{34} is universal in the sense that every meaningful sentence can be equipollently translated into it. Is Carnap's opinion correct? It is impossible to answer the question as long as (1) the stock of basic physical concepts in L_{34} has not been specified, and (2) the "total scientific language" V and its "postulates" P have not been made available for an effective survey. (Concerning the purely mathematical misgivings as regards the idea of a universal formalized language, (cf. p. 280).) It is interesting to note the difference between the claims to universality made on behalf of L_{28} and of L_{34}. L_{28} claims a sort of "absolute" universality based on the idea of extensional translatability. Given the set of meaningful sentences, L_{28} either is or is not universal in this sense, independently of how other factors might vary. But the universality for which L_{34} is a candidate, is relative to the contents of scientific theory. The richer those contents become, the stronger presumably the principles P are, and the greater is the chance for L_{34} to be universal. It would have been interesting to know which state of science Carnap had in mind in 1934. The state of what dreamt-of future?

Unless one places additional demands on the basic concepts of L_{34}, even assertions which would not normally be considered to be "physical" can be expressed in that language. For instance, one could introduce a function g by means of the conditions:

$g\,(0, 0, 0, 0,) = 1$ if and only if God exists.

$g\,(0, 0, 0, 0) = 0$ if and only if God does not exist.

The expression:

$(\alpha)\, g\,(0, 0, 0, 0) = 1,$

would then be a formulation in L_{34} of the religious belief in God. I suppose that in 1934 Carnap would have rejected (α) on the ground that it has no empirical content. But in *The Logical Syntax of Language* (in which the discussion of physicalism plays only a subordinate role) he pays no attention to the question as to when a concept is to be accepted as having empirical significance.

In *Testability and Meaning* (1936-7) this question is at the very centre of Carnap's interest. Here he sketches an "empirical" language, let us call it L_{36}, whose empirical character is guaranteed by the manner in which all its predicates are ultimately tied to "observation predicates".

A predicate P is said to be observable for an organism O, if O (for a suitable object a, and under suitable conditions) can, with the help of a few observations, obtain evidence for, or against, the sentence "a has P", sufficiently strong to enable O to accept or to reject the sentence. Among examples of observable predicates Carnap names the common colour predicates.

In an early phase, Carnap and other logical empiricists shared Hume's view that it would be possible, by means of explicit definition, to reduce all legitimate terms to observation terms. In *Testability and Meaning* Carnap rejects this view. The demand for explicit definability is replaced by a weaker demand. The predicates in L_{36} are thought to be ordered in a series, $P_1, P_2, P_3, \ldots$ in such a manner that every term P_n fulfils at least one of the following conditions:

(a) P_n is an observable predicate.

(b) P_n is explicitly defined on the basis of earlier terms in the series.

(c)   The scientific theory formulated in L_{36} contains theorems which "reduce" P_n to earlier terms in the series. If we interpret P_n as the name of a set, then such theorems, so-called reduction sentences, can be written in the following manner:

(i) X is a subset of P_n,

(ii) P_n is a subset of Y,

where X and Y are names constructed entirely with the help of earlier terms in the series.

The sense of such reduction sentences can be illustrated by the Venn diagram (I).

(I)

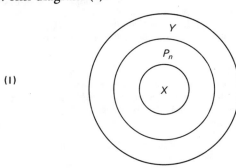

Condition (i) states a lower bound, for the set P_n, while (ii) states an upper bound.[8]

In case (c) Carnap demands that scientific theory state both a lower and an upper bound, and that these bounds not be trivial, i.e. that the theory does not declare X empty and Y universal. As science develops, the bounds may be displaced. The theoretically possible eventuality that given bounds are trivialized, and that P_n must therefore be eliminated from the vocabulary, has perhaps a minor practical relevance. The opposite eventuality is that the bounds are brought to coincide. The reduction sentences, which are regarded by Carnap as a sort of "partial definition", would then be transformed into an explicit definition of P_n, and an instance of case (c) would be transformed into one of case (b).

The changes in points of principle in Carnap's ideas of 1936, are *first*, that he now allows terms into the universal language which have no empirical interpretation and which are only theoretically coupled with empirically interpreted terms; and *second*, that the legitimacy of term is again made explicitly dependent on the contents of scientific theory. What is meaningful (empirically, or scientifically meaningful) at a given moment of time will depend on what theories the scientists happen to believe in at that moment. What is meaningful today can become meaningless tomorrow and vice versa, solely on the ground that prevailing scientific hypotheses have changed.

In his publications after 1936 Carnap continued along the

---

[8] It was primarily in connection with so-called dispositional predicates that Carnap introduced such boundary statements. An example of a dispositional predicate is 'soluble in water'. If an object is sunk in water and dissolves, then, Carnap thinks, it is soluble in water. Let 'soluble in water' be P_n, 'sunk in water' be P_i ($i < n$), and 'dissolves in water' be P_j ($j < n$). We can then express this thought of Carnap's as follows:

(i') If P_i, then if P_j then P_n.

If we let X be the product of the sets defined by P_i and P_j, then it is easily seen that (i) and (i') say the same. Further, according to Carnap, if an object is soluble in water, then it is not sunk in water without dissolving, i.e.:

(ii') If P_n, then if P_i then P_j.

If we let Y equal the sum of the set defined by P_j and the complement of that defined by P_i, we find that (ii) and (ii') say the same.

same line of thought, further liberalizing his demands upon the manner in which observation terms are coupled to the remaining legitimate terms. For those terms which neither themselves are observations terms nor can be explicitly defined on the basis of these, the later writings of Carnap employ the expression "theoretical terms". A central theme in his later philosophy is the place of theoretical terms in science. This theme is dealt with from different perspectives in *Foundations of Logic and Mathematics* (1939), "Empiricism, Semantics and Ontology" (1950), "The Methodological Character of Theoretical Concepts" (1956), "Beobachtungssprache und theoretische Sprache" (1959), and "On the use of Hilbert's ε-operator in scientific theories" (1961). The common tendency in these writings is to regard the language of science as divided into two sections, firstly the observation language which appears to have a sturdy empirical meaning, and secondly the theoretical language which in itself is a formal calculus without empirical interpretation, but which has deductive connections with the observation language by means of "rules of correspondence" ("rules of evaluation"). The legitimacy of a term in the theoretical language depends on whether or not it is empirically useful. Depending on whether, roughly speaking, deductions that lead from the theoretical language down to the level of observations are, or are not, influenced by the presence or absence of a term, that term is empirically useful, or useless. For this kind of usefulness Carnap now employs the phrase "empirical significance".

33. ANALYTIC AND SYNTHETIC, *A PRIORI* AND *A POSTERIORI*

A. *The general point of view*

Logical empiricists accepted, in principle, Wittgenstein's division of the sentences of a language into the three categories, analytic, synthetic, and contradictory, a division which sprang from an old epistemological tradition. It plays a decisive role in a number of the logical empiricists' most fundamental doctrines. We have already seen that some of the formulations of the verification principle presuppose the division. The division was made in various ways within logical empiricism. Independently of the particular formulation of the principle of division chosen, logical empiricists held fast to some basic theses, found in Wittgenstein's *Tractatus*:

(a)   The truth-value of a sentence can be determined *a priori* only if the sentence is a tautology or a contradiction.

(b)   Synthetic sentences must be verified or falsified *a posteriori*, on the basis of experience.

(c)   Tautological sentences say nothing about the nature of reality; they are compatible with every possible world, with every conceivable outcome of an empirical investigation.

(d)   No synthetic sentence has characteristic (c).

The verification principle admonishes us to ignore in scientific discussion all sentences which do not have the verifiability intended by the principle. (b) adds the exhortation to put all synthetic sentences to the test of experience (c) and (d) can be interpreted as a kind of motivation for (a) and (b).

Thesis (b) goes against Kant's theory that there are synthetic *a priori* judgements in science. The truths to which Kant granted this status were:

1.   The truths of arithmetic,

2.   The truths of Euclidean geometry,

3.   Certain propositions which Kant considered to be of fundamental importance for the natural sciences, for example the principle of causality.

4.   The principles of morals.

When the logical empiricists rejected the Kantian theory of a synthetic *a priori*, they could point to the fate which these classical candidates to the title seemed to have suffered. Concerning the truths of arithmetic, the logical empiricists agree with the view of Frege and Russell that they are analytic and *a priori*. Through the discovery of non-Euclidean geometries and the use which they had found in physics, Kant's doctrine about Euclidean geometry had become antiquated. The classical formulations of the so-called principle of causality are, as shown, for example by the logical empiricist Philipp Frank in *The Law of Causality and Its Limits* (1932), generally so vague that the question of truth cannot even be raised. If they are clarified sufficiently, they become either idle analytic propositions or empirical hypotheses which experience may falsify. Further, as is well known, certain results in atomic physics (Heisenberg's uncertainty principle) have been interpreted as showing that the principle of causality (in what formulation ?) is incorrect. Concerning the principles of morals, finally, many logical empiricists adopted a theory according to which value statements and normative statements have an emotive meaning. (a) and (b) could perhaps be regarded as inductive generalizations arrived at by critically scrutinizing those sentences which in the history of philosophy have been presented as synthetic *a priori*.

If the epistemology of logical empiricism, as I have just formulated it, is to have a definite content, one must clarify the classifications which it involves:

(i)   *a priori/a posteriori*.
(ii) analytic/synthetic/contradictory.

Logical empiricists never showed more than a minimal interest in the meaning of dichotomy (i). They seem to have been under the impression that it was sufficiently clear by itself. (Their contributions to the clarification of (i) were all indirect; these are to be found in their discussions concerning "experience" and "observation", "observation sentence" and "empirical verification".)

Concerning the tripartite classification (ii), we have already seen that, in the course of time, philosophers have explained it in many ways, and also that they have differed as to what sentences ought to be placed in what category. Obviously (ii) is vague, and obviously it can be rendered more precise in many distinct but equally reasonable ways. The precise formulation which a logical empiricist eventually chooses ought to be such that, together with a clarification of (i), it gives a reasonable and interesting meaning to the methodological recommendations of logical empiricism. If the recommendations are to be of any value, it should be possible to decide fairly often whether or not a theoretical procedure agrees with them. This in turn presupposes that one can fairly often decide to which category a given sentence belongs. In other words, the clarifications ought to make it possible actually to apply the clarified concepts to given sentences, in science and perhaps also in other fields of human thought. As early as in the 1920s, a series of semantic concepts crystallised within Hilbert's metamathematical school, concepts which have an obvious kinship to the time-honoured classification (ii). Quite independently of the problems of logical empiricism, logical research has continued along the lines laid down by Hilbert, and today logic can exhibit a rich collection of concepts which must be taken into account by those who wish to give a more precise meaning to (ii).

Among logical empiricists, Carnap is the one who was especially interested in clarifying (ii). Here I shall limit myself to considering some of his many thoughts on this question. Given a definite, natural, or formalized language L, one can attempt to determine the boundaries between the different categories of sentences in L. Many of Carnap's definitions are of this sort, and these definitions are perhaps the most valuable results of his thinking in this area. However, these definitions cannot be understood without a detailed acquaintance with the languages concerned, and here I must pass them by. One can also seek a clarification of the concept "analytic in L", where L can be any arbitrarily chosen language. (Compare the distinction between defining "divisible by 3" and defining "divisible by n", where n is an arbitrary number.) Carnap has sketched at least, conceptual explanations with this general scope, and it is these explanations I shall now discuss.

B. *The argument in The Logical Syntax of Language*

According to the position in *The Logical Syntax of Language*, a "language" L is approximately what I shall call in Chapter VII an "effective calculus":

$$L = (A, S, P, R),$$

where A is the set of "simple signs" of the language, S is its set of "sentences", P are the "postulates", and R is the set of "direct consequence relations" (cf. section 36). On the basis of this notion of language—which has little in common with what linguists mean by a language—Carnap develops a classification of sentences which can be illustrated by diagram (J).

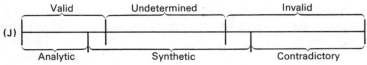

If a sentence can be obtained from a given set of sentences through the iterated use of the direct consequence relations, the sentence is said to be a consequence of the set. A sentence is valid if it is a consequence of the postulates; it is invalid if every sentence is a consequence of it; and it is undetermined if it is neither valid nor invalid. In order to delimit the analytic sentences among the valid and the contradictory sentences among the invalid, Carnap uses an idea which is reminiscent of certain ideas in Bolzano's logic of variation.[9]

Carnap's definitions, the content of which has been roughly sketched, have an admirable subtlety. At the same time, it is impossible to close one's eyes to the fact that they do not contribute at all to the clarification of concepts which could be used in the description of given linguistic material. Suppose that we are interested in deciding whether or not a given sentence, say, Kant's "$7 + 5 = 12$", is analytic. If one tries to use Carnap's definitions, one has first to transcribe the sentence into a definite formalized language. When this step has been taken, when, say the sentence has been formulated in L_1—it may turn out that the sentence is analytic in L_1. If, however, the formulation has been done within a different language L_2, the result might have been that it is not analytic in L_2. To which L should the sentence be referred, in order that the answer to the question "analytic in L?" can be made the basis for a correct application of the empiricist epistemology? And how should one adequately identify the "postulates" and the "direct consequences relations" of a given language? Carnap says nothing about

[9] Bolzano's distinction between "logical" and "non-logical" concepts has its counterpart in Carnap's distinction between logical and descriptive signs. How Carnap defines this distinction must be ignored here. Two expressions in the language are isogenous if the one can always be exchanged for the other in a given sentence without the sentence character being lost. We can say that sentence A is a variant of sentence B if A results from B when the descriptive expressions in A are uniformly replaced by isogenous expressions. Then, according to Carnap, analytic sentences are those valid sentences all of whose variants are valid, contradictory sentences are those invalid sentences all of whose variants are invalid, and synthetic sentences are those which are neither analytic nor contradictory.

these questions. The definitions in *The Logical Syntax of Language* leave empiricist epistemology just as indefinite as it was before.

C. *Some semantic notions*

According to Carnap's later, semantical, point of view, the purely syntactical concepts which he presented in 1934 are too poor to do justice to linguistic reality. He now points out that an actual language also has a semantical aspect: its expressions have a meaning, and its sentences have a truth-value which normally depends on the meaning as well as on the actual state of the world. If one wishes to specify a language completely, then one must, with the help of "semantical rules", state that meaning. According to a classical philosophical view, an analytic (contradictory) sentence is one whose truth (falsehood) depends only on its content. A synthetic sentence on the contrary, is, according to the same view, a sentence whose truth-value cannot be decided by a study of its meaning: a study of the facts is also required. During his semantical period Carnap has occasionally suggested that these traditional ideas could be clarified by saying that an analytic (contradictory) sentence is one whose truth (falsehood) follows from the semantical rules of the language. Does this proposal amount to a useful explication of the concepts? Let us imagine a philosopher who is already acquainted with the classical epistemological ideas with which Carnap is dealing, but who is doubtful about how to classify a given sentence, say again "$7 + 5 = 12$". He studies Carnap's semantics and tries to apply it to the sentence. First he must formulate suitable semantical rules.

According to one of Carnap's ideas, the semantical rules of a language L imply for every sentence A of L, a condition of the form:

(i)   "A" is true if and only if B,

where B is a "translation" of A into the "metalanguage" in which the rules are formulated. If L is a part of the metalanguage, then A and B may coincide. Let us suppose that the latter is the case. Our philosopher thus formulates semantical rules which imply:

(ii) "7 + 5 = 12" is true if and only if 7 + 5 = 12.

If he were convinced that the sentence:

(iii) 7 + 5 = 12,

is true on logical grounds, then he could use (iii) to derive from (ii):

(iv) " 7 + 5 = 12" is true.

With this derivation in mind he could establish that:

(v) "7 + 5 = 12" is an analytic sentence.

But what is required of (iii) in order that it be true on logical grounds? Is it not required just that it be analytic? But then our philosopher's attempt to employ Carnap's clarification of 'analytic' leads him into a circle.

If the demand that B in (i) is to be a "translation" of A, is dropped, the situation becomes even worse. If, for a semantical rule such as (i) we expect merely that it should be correct, then we must be prepared to accept, say this rule:

(vi) The sentence "Piccadilly Circus is in London" is true if and only if 2 = 2 or 2 ≠ 2,

provided that, like Carnap, we understand "if and only if" as expressing material equivalence (identity of truth-value). From this we can infer, on the strength of the law of the excluded middle:

(vii) The sentence "Piccadilly Circus is in London" is true.

To conclude from this that the sentence is analytic, would be absurd!

The result is equally queer if we think of the semantic rules, not as a description of a pre-existing distribution of truth-values among the sentences of a language, but as conventions by which, in some sense or other, we "impart" truth-values to them. (Carnap hardly ever made it quite clear what view he took on this matter.) Of course, by saying that a sentence is true (or false) we do not render it true (or false), just as little as we make, say, a horse into a cat by saying that it is one. But the semantic rules could be looked upon as prescribing that sentences of a language should be given some interpretation, by which the rules are verified. If the rules merely define a distribution of truth-values, there will always exist infinitely many interpretations which lead to that distribution and, hence, verify the rules. With regard to a given distribution, it is inessential whether a sentence be merely factually true (false) or analytic (contradictory) under that interpretation.

Following Quine, Carnap occasionally distinguishes between "logically true sentences" and "analytic sentences". Logically true sentences are (primarily) all true sentences which contain only logical terms, for example the sentence:

(viii) $a = a$.

In addition, those sentences are logically true which are substitution instances of sentences of the first type, for example:

(ix) Red = Red.

All logically true sentences are also analytic, but not conversely. Sentences which are analytic but not logically true are, for example:

(x) All bachelors are unmarried.

In order to define the wider concept "analytic sentence", Carnap introduces the concept of "meaning postulate". The meaning postulates of a language are, according to Carnap, those "fundamental" analytic sentences, of which all the analytic sentences of the language are logical consequences. (x) could serve as a meaning postulate for the English language. Carnap assumes that there are only a finite number of meaning postulates for a given language, and that we can thus form the conjunction of them. Let M be the conjuction of the meaning postulates for language L. Carnap now proposes the following definition:

The sentence S is analytic in L = df The conditional 'If M then S' is logically true in L.

This definition does not give us a useful explanation either.

The concepts "logical term" and "logically true sentence" are vague and problematic, but let us ignore that. In order to determine whether or not a given sentence is analytic, in the sense of the present definition, one must discover the meaning postulates of the language. To search for the meaning postulates is to seek a finite set of analytic sentences of which all other analytic sentences in the language are logical consequences. We are again invited to engage in circular reasoning.

D. *Two tendencies in Carnap's epistemology*

At the outset, logical empiricists were convinced of the validity of a number of linguistic-epistemological distinctions, like: meaningful/meaningless. analytic/synthetic/contradictory; *a priori/a posteriori*. Little by little these distinctions showed themselves to be extremely problematic. Carnap's own attitude to the concepts discussed in this chapter has changed over the years. In the 1920s his attitude seemed to be absolutist. But in *The Logical Syntax of Language* (1934), he added an important reservation to traditional empiricist epistemology. As long as we "accept" a language-system $L = (A, S, P, R)$,—in this manner we could perhaps restate his position—the analytic sentences of L are *a priori*, while the synthetic sentences of L must be established on the basis of experience. But, in the final analysis, even the "acceptance" of the consequence relations R and the entire logical apparatus of L based on them, is hypothetical. Writing about the language of physics, Carnap says, "No rule of the physical language is definitive; all rules are laid down with the reservation that they may be altered as soon as it seems expedient to do so." This applies even to mathematical rules: "In this respect there are only differences in degree; certain rules are more difficult to renounce than others."[10] One can say that at this point Carnap sharpens the empiricist epistemology adopted from Wittgenstein. *All* sentences and rules must eventually be empirically established; it is only that, in the case of a conflict between theory and experience, certain sentences and rules, among them the so-called analytic sentences, are more resistant than others. In the same

[10] Carnap, R., *The Logical Syntax of Language*, p. 318

relativistic spirit Carnap here expresses his (already cited) "principle of tolerance".

However, some years later, in *Foundations of Logic and Mathematics* (1939), Carnap deprived this principle of most of its edge. If a language is regarded as a game with signs without meaning, as a pure calculus, then the rules of the language can be established arbitrarily. But if one has given a meaning to the signs, it is already determined which sentences constitute logical truths.

The result of our discussion is the following: logic or the rules of deduction (in our terminology, the syntactical rules of trans-formation) can be chosen arbitrarily and hence are conventional if they are taken as the basis of the construction of the language system and if the interpretation of the system is later superimposed. On the other hand, a system of logic is not a matter of choice, but either right or wrong, if an interpretation of the logical signs is given· in advance.[11]

During the 1950s the most energetic critic of the later Carnap's absolutism was Quine. The position which Quine adopted is intimately related to Carnap's own relativism of 1934. A very natural objection to Carnap's absolutism is the following.

In the language which I have already mastered, we can call it *L* (it may, for example, be current English), I have in one sense or another accepted a logic. Let us assume that I wish to define a new artificial language *L'*, the meaning of which is to be established by translation into the original language *L*. By means of the translation the given logic is projected on to the new language *L'*, and I can explicitly formulate the logical relations which will hence obtain in *L'*. If *L* and the method of translation are sufficiently unambiguous, the proposed formulation of the logic of *L'* will be either correct or incorrect. In this Carnap is undoubtedly right. But this says nothing about the epistemological status of the logic of *L*. Thus, Carnap's semantical motivation for his absolutism does not carry conviction.

The conflict in Carnap between absolutism and relativism was never, it seems, completely resolved.

[11] Carnap, R., *Foundations of Logic and Mathematics* (Chicago: University of Chicago Press, 1939), p. 28.

34. INSTRUMENTALISM

A. *Instrumentalism in modern science*

A person can be said to have an instrumentalist view on a scientific question if he thinks that the question is one of expediency, rather than one of right or wrong. The greater the number, and the more fundamental the character, of those questions of which an epistemologist takes this view, the greater is the justification for labelling him an instrumentalist.

Carnap's instrumentalism has deep roots in the history of philosophy, but I believe that it ought to be viewed primarily as a philosopher's speculative stretching of ideas which occur in a less definite form in modern science, especially in theoretical physics. A physical theory cannot, as has often been pointed out, be directly verified through experience. At best, it can be inductively confirmed by experience, in the same manner as the sentence "All men are mortal" is inductively supported by our observing that a is a man and dies, b is a man and dies, and so on. Many theories of modern science do not admit of such induction simply because the concepts with which they deal are not accessible to direct observation. An "abstract" theory T of this sort is confronted with experience by our deriving from it some sentence S which can be tested by observation. If S is verified, then T has been confirmed in this instance; if S is falsified, then T has been refuted. That a theory is confirmed in one case does not preclude that it will be refuted in another case. That a theory has, to the best of our knowledge, been confirmed without exception until today, does not preclude that it will be refuted in the future. That one theory T has thus far been confirmed without exception, also does not preclude that another, logically incompatible theory T' can also be confirmed without exception. Although T and T' are logically incompatible, they might result in exactly the same set of empirically decidable sentences. This situation has caused a kind of scientific resignation and via resignation a form of instrumentalism. With very good luck it might happen that a theory which we accept actually gives a true picture of reality. But the probability of such luck seems small. What we can actually *know* is not that the theory gives a true picture of reality, but that such and such a set of derived observation sentences has been verified. A reasonable goal for science in fields where this situation obtains would seem to be, not literally true theories, but theories whose verifiable consequences agree with our observations. When our imagination suffices to create several competing theories, the choice between them becomes a question of expediency. One principle of choice is "the degree of simplicity". Within many areas of theoretical physics, for example in quantum mechanics or in the theory of relativity, scientists today generally work, I believe, in that spirit.

In the preceding paragraph I supposed that the theories among which we have to choose, *are* literally true or false, approximately as the sentence, "Stockholm has more than a million inhabitants", is true or false. I suppose that the theories have a definite truth-value, but that their truth-value eludes our knowledge. However, in the case of modern science these assumptions are in many cases unrealistic. Certain theories of physics involve basic concepts for which it seems impossible to provide genuine interpretations. The basic concepts are a kind of abstract parameter upon which the theories impose certain general conditions. To ask whether the theories are true or false seems meaningless. This is a new reason why the only plausible demand upon such theories seems to be that their verifiable consequences be correct.

What has just been said could be more schematically expressed as follows. Let T be some "abstract" theory, and let E be some class of "empirically decidable" statements, a class which does *not* contain all the statements of T. The question, "Is T true?", has in many cases been pushed into the background in modern science, and in its place have appeared the instrumental questions. "How correct are the statements in E which can be derived from T? How wide a field of phenomena do they account for? And how simple is the derivation?" When a modern scientist formulates T as his hypothesis, his "primary" hypothesis, this does not imply that he, even if only tentatively, presents T as a "truth about reality". The truth which he tries to establish is only that of the hypothesis: "T makes possible the derivation in a simple

way of *E*-statements in satisfactory number and with satisfactory correctness", or of some similar "secondary"
hypothesis about the instrumental worth of *T*. This is one
reason why one must observe the greatest caution when
trying to read into the theories of modern science something
like a world-view. The primary hypotheses are often not
completely seriously intended, and the secondary hypotheses
about the instrumental worth of the former obviously do not
imply what we naturally mean by a "picture of the world".

B. *Carnap's instrumentalism*

"Is Theory *T* a good instrument for the derivation of correct
sentences of the set *E*?" Let us say that for those who allow
the answer to this instrumental question to determine their
evaluation of *T*, *E* constitutes the verification base, or simply
the base, for *T*. If Carnap's instrumentalism can be characterized in a few words, the first point in that characterization
could read:

(A) There is *one* set of sentences, namely the sentences
of the so-called "observation language", which is, or ought
to be, the common ultimate verification base for all empirical theories. (The basis thesis.)

When the instrumental question is raised in modern
science, *T* is usually an "abstract" theory whose sentences
are incapable of "direct" empirical proof, while the sentences
in *E* seem capable of empirical test, if not "directly", at least
"more directly", than the sentence in *T*. It is not self-evident
that the base for all theories and all scientists is one and the
same, not even that the ultimate base is. Perhaps, even the base
for *one* and the same theory does not have to be the same
for all scientists. It may also be questioned whether a given
scientist always uses the same base for judging a given
theory. Carnap's idea (A) implies a kind of convergence
principle for the base relation, formally resembling those convergence principles on which Thomas Aquinas based his
proofs for the existence of God. Obviously (A) agrees with
well-known ideas in classical British empiricism, and Carnap
seems to find (A) more or less self-evident. Those who do
not share his attitude must ask themselves: In so far as (A)

is descriptive of scientific practice, would a careful and objective study of science confirm it? Further, in so far as (A) is a methodological recommendation, what is gained by following it?

(B)   Only the sentences of the observation language have a genuine meaning. Only they are "fully interpreted", or "fully understandable". The sentences of theoretical languages have had a kind of "incomplete" or "indirect interpretation", and this they obtain exclusively through their deductive connection with the sentences in the observation language. It is only because of the so-called "correspondence rules" which make inferences possible from the theoretical level to the observation level and vice versa, that the concepts in the theoretical languages have meaning. If these rules are discarded, all that remains of a theoretical language is a game with signs, a pure calculus. (The formalistic thesis.)

The third and last point in my schematic characterization is this:

(C)   A theory which cannot be expressed in the observation language ought to be regarded as an instrument for one purpose or another. The purpose for which such theories are put forward in empirical science is to make possible the deduction of (correct) statements of the observation language. Every instrument can be more or less suitable with regard to its purpose; this holds for theories of empirical science, too. On the other hand, to ask about the objects which are postulated by a theory, whether or not they "actually exist", whether the theory gives "a true picture of them", and so on, is metaphysical nonsense. (The anti-metaphysical thesis.)

Theses (B) and (C) are tied up with Carnap's conviction that meaning is connected with verifiability. It is especially through (B) and (C) that Carnap paradoxically sharpens the somewhat vague instrumentalistic tendency of modern science. Concerning some given "abstract" theories one can agree that the question of their absolute truth is undecidable and that it ought suitably to be replaced with the question of their instrumental value in relation to some set of empirically decidable sentences *E*. But one need not therefore, agree with

Carnap's much more radical and dogmatic views (B) and (C). Although aware that speculations about "the nature of reality" must always remain empirically unprovable, one could still consider them to be meaningful, philosophically interesting, and of great human value.

Consider Diagram (K). From Carnap's point of view, B as well as A has a "complete interpretation", and the statements

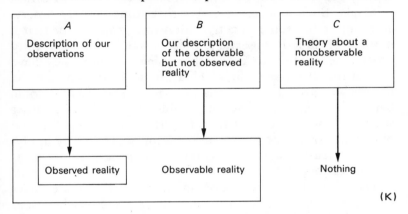

(K)

which are parts of B are literally true or false concerning observable reality. The assumptions which are parts of C have, on the contrary, no corresponding reference to a reality: they constitute *either* a scientifically expedient calculus coupled to A and B by rules of correspondence, *or* metaphysical nonsense. One may well put the following questions:

(i) We construct B through a variety of arguments from A. Are the steps which take us from A to B different in principle from those which lead scientists from A + B to C? If not, what right do we have to accept B as a meaningful existential hypothesis but deny this status to C?

(ii) Is the observable world in itself something consistent, complete, and self-sufficient? Is it at all intelligible as an isolated reality? Must it not be complemented by something non-observable, that is, be considered to be embedded in a larger, partly non-observable, totality in order to become intelligible? Carnap would probably reject these questions as metaphysical nonsense. But *are* they?

C. *What is the observation language?*

Carnap's instrumentalism, described by (A), (B), and (C), remains a mere schema as long as the intended nature of the observation language has not been explained.

The simplest sentences of the observation language are the "observation" or "protocol" sentences which we have already encountered in connection with the verification principle. Such a sentence states that some directly observable object has some directly observable property, or that a number of directly observable objects stand in some directly observable relation to each other. Linguistically, they have the form of a sentence in which a predicate, designating the observable property or relation, is predicated of some name(s), designating the observable object(s). The other sentences of the observation language are thought to be obtainable from the simple observation sentences by applying the truth-functional sentential connectives, such as quantification, etc.

The idea of an observation sentence, in this sense, gives rise to a number of intricate questions. Exactly when does the following relation obtain:

(I) X is directly observed by Y?

Is Carnap thinking only of human observers on earth, or only of us, present-day half civilized men? Or of all observers in the universe, including whatever extraterrestrial beings there might exist? (Can we form any notion at all of their way of observing, and of the phenomena that may be accessible to them but not to us?) If we, to start with, limit the discussion to present-day human observers, Carnap and you and me, *what* is it that we directly observe? All the problems discussed in the history of epistemology since antiquity present themselves here, but they have never received a well-considered answer from logical empiricists. For instance, is the observation of molecules through an electron microscope direct? Is the observation of astronomical phenomena through a telescope direct? Is the observation of the planet Mars through a rocket-transported automatic television-apparatus direct? Is direct observation irrevocably connected with our outer senses, with sight, hearing, touch and so on?

Or are there other sorts of direct observation? Are a tooth-ache, a stomach-ache, an itch on one's skin, etc. forms of direct observation of something? What about "ideas" as opposed to "impressions", to speak with Hume? Do fantasies, dreams, thoughts, contain any direct observation or not? what is the place of so-called introspection? Can there be any direct observation of abstract entities?

However, suppose that we have adequately clarified the fundamental relation (I). The task remains to clarify the derivative concept:

(II) X *can* be directly observed by Y,

or:

(II')   It is *possible* that X can be directly observed by Y.

Logical empiricists often pointed out that they were not thinking about the technical possibility of making observations. In the 1920s, and 1930s, before the construction of moon rockets, observations of the far side of the moon were often cited as examples of observations possible in principle but then technically impossible. It is the possibility in principle which is spoken of in (II'). Occasionally it was said that the intended possibility meant consistency with "the laws of nature". But what are "the laws of nature"? Such and such sentences in such and such currently accepted textbooks? Or certain sentences in some divine textbook?

Suppose that we have satisfactorily clarified (II) as well as (I). The task still remains of answering another group of equally complicated questions. The observation language contains predicates and names. Let us take a look at the names. They are supposed to designate objects that are observable directly. What, then, is the exact sense of the relation:

(III) X is a name of Y?

Suppose that Y is an object which can (could) be "directly observed", say, Socrates. We can designate him in practically an infinite number of different ways. Some designations of Socrates are the following:

(1)   Socrates,

(2) The Athenian philosopher who is the leading character in most of Plato's dialogues,

(3) The philosopher who drank a cup of hemlock in 399 BC in Athens.

With a little imagination one can produce any number of designations of Socrates like (2) and (3). (They are what Russell called definite descriptions.) Are all these designations of Socrates also "names" of Socrates in the intended sense? Or, are only some of them names? If so, which ones? Is (1) but not (2) or (3) such a name? However, as Bolzano, Frege, and Russell have taught us, (1) can very well serve as shorthand for a description like (2) or (3).

If we admit object names into the primitive vocabulary of the observation language, there seems to be a choice between three policies:

(i) All designations of directly observable objects, even those which are, or are synonymous with, descriptions, are allowed.

(ii) Only those designations of directly observable objects which have no descriptive content (which are "logically proper names" in Russell's sense), are allowed.

(iii) Designations with descriptive content are allowed into the observation language, but the descriptive content must then be of a special observable sort.

Let us glance for a moment at these three policies. If (i) is adopted, any concepts whatsoever could sneak into the observation language by a back door, as elements of the descriptions. The following would, for example, be an admissible designation of Socrates in the observation language:

(4) The philosopher who drank the hemlock in Athens in 399 BC, and who lived in a world where $E = mc^2$.

Obviously, this goes against Carnap's intentions, and I think we may rule out policy (i).

It seems conceivable that Carnap may at some time have intended policy (ii). Yet one can ask whether there are any "logically proper names" in Russell's sense. Russell himself, as is well known, recognized as such primarily the demonstratives "this" and "that", in a certain use and names of sense qualities. In *Meaning and Necessity*, Carnap adopts a form of Frege's semantics, according to which all names have descriptive meaning. In so doing he deprived himself of the opening (ii). Thus it seems that (iii) is the only policy which is available to Carnap. Perhaps he would admit a designation *A* of a directly observable object to the observation language only if "direct observation" can tell whether *A* is applicable to an observed object, or whether "this is *A*" is the case, where "this" points to an observed object. It would be easy to show by means of critical examples how problematic such a demarcation would be.

Actually an idea of Quine's suggests a fourth conceivable policy, namely:

(iv) No designations, names or otherwise, of objects are allowed as primitive terms of the observation language.

If we presuppose that every name is synonymous with a description, then we can achieve this by (a) replacing every name with the synonymous description and (b) eliminating the descriptions, for example through Russell's method. The result would be an observation language where the designating function has been taken over entirely by variables and predicates. (In the earlier work *The Logical Structure of the World*, Carnap explored a "structuralist" line of thought which is closely related to (iv).) But, then, would not the predicates give rise to the same problems which the names of objects presented us with? The discussion has clearly not been brought to a satisfactory end.

Carnap never made any serious attempt to unravel these questions. The observation language, in the sense of Carnap and logical empiricism, appears to be one of the many nebulous shapes in which the history of philosophy is so rich. Carnap's instrumentalism is, I believe, as indefinite as it is radical.

D. *Philosophy as critique and construction of languages*

It is the task of science to study and describe the world. The end product of scientific labour is the formulation of sentences about the world. It is the task of philosophy "to analyse logically" this product, the sentences of science, the language of science.

This philosophical programme, which Carnap inherited from Wittgenstein's *Tractatus*, and to which he always held, he thought he could justify as follows.[12] If one investigates the traditional problems of philosophy, one finds that they can be divided into three categories: (i) questions about objects of the special sciences; (ii) questions about imaginary objects which are not dealt with in any of the special sciences (the thing-in-itself, the absolute, and so on); and (iii) questions of logic. Questions of type (i) properly belong to the special sciences, not to philosophy. Questions of type (ii) are illusory. Thus, only questions of category (iii) remain as the legitimate province of philosophy. This argument takes the Plato–Wittgenstein distinction between "science" ("special science", "empirical science") and "philosophy" to be so self-evident that it does not even have to be stated, much less supported by reasons. It also presupposes that all there is falls within the proper realm of some "scientific" study. (Since Carnap cannot reasonably have had any existing university organization in mind, he seems to have envisaged the organization of some future, or heavenly, all-embracing university.) The argument also presupposes that the logical study of the language of science is, in some respect, essentially different from studies of other things. Otherwise the study of the language of science would also fall to some special science. Even if these vague and disputable presuppositions are accepted, the conclusion is surprising. Why should philosophy be identified with the logical analysis of the language of *science*? Do not languages exist outside of science? Is it that they cannot be "logically analysed"? Or is there some other unexpressed reason? (Occasionally one receives the impression that, by identifying philosophy with the logic of *science*, Carnap wishes to give to philosophy the prestige of science as well as of logic.)

Carnap assigns two closely related tasks to the logic of science, one constructive and the other descriptive. The constructive task is to formulate precise languages which are

---

[12] Carnap, R., *The Logical Syntax of Language*, pp. 277–8.

suitable instruments for science. In *The Logical Syntax of Language* Carnap thinks of language construction as a purely syntactical affair. To construct a language of arithmetic is, for example, to enumerate the simple signs with which the sentences of arithmetic are to be built, to state the rules according to which sentences are manufactured from these signs, and the rules according to which sentences can be derived from other sentences. Let *A* be such a language for pure arithmetic and let it contain sentences of the type "2 + 2 = 4", but not sentences of the type "There are two men in the room." To explain the concrete application of arithmetic is not a new task beyond the syntactical one. What is required is to expand the syntactical construction so that inferences of the following type are made legitimate: ·

(v) Karl and Peter, and no one else, are in the room. Thus, there are exactly two men in the room.

In other words, the supply of primitive signs has to be suitably enriched, the rules of sentence construction must be enlarged so as to admit sentences like (v) (or suitable transcriptions of them) into the language, and, finally, the rules of derivation must be extended to cover inference of type (v). A proposal for a complete solution of all the philosophical problems of arithmetic would be given if, in this syntactical way, one had constructed a total language for all of science.

Carnap was brought later on to acknowledge that purely syntactical conventions were inadequate for the complete specification of a language for science. One also requires semantical conventions, "semantical rules", which indicate the meaning of the sentences of the language. According to an early (1942) line of thought, semantical rules ought to be stated in the form of a definition of the concept "true sentence". The definition should be such that for every sentence "..." in the language, it implies a truth condition:

"..." is true if and only if ... ,

where "..." expresses some statement or other which we already understand. In *Meaning and Necessity* (1947) Carnap took a further step and advocated that to the rules determining truth-values should be added rules determining meanings.

In the paper "Empiricism, Semantics, and Ontology" (1950), Carnap seems to think that, in addition to the making of syntactic conventions, language construction comprises the statement of rules determining under what circumstances a sentence shall be "accepted" or "rejected". He considers these rules to belong to what he calls "pure epistemology". In this paper he apparently does not regard semantical rules as an independent factor in the construction of a language.

When a language has been constructed, in one way or another, the question arises as to whether or not the language is a suitable tool for some scientific purpose. Is it possible to discuss this question—I ask again—without resuming consideration of what are, in Carnap's eyes, the suspect philosophical questions from which concentration on logical analysis was to free us? For instance, is the expediency of a physicalistic language proposed as a universal language, independent of such traditional philosophical problems as that of "mind and body"? Is the expediency of a solipsistic, phenomenalistic language (like the one sketched in *The Logical Structure of the World*) independent of the classical problems of solipsism and phenomenalism? True to his instrumentalistic convictions, Carnap would probably reject these misgivings out of hand, as groundless.

A constructed language L' can often be seen as a "rational reconstruction" of an existing, more naturally grown language L. This is the case when L' and L are in such essential agreement that L' can be used in place of L in science and L' is also, in some respect, "better" than L. According to Carnap, it is just through the rational reconstruction of already given languages that philosophy can fulfil the task, which Wittgenstein laid upon it, to "make thoughts clearer".

VII

Formalization

35. INTRODUCTION

Today's philosopher of a logico-analytical bent often imposes an axiomatic discipline upon himself; first presenting his fundamental assumptions, his axioms or postulates, and then deducing from them whatever else he wishes to assert. Further, he often expresses himself with the help of formulae. Where philosophers in the good old days said:

All men are mortal,

he instead says *à la* Russell:

$$(x) \ (x \text{ is human} \supset x \text{ is mortal}),$$

or in an even more formalized manner:

$$(x) \ (H(x) \supset M(x)).$$

Axiomatizing and formalizing are two characteristic features of large sections of modern philosophy, with the result that much philosophy today looks like mathematics. In order to understand it one must submit to a technical training of the same sort as that required for the understanding of mathematical texts. How did this happen? What is gained from the point of view of knowledge by axiomatizing and formalizing? Is the gain so great that it justifies this summons of symbolic technique? What exactly does formalizing signify? In this chapter, which is not concerned with any specific philosophical school but with a general feature of many contemporary philosophical approaches, I will try to shed light on these and similar questions.

Axiomatizing and formalizing are, to a certain extent, philosophically neutral processes. They determine the manner of presentation but not the content which is presented. Theology and metaphysics can be axiomatized as well as arithmetic, geometry, the theory of relativity in physics, or certain logical theories. What is not philosophically neutral, but on the contrary a matter of sometimes heated dispute, is the question as to the philosophical value of axiomatizing and formalizing.

On the one hand there are philosophers who claim that clarity and precision are the highest virtues of a philosopher, and that axiomatization and formalization are necessary conditions for achieving them. Rudolf Carnap and some other logical empiricists belong to this group.

On the other hand there are also philosophers who see in axiomatization and formalization something extraneous to philosophy. The later Wittgenstein, the author of *Philosophical Investigations*, as well as many Oxford philosophers, can be listed here. The opposition to the formalistic approach in philosophy has made the following points:

(a)   The generally acknowledged principle "garbage in— garbage out" holds for calculuses (formalized theories) just as for computers. When the ideas which are initially fed into the calculus are fuzzy or uninteresting, all the precisely proved theorems will have the same fuzziness and lack of interest. The opponents of formalization can point to many examples in which the work devoted to the formal apparatus has no counterpart in an equally thorough elaboration of the content to be formalized. Indeed, the interest in calculuses seems to compete in certain weaker minds with free and thorough intuitive thinking. Objection (a) is not one of principle, but is directed against various sham varieties of formalizing.

(b)   On the whole, we think and speak in non-formalized languages. When formalistically oriented philosophers wish to discuss epistemological and linguistic problems, they often imagine that the non-formalized languages which are actually used have been translated or transformed into formalized languages. According to the critics the distance between the two kinds of language is so great that this transcription implies, in important respects, a distortion of the problems.

(c)   A third objection to one-sided formalism in philosophy is that formalized languages and theories are a possible and suitable intellectual tool mainly in those areas in which axiomatization, in a more traditional sense, is possible and suitable. Large areas of philosophy are not of this sort, and must be studied with a more descriptive and empirical method.

After presenting a very simple model of a formalized language (with a built-in theory) (in section 36), I shall attempt to clarify in general terms what is meant by a formalized language (37). Against the background of this explanation, I shall discuss the role which such languages play, as tools of thought and means of communication (38), and as objects of study (39).

36. AN EXAMPLE OF FORMALIZATION

A. *Language M*

The example is a very simple arithmetical theory which is actually nothing but the addition and multiplication tables in a disguised form. The non-negative integers, 0, 1, 2, 3, . . . , will be assumed to be generated through the successive addition of 1, as follows:

$$0, 0 + 1, (0 + 1) + 1, ((0 + 1) + 1) + 1, ...$$

Instead of writing $n + 1$ we shall, more briefly, write n', whereby the series takes the form:

(i) $0, 0', 0'', 0''', ...$

In this new symbolism, the sentence "$(5 + 7) = 12$" is transformed into:

(ii) $(0''''' + 0''''''') = 0'''''''''''''$.

The sentence "$(2 \times 3) = 6$" becomes:

(iii) $(0'' \times 0''') = 0''''''$.

(ii) and (iii) are examples of sentences belonging to our formalized language and, at the same time, of theorems provable in our formalized theory. From any normal point of view, this new manner of writing is very impractical. The reason for introducing it is that the structure of our formalized language thereby becomes more easily describable. (In formalized languages, simplicity of structure often stands in inverse proportion to practicality.)

Let M stand for the language to be specified. This language is based on an alphabet which has little similarity with, say, the English alphabet, but which serves the same purpose. M's alphabet, which we shall call A, will consist of the seven signs: 0, ', +, ×, (,), =. If we wish we can formally define:

D1. A sign belongs to alphabet A if and only if it is either "0", or "'", or "+", or "×", or "(", or ")", or "=".

From these signs we can form finite sequences in an infinite number of ways. Some randomly chosen sequences are the following: $(++)() = × = 0', +0+0++0+0+ × × × × × ×$, 00000000, $0 = 0'$.

Some of the sequences become abracadabra in our language, but others will play the same role as words and sentences in customary language. We shall define three sets of meaningful sequences, namely the set of "numerals" (D2), the set of "terms" (D3), and the set of "sentences" (D4).

As numerals (N) we consider all expressions which can be formed from "0" by means of successive applications of the prime, thus all which occur in series (i). The numerals can be defined by the following inductive (or recursive) definition:

D2. (a) "0" is a numeral.

(b) If an expression a is a numeral, so is the expression a' (i.e. the expression which consists of a followed by the prime).

(c) Nothing is a numeral save by virtue of (a) and (b).

Since according to (a) "0" is a numeral, "0'", "0''", "0'''", etc. are numerals according to (b); and according to (c), all numerals must occur somewhere in this series. Given an arbitrarily chosen sequence of signs from the alphabet A, we can always decide in a routine manner whether or not the sequence is a numeral.

Terms (T) are all expressions which arise when we add and multiply numerals, sums and products of numerals, and so on. Terms can be inductively defined as follows:

D3. (a) Every numeral is a term.

(b) If a and b are terms, then $(a + b)$ and $(a \times b)$ are terms.

(c) Nothing is a term except by virtue of (a) and (b).

($a + b$) is here the expression which results when one writes in immediate sequence: the left parenthesis, expression a, the plus sign, expression b, the right parenthesis. ($a \times b$) is the same expression with the plus sign replaced by a multiplication sign. According to (a), the numerals "0" and "0′″" are terms. According to (b), "(0 + 0″)", and "(0 × 0″)" are also terms. Etc. Given an arbitrarily chosen sequence of signs from the alphabet, we can, as it were, mechanically decide whether or not that sequence is a term.

Sentences (S) are defined as follows:

D4. A sequence is a sentence if and only if it has the form, $a = b$, where a and b are terms.

Since "(0 + 0″)" and "(0 × 0″)" are terms, "(0 + 0″) = (0 × 0″)" is a sentence. The question whether or not a given sequence is a sentence can also be decided in a routine manner.

B. *Theory M*

We have described the sorts of expressions which belong to our language. Now we shall introduce an axiomatized theory formulated in M. Henceforth the letter M will also designate this theory. Let us first state the axioms or postulates (P). The theory has five infinite sets of axioms, $P1$–$P5$.

P1. Every sentence of the form $a = a$, where a is a term, is a postulate.

Two postulates from class $P1$ are: "0 = 0", "(0′ + 0″) = (0′ + 0″)". In the description of the remaining postulates I will give only the sentence form, with the understanding that all sentences of that form are postulates; a and b are supposed to be any terms:

P2. $(a + 0) = a$,
P3. $(a + b′) = (a + b)′$,
P4. $(a \times 0) = 0$,
P5. $(a \times b′) = ((a \times b) + a)$.

The following sentences exemplify these four sets:

(P2). $(0 + 0) = 0$
(P3). $(0′ + 0″) = (0′ + 0′)′$

(P4). $(0''' \times 0) = 0$
(P5). $(0' \times 0'') = ((0' \times 0') + 0')$

The set of postulates can be explicitly defined as follows:

D5. A sentence is a postulate if and only if it belongs to one of the sets *P1–P5*.

Given an arbitrarily chosen sequence of signs from the alphabet, we can obviously always decide in a routine manner whether or not it is an axiom.

The idea of formalization involves the requirement that one should explicitly state, not only the postulates on which the theory is based, but also the rules according to which theorems may be derived from them. We decide that the simplest, most direct logical step in *M* will always be of the form:

$$\text{(iv)} \quad \frac{a = b \qquad Y(a)}{Y(b)}$$

where *a* and *b* are terms, $Y(a)$ is a sentence which contains *a* at some place or places, and $Y(b)$ is the sentence which results when *a* is replaced with *b* at one or several (possibly all) of the places where *a* occurs in $Y(a)$. If three sentences *X*, *Y*, *Z* stand in that relation to each other in which the three sentences $a = b$, $Y(a)$, and $Y(b)$ stand to each other in (iv), we shall say that *X* and *Y* (or the set $\{X, Y\}$) have the relation of direct derivability *R* to *Z*. The rule of derivation can be formulated as follows:

Rule. If sentences *X* and *Y* stand in the relation *R* to sentence *Z*, then *Z* can be (directly) derived from *X* and *Y*.

In order to illustrate how the axioms and the rule are used, let us prove the sentence:

$(0'' + 0') = 0'''$.

The proof can run as follows:

(1) $(0'' + 0') = (0'' + 0)'$ (postulate from *P3*).
(2) $(0'' + 0) = 0''$ (postulate from *P2*).
(3) $(0'' + 0') = 0'''$ (from (1) and (2) using the rule).

We shall take the theorems in M to consist of all sentences which can be derived in this manner from the postulates P:

D6. (a) Each postulate is a theorem.
  (b) If X and Y are theorems and if X and Y stand in R to Z, then Z is a theorem.
  (c) Nothing is a theorem save by virtue of (a) and (b).

One can also say that a sentence is a theorem if there is a proof of the sentence. The concept of proof can be defined as follows:

D7. A sequence of sentences, $X_1, X_2, \ldots, X_n$ is a proof (of X_n) if and only if every sentence X_i $(1 \leqslant i \leqslant n)$ fulfils one or the other of the two conditions:

  (a) X_i is a postulate,
  (b) Two sentences X_k, X_l $(k, l < i)$ have R to X_i.

Given any arbitrarily chosen sequence of sentences one can always check mechanically whether or not that sequence is a proof (of its final sentence).

As one could easily show, theory M has the stronger property that it can be decided mechanically whether or not there is proof of an arbitrarily chosen sentence X. This characteristic, the so-called decidability of the theory, does not belong to all formalized theories.

So far we have not explicitly given a meaning to the expressions in M. The interpretation which I have in mind is obvious, but let us nevertheless state it formally through the following conventions:

T 1. The sign "0" designates the number zero.
T 2. If a term a designates the number n, then the term a' designates the number $n + 1$.
T 3. If a term a designates the number m and a term b designates number n, then the term $(a + b)$ designates the number $m + n$, and the term $(a \times b)$ the number $m \times n$.
T 4. If the term a designates the number m and the term b designates the number n, then the sentence $a = b$ expresses the statement that m is the same number as n.

By virtue of T 4 and upon a natural understanding of 'truth', the following then holds:

T 4'. $a = b$ is true if and only if the terms a and b designate - the same number.

It is easy to see that theory M has the following properties:

I. All axioms are true.
II. If X and Y are true and have R to Z, then Z is true.

A corollary to I and II is:

III. All theorems are true.

It would also be rather easy to show:

IV. All true sentences (from our stock of sentences S) are theorems.

C. *Instances and forms of expression.*
   A problem of existence

Definitions D1–D7 are formulated in a manner which is customary in modern formalizations. Upon reflection, the sense of these definitions appears far from evident. An attempt to clarify them brings us into contact with some very subtle and intriguing problems, first observed by Tarski.
   On the next line,

   0 0 0 0,

there are four particular instances of the same form of expression, namely the one we call the sign-form "0". A form of expression is something which is shared, or could be shared, by several concrete linguistic expressions, spoken, written, or produced in some other way. The concrete expressions are said to be so many instances of their common form. Let us say that a form manifests itself in its instances, and is manifested if it has any instances at all. Instead of using such cumbersome constructions as "numeral-instance", "sentence-instance", etc., I shall in what follows frequently use the more natural expression 'concrete numeral', 'concrete sentence', etc.
   Now one can ask: Do the above definitions deal with

instances or forms? On this point I shall decide on a systematic but, I think, innocuous ambiguity. I shall apply all the concepts previously introduced to forms as well as to their instances. Both the form "0" and each separate instance of that form is a sign in our alphabet, a numeral and a term. The form "0 = 0" as well as each distinct instance of it is a sentence, and so on.

With the distinction between instances and forms in mind, let us look more closely at, for example, condition (b) in D2. It reads:

(v) If an expression a is a numeral, so is the expression a'.

What exactly is said by this? Taking (v) to refer to instances, the following is a possible, very weak interpretation:

(vi) If a concrete expression b consists of a concrete numeral a followed by a concrete prime, then b is a numeral.

(vi) says nothing about what concrete numerals there are. Such knowledge is irrelevant to someone who uses M in a pedantic way, taking no short cuts, and lets himself be absorbed in the use of M without being concerned about its scope. However, a formalized theory becomes absurdly unwieldy unless one allows short cuts, in the assurance that if sufficient time had been spent the complete task could have been done. To work with a theory without forming any idea about its scope is also unnatural. We have, for instance, already established that all true sentences are theorems in M (proposition IV, p. 258). What has thus been established could be understood to signify that if a concrete true sentence belonging to M is produced, we *can* always produce a sequence of concrete sentences which constitute a proof of the given sentence. With special application to numerals, this line of thought seems to suggest the following postulate:

Existence postulate I. Given a concrete numeral a it is always *possible* to produce a concrete numeral which consists of an expression which has the same form as a followed by a concrete prime.

A postulate of this sort would seem to be presupposed, for example, by Hilbert when he attempts to prove the consistency of formalized arithmetic by so-called finite, concrete considerations. Our postulate says something which can be correct or incorrect. Is it correct? However large a numeral we are confronted with, we can, if the postulate is true, write an even larger (and hence longer) one. If *a* is the largest numeral ever produced in the history of the universe, we are still, the postulate asserts, *able* to produce the larger *a'*. But suppose the world is too small for *a'*? In one sense of "possible", the postulate is clearly false. In what other sense is it true?

For many (apparently legitimate) purposes of proof theory, postulate I is too weak in spite of the misgivings it generates. In his pioneering work "The Concept of Truth in Formalized Languages" ("Der Wahrheitsbegriff in den formalisierten Sprachen", 1936), Tarski makes a syntactical assumption which, in our special case, corresponds to the postulate:

Existence postulate II. For every concrete numeral *a* there is a concrete numeral which consists of an expression of the same form as *a* followed by a concrete prime.

Granted that a concrete zero exists, postulate II implies the existence of infinitely many concrete numerals, or more precisely the existence of at least one concrete numeral representing each number. If a concrete numeral is to be a product of human activity, postulate II is obviously false. One could, in accordance with a proposal of Tarski's in the work cited, imagine the concrete numerals to be "all physical bodies of a definite shape and size". On Tarski's view, postulate II is then turned into "a special consequence of the hypotheses which are normally accepted in physics or in geometry".[1] To make the formalization of theories dependent in principle on the contingent outlook of physics or (physical?) geometry does not seem satisfactory.

In order to guarantee the existence of all conceivable numerals, terms, sentences, and proofs, without openly lying or resorting to insecure hypotheses, we are thus led to let our postulates of existence concern only forms of expression, not instances. Considering only the numerals we state:

[1] Tarski, A., *Logic, Semantics, Metamathematics* (Oxford, 1956), p. 174, footnote 2.

Existence postulate III. If form a is a numeral, then the form a' (composed of the form a and the prime form) also exists.

In the world of forms there are, we assume, all the infinitely many numerals, terms, sentences, and proofs. Which of these forms happen to be manifested in concrete expressions is, we are bound to acknowledge, an empirical contingency and something which largely eludes our knowledge.

Is not to assume the existence of non-manifested forms, to side with Plato and the medieval conceptual realists in asserting the existence of *universalia ante res*? With this assumption, does not formalization become a very fragile speculative enterprise? For those who have no qualms about the existence of the integers, the assumption can be made acceptable by means of a simple device. As Gödel first showed, forms of expression can be described through numbers, their so-called Gödel numbers. The Gödel numbers for the language M can be defined in a very simple manner. The concrete expressions which occur in the list below will play approximately the same role as the standard metre in Paris:

(vii)

1	2	3	4	5	6	7
0	'	+	×	(	)	=

The concrete zero in the list is the standard zero, the prime is the standard prime, and so on. We can now say that a series of concrete alphabetic signs, $t_1 t_2 \ldots t_n$, has the form, $a_1 a_2 \ldots a_n$ (where each a_i is one of the numbers from 1 to 7), if and only if for every i ($1 \leqslant i \leqslant n$), the sign t_i has the same form as the standard sign with the number a_i in our list (vii). The form of this inscription: $(0 + 0') = 0'$, is thus 513126712. We take forms of expression to be just those numbers whose representation in the decimal system employs only the numbers from 1 to 7. Our language and theory M then becomes primarily a numerical structure which only in part manifests itself in concrete linguistic expressions.

37. WHAT CHARACTERIZES A FORMALIZED LANGUAGE?

To state in general terms what characterizes a formalized, as opposed to an unformalized language, is almost as difficult as to explain in general terms the difference between mathematical and non-mathematical theories. Formalized languages constitute, to borrow a term from the later Wittgenstein, a "family" whose members are united through a complicated net of similarities. But there is no one characteristic which belongs to all the members. Whichever characteristic *C* we use to identify formalized languages, we run the risk that a linguistic structure already exists which lacks *C* but which is nevertheless so intimately related to those languages which are generally accepted as formalized that it ought to be included among them. At any rate one runs the risk that someone will suggest such a structure tomorrow. Many of the terms with which one might wish to explain the concept of a formalized language, are seen, upon closer examination, to be painfully vague. Much of what is said in this section should therefore be taken with a large pinch of salt.

A. *Some conventions*
The following conventions are introduced in order to simplify the discussion.

(1) We shall consider only *linear written languages*, and "language" will be used as a synonym for "linear written language". The limitation to written languages is, of course, inessential. Spoken languages can also be formalized. But it is doubtful whether a language in which objects are named, say, by pointing to them could be formalized in any interesting sense. A linear written language is a written language in which the signs follow each other like dots on a line. Since such apparently non-linear languages as, for example, Frege's concept language can be easily rewritten in linear form, the demand for linearity is not a serious limitation.

(2) The expressions of a language are considered to be sequences of certain signs which we shall call *simple signs*. We presuppose that every expression can be analysed in exactly one way as a sequence of simple signs. A special

case of this presupposition is that no simple sign is itself a sequence of several simple signs. What is written with, for example, an ordinary typewriter satisfies this demand. One could imagine a formalized language which did not satisfy it, but consideration of languages of this sort would introduce an uninteresting complication.

(3) A language always has, we assume, a *finite supply of simple signs*, or a finite *alphabet*. To allow a denumerably infinite stock of simple signs, say $a_0, a_1, a_2, \ldots$, would, from one point of view, be no essential generalization. For the denumerably infinite stock of signs could be construed as built from, for example, the finite alphabet a, b, as follows: $a, ab, abb, \ldots$. (Only if the denumerably infinite alphabet is taken to be generated in some such manner from an underlying finite alphabet, can the language fulfil the demands of effectiveness which will be stated below. To allow a more than denumerably infinite supply of simple signs would, on the contrary, be an essential generalization. An alphabet which is more than denumerably infinite cannot be generated from an underlying finite alphabet, and a language with this sort of alphabet thus cannot satisfy the demands of effectiveness which are to be stated.)

(4) Every expression in a language is, we shall suppose, a *finite sequence* of its simple signs. One can, of course, allow infinite sequences of simple signs to be expressions in the language. Languages with infinitely long expressions have become interesting objects for mathematical study, but they cannot be used as languages: we can only write finite expressions. An infinite decimal fraction can never be written out, but only described, through a finite expression. (The occurrence of infinitely long expressions in a language also means that the demands of effectiveness cannot be fulfilled.)

In what follows, formalized languages will be identified with those linear written languages which are based on a finite alphabet (supply of simple signs), and all the expressions of which are finite sequences of the signs of the alphabet. Language M was of this sort.

Of a formalized language one primarily expects certain syntactical properties, i.e. properties which concern the construction of the expressions from the simple signs of the alphabet, and we shall start our examination with the syntactical aspect.

B. *Languages as systems of instances of expressions*

A written language first presents itself as a collection of marks on paper or some other writing material. When we take these marks to be manifestations of a language, we classify them in various ways. One fundamental classification occurs when we regard distinct concrete inscriptions as instances of a common *form* of expression. We can make a first division of languages into *distinct* and *indistinct* languages. A language which is presented as a collection of expression-instances and expression-forms is indistinct to the extent that it is difficult or impossible to decide which form is exemplified by which instance. A language is distinct to the extent that it is not indistinct. One expects a formalized language to be distinct. This is so trivial that it is hardly worth mentioning, but at the same time it is a problematic statement: cannot a formalized language be written in an illegible hand?

"Formalized" in "formalized language" comes from "form", which can be interpreted in this context as a synonym for "expression-form" (*Gestalt*, structure). We can say that a set of concrete expressions is a formally determined set if the form of a concrete expression determines whether or not it belongs to the set. If K is a formally determined set of instances, if a belongs to K, and if a has the same form as b, then b belongs to K. In an analogous manner we can introduce the concept of a formally determined relation between instances. If R is a formally determined relation, which obtains between the instances a and b, and if a has the same form as c, and b the same form as d, then R also obtains between c and d.

In a formalized language, certain sets of, and certain relations among, concrete expressions, sets, and relations which are important from the point of view of communication, should be formally determined. This holds especially for the concept of "sentence" (or as logicians often say: "formula" or "well-formed expression"). The definitions of sentences in linguistics are many, indeed they are legion.

Philosophers and logicians often take this concept, which is so problematic for linguists, more or less for granted. Reasons of space compel me to speak like a logician. With this important reservation, it may be said that in English one occurrence of an expression can be a sentence while another occurrence with the same form is not a sentence. When the policeman says "Stop!" to the pedestrian, his "Stop!" is by itself a complete imperative sentence. When the pedestrian asks the policeman: "Where is the nearest bus stop?" his "stop" is not a complete sentence. If this is granted, the set of sentences is not formally determined in English. A language can have or not have a formally determined concept of sentence. (The critical reader may justifiably object that the grammarian, not the language, determines the concept of sentence, and while one grammarian defines 'sentence in English' so that it *is not* formally determined, perhaps another defines it so that it *is*. My presentation is necessarily superficial.) A formalized language is expected to have, like *M*, a formally determined concept of sentence.

C. *Formalized languages as systems of expression-forms*

Within a given language, I have so far distinguished the concrete expressions (or expression-instances) from the expression-forms, and among the former I have drawn attention to a certain set, the set of concrete "sentences". Since the concept of sentence is formally determined in a formalized language, we may take sentences to be the forms of concrete sentences. All formally determined concepts which are applicable to concrete expressions can in the same trivial manner be transposed to expression-forms. This transposition corresponds roughly to the shift from what the linguist Saussure called "*la parole*" to what he called "*la langue*". I shall presuppose below that this shift has occurred; henceforth I shall treat forms, not concrete instances, as the basic level of language.

The notion of a 'formal' property of, and a 'formal' relation between, expression-forms will now be introduced. It is, of course, entirely distinct from that notion for which the phrase 'formally determined' has already been used. In studying expression-forms we may, for certain purposes, restrict our attention exclusively to the manner in which complex forms are built from the simple signs (sign-forms) of the alphabet. Such a study will be called a formal study, and the properties of, and relations between the forms which are encountered in the formal study will themselves be called formal. That, for example, the form *Sit tibi terra levis* is cut into a certain Roman tombstone, is not a formal property of that form. That the same form contains four occurrences of the letter *i*, is a formal property. All properties, relations, etc. of forms that will be discussed in the sequel will be formal in this sense.

There are vague concepts and sharp concepts. The classical example of a vague concept is bald-headedness, since the boundary between bald and not-bald is indefinite. The concept of prime number is a standard example of a sharp concept. The concept of sentence can be either vague or sharp. In a formalized language the concept of sentence ought to be, not only formally determined, but also perfectly sharp.

By an exact notation I shall mean a linguistic structure:

(i) $N = \langle A, S \rangle$,

in which A is a finite set of simple signs (now understood as sign forms), and S is a sharply delimited subset, "the sentences", of the total set of finite sequences of these signs. The first demand on a formalized language is that it contain an exact notation.[2] Language M does so.

A formalized language is further expected to possess an *effective concept of sentence*. What is meant here can be illustrated as follows: Let $N = \langle A, S \rangle$ be an exact notation, and let T be the set of all finite sequences which could, in principle, be formed with the signs of the alphabet A. S is then a given subset of T. S is effective in T if and only if it is theoretically possible to program a computer (without the limitations of actual computers) so that, given any sequence from T, it can always calculate whether or not that

[2] In *Introduction to Symbolic Logic* (1951), Carnap proposed that "language" (in the sense of "formalized language") should be used as a synonym for what might be called, in terms of the vocabulary developed here, "an exact notation in which every simple sign occurs in some sentence".

sequence belongs to S. If S is effective in T, then we can call N an *effective notation*. A formalized language is generally assumed to include an effective notation.[3] In language M the set of sentences S is effective, and $\langle A, S \rangle$ is thus an effective notation.

In many formalized languages, formal character, precision, and effectiveness belong not only to the concept of sentence but also to a number of other concepts which, in part, play the role of auxiliary concepts in defining the concept of sentence. When describing language M, we introduced two such effective formal auxiliary concepts, viz. numeral (N) and term (T). One can, of course, think of languages which would merit being called formalized, but which would not contain anything one would wish to call "sentences".

D. *Formalized theories as effective calculuses*

A formalized language usually contains a formalized theory, i.e. certain sentences are explicitly listed as postulates or axioms, and in addition certain formal rules of derivation are laid down. A direct inference usually has the form:

(ii) $X_1, \ldots, X_n$; therefore Y,

in which $X_1, \ldots, X_n$, and Y are sentences and n is a finite number greater than or equal to one. A formal rule of derivation says that if a set of sentences $\{X_1, \ldots, X_n\}$ stands in a given formal relation R_i to a sentence Y, then (ii) is an admissible or correct inference. A rule of derivation of this sort thus involves a certain formal relation R_i between non-empty finite sets of sentences on the one hand and particular sentences on the other hand.[4] A relation of this sort is often

---

[3] The effectiveness in question concerns only languages with a formally determined concept of concrete sentence. In a language in which this concept is not formally determined, it may still be possible to decide effectively (in another sense) whether or not a given concrete expression is a sentence! The speaker could, for example, raise his arm if and only if what he utters is a sentence. When Alonzo Church, in *Introduction to Mathematical Logic*, vol I (1956), says that a language which lacks an effective formal concept of sentence-form is not fit for communication, this is obviously and fortunately a mistake.

[4] The concept of inference rule and inference relation can be generalized in many ways. As for the set of premises, one could allow that it be empty, or also that it be infinite. The former is a non-essential but practical convention for certain purposes. (Instead of introducing the set of postulates P as a primary

called a "direct inference relation". If $R_1, \ldots, R_q$ are the direct inference relations in a language L, we can form their logical sum:

$$R = (R_1 \text{ or } R_2 \ldots \text{ or } R_q)$$

and regard R as the direct inference relation in L. A formalized language which contains a formalized theory as a constituent can then be regarded as a structure:

(iii) $\langle A, S, P, R \rangle$

in which (as before) A is the finite alphabet and S is the set of sentences, also P is the set of postulates or axioms and R is the direct relation of inference. One often requires of a formalized language that not only S, but also P and R be effective. One can call a linguistic structure of type (iii) which satisfies this requirement, an *effective calculus*.

Every sentence which can be obtained, starting from P, through iterated application of R is called a *theorem*, or a *provable sentence*, in the calculus. One can equivalently define 'theorem' as follows (cf. p. 257). Let us say that a finite sequence of sentences from S, for instance:

(iv) $X_1, X_2, \ldots, X_n$ $(n \geqslant 1)$,

is a proof of its final sentence X_n provided that:

(v) Each X_i satisfies at least one of the two conditions:
(a) X_i belongs to the postulate set P.
(b) The inference relation R obtains between a set of sentences which all occur in (iv) to the left of X_i, and X_i.

A sentence can then be said to be a theorem if there is a proof of that sentence.

The set of proofs in an effective calculus is itself an

datum in the calculus, Carnap occasionally chose to introduce a direct inference relation which obtains between the empty set of sentences and each sentence in *P*.) The latter is an essential generalization, through which the inference relation loses its effectiveness. As the second term of an inference one could allow not only individual sentences but also sets of sentences. One can imagine a long series of further variations of the notion of a calculus. In Gentzen's system of so-called natural deduction, among the premises of certain inferences there occur not merely particular sentences, but also entire derivations.

effective set: if a sequence of sentences is given, a computer can always, in principle, decide whether or not the sequence constitutes a proof, since the postulate set P and the inference relation R are effective. Assuming that there is a proof of a certain sentence X in S, a computer can, in principle, always find such a proof: the computer can enumerate the sequences (iv) of sentences in alphabetical order (like the words in a dictionary), and for each given sequence the computer can decide whether or not it is a proof for X. When there is a proof of X, the machine will come upon it sooner or later and establish that it *is* a proof of X. (This holds in principle only. Much work is being done toward devising mechanical proof-procedures that existing computers may be capable of handling.)

If there is no proof of a given sentence X, a computer cannot always establish that none exists: the successive checking of the alphabetically listed sequences of sentences never leads to the conclusion that no as yet unchecked sequence is a proof. The set of theorems is thus effective only in exceptional cases. When it is, the calculus (iii) is said to be a *decidable calculus*. As we have already observed (p. 257) our language M contains a calculus of the decidable kind.

E. *The symbolic and artificial character of formalized languages*

Two superficial but conspicuous features of customary formalized languages are their symbolic and their artificial character.

In a formalized language something resembling ordinary words and statements seldom or rarely occurs. In place of words and statements there are symbols and formulas with a mathematical appearance. By symbols and formulas one can often express one's thoughts more briefly and perspicuously (often also with greater prolixity and less perspicuity!) than with words. The symbolic apparatus is not theoretically essential for a formalized language. An effective calculus could, in principle, be formulated just as well with ordinary words and sentences.

The other feature is the artificiality. By a "natural language" one usually means a language which existed before any grammarian or logician formulated the rules for it. In an artificial language the use of the language is the conscious application of rules given in advance. The boundary in the history of language between natural and artificial languages is not sharp, but one can still assert that formalized languages have, hitherto, on the whole been artificial. *A priori* there is nothing to prevent a natural language from containing an effective notation ((i)) or an effective calculus ((iii)), or to prevent a formalized language from eventually becoming natural in some intellectual circles.

F. *The interpretation of formalized languages*

By specifying an effective notation ((i)) or an effective calculus ((iii)), we have obviously not defined an actual language. If someone writes an element from the set S of sentences, it means nothing to us. In order for a calculus to function as a language, we must in some way associate a meaning with the elements in S. The formalized languages developed thus far are generally designed to express what one could vaguely call "theoretical statements"—the sciences are thought to consist of such—as opposed to prayers, imperatives, interjections, questions, etc. If we ignore conceivable or already undertaken formalizations beyond the domain of theoretical statements, we can say that a calculus does not function as a language before we let elements in S express some sort of assertion. To accomplish this association is to give the calculus an interpretation. What it actually means to interpret a calculus cannot, I think, be adequately explained by anyone today. We have previously met the views of Bolzano and Frege: the assertion (Bolzano: the proposition-in-itself; Frege: the thought) is an abstract, Platonistic entity which we intellectually associate with the linguistic sentence. We have also met Carnap's instrumentalistic conception of the language of science. An instrumentalism related to but not identical with Carnap's will be encountered in Wittgenstein's *Philosophische Untersuchungen*. (Many logicians and epistemologists today think that within the prevalent scientific languages one must distinguish between a layer of sentences which, so to speak, "actually express theoretical assertions", and a layer of sentences which function only as a useful but content-less calculus. If a formalized language is interpreted through translation into a language with this stratification, then the formalized language itself will obtain the same stratification.)

One manner in which one in practice provides an interpretation for the sentences of a calculus is to consider these sentences as translations of sentences in a language which we already have a command of and understand. Usually, the translation is not into what we might call a raw portion of a natural language, but into a portion which has been intellectually refined in advance through various methods. Our interpretation of *M* was done through a translation into our customary arithmetical language. Through the given interpretation, *M* thus becomes just as clear or obscure, as comprehensible or incomprehensible, as that customary language; indeed, in many respects the two languages become completely identical.

G. *Some special demands on the interpretation*

One often places special demands on the interpretation of a formalized language. Five such demands will be indicated here.

(1) In natural languages, the assertion which is expressed by a concrete sentence is not uniquely determined by the form of that sentence. In many cases, which assertion an instance expresses depends on the linguistic context in which the instance is found. Often it also depends on factors in the non-linguistic surroundings of the concrete sentence, for instance upon who writes (or utters) it, at what time it is written (uttered), and so on. In "Now I am here", the sense of "I" depends on who is speaking, of "now" on when he speaks, and of "here" on where he is.

Of a formalized language we often demand that the meaning of its sentence instances be uniquely determined by their form and thus be independent of context. An interpretation which satisfies this condition can be called a formal interpretation. Our interpretation of *M* is formal. It should be added at once that it is possible to conceive of formalized languages for which the meaning of the sentence instances systematically varies with factors other than their form. In so-called tense-logic, first developed by A. N. Prior, the meaning of sentence instances is dependent on the time at which they are written (uttered).

(2) The sentence-forms of a formalized language should have a meaning which is "clear", "sharp", "precise", or "exact". What is meant by these words may be felt, but has not, to my knowledge, been satisfactorily clarified by anyone. If the meaning of a formalized language is given through the method of translation, the meaning will be of the same degree of clarity as the meaning of the language into which the translation is done.

(3) A formalized language should be *sound* in relation to its intended interpretation. By this is meant that the interpretation should have the effect that the postulates P express true statements, and that if a sentence Y is directly derivable from sentences $X_1, \ldots, X_n$ (i.e. the set of sentences $\{X_1, \ldots, X_n\}$ has the relation R to Y), then the truth of the statements which $X_1, \ldots, X_n$ express, implies the truth of the statement which Y expresses. (The strength of this demand naturally varies with the strength of the relation "imply" which is involved here.)

Language M is, in an obvious sense, sound in relation to its given interpretation.

(4) A formalized language can be said to be more refined, or, to use a word with many philosophical connotations, more analytic in relation to its intended interpretation, the more the logical relations among statements are mirrored in formal and simply definable (for example with the help of elementary arithmetic) relations among those sentences which express these statements. We naturally wish to make our formalized languages as analytic as possible. In particular, one usually desires that the logical consequence relations among the statements be reflected, to a high degree, in formal and simply definable relations of derivability among the sentences. A desirable but often unattainable goal is to mirror the logical relations among the statements in formal sentence relations which are also effective.

(5) We have said that a formalized language should have a formal interpretation. Often one makes a stronger demand, which could be called the demand for organic formal interpretation. It is not only the meaning of the concrete sentences which ought to be formally determined, but also the meaning of certain parts of sentences ("names", "predicates", "logical constants", and so on). The demand for an organic formal interpretation is closely connected with the demand for analytic refinement; only to the degree that the interpretation of a language is formal and organic can the logical relations among the statements be reflected in simply definable formal relations among the sentences.

H. *The formalization of statements and theories*

We have dealt with the concept of a formalized language. One can also speak about formalizing a statement or a theory.

To formalize a statement is to express it by means of a sentence of formalized language, the assumed interpretation of which makes this sentence express the same as this statement. If the statement is indefinite in one way or another, formalization can sometimes result in a clarification of it.

To formalize a theory could be simply to formalize the statements of that theory. Customarily, however, it means to create an effective calculus with an interpretation which makes the theorems of the calculus express exactly all the assertions of the theory. The formalization of a theory contains a formalization of its particular assertions and can thereby involve a clarification of them. The formalization of a theory can imply also another kind of clarification: the set of assertions belonging to the theory may initially be rather vaguely delimited, but the formalization draws the boundaries sharply.

38. FORMALIZED LANGUAGES AS TOOLS AND MEANS
    OF COMMUNICATION

Why do so many philosophers today take such a lively interest in formalized languages? One can point to the fact that formalized languages are good for one purpose or another, and that is the type of answer to the question that will be given here. But the question is psychological and an answer of this type is certainly incomplete: "What is the interest of *A*? *A* is good for *B*. What is the interest of *B*? Well, ..." This series of questions must end eventually. There are things which people simply take an interest in, and at present formalized languages belong to what interests many philosophers (especially in the Anglo-Saxon countries and in Scandinavia) and many mathematicians, the world over.

When an intellectual domain is new, it is often studied with a view to its consequences for other fields which are regarded as interesting in themselves, and then, when the domain reaches a respectable age, this kind of motivation fades into the background. Something like this is now, regrettably or not, happening in the study of formalized languages. When deliberating whether to engage upon the formalization of a theory, the philosopher should always, I think, ask himself what is to be gained by the formalization. The philosophers of a wiser posterity will probably look upon much of the formalization done today as a form of solitaire, the main value of which was to fill out idle hours. Formalization has a dangerous appeal to philosophers who have wearied themselves by brooding over speculative questions where certainty is impossible and whose respectability is perhaps questioned by scientific colleagues. Formalization is to them an oasis where certainties comparable to "There are two *p*s in *perhaps*" abound, and where everything has an awe-inspiring "scientific" appearance.

A formalized language can be used as a tool in intellectual work and as a means of communication. But it can also be treated as an object of study. In this section I shall discuss formalized languages as tools and means of communication, and in the next section, I shall add some considerations concerning their role as objects of study. These two aspects are so intimately connected that the distinction I am making is tinged with some artificiality.

A. *Roots of formalization in mathematics and philosophy*

Formalization has deep roots in the history of philosophical and scientific ideas, especially in mathematics. The entire apparatus, the symbols and formulas, which serve as a shorthand, allowing brief formulation of complex ideas, is inspired by mathematics. The formal interpretation of the symbolic apparatus is in line with the striving of science for a mode of expression which cannot be misunderstood. When the interpretation is formal, and thus independent of context and milieu, the expression can, as it were, be freely transported from context to context, and milieu to milieu, without its content undergoing any change.

Formalization in an effective calculus is, as Frege observed, a natural development of the ideal of axiomatization: having explicitly specified the axioms from which we wish to derive our theory, it is natural to proceed to a specification of those inference rules by which the theory is to be derived from the axioms. Theories formulated as effective calculuses have an even higher degree of that intellectual charm which axiomatized theories possess: the principles of an effective calculus (especially its postulates and inference rules) are like an instrument board through which the entire theory, no matter how complex it may be, can be mastered. The effectiveness of the concept of proof in a formalized language can be seen as meeting the old mathematical demand that it be possible to check the correctness of a proposed proof in a routine manner.

Formalized languages also open great possibilities of replacing freely seeking, intuitive thinking by mechanical methods in areas which lie well outside the traditional domains of mathematics. To mention just one of many similar examples, with his so-called "deontic logic" the Finnish philosopher Georg Henrik von Wright (b. 1916) has rendered it plausible that sound methods of calculation can be introduced even in moral philosophy. The ancient philosophical interest in the analysis of meaning (conceptual analysis, logical analysis, etc.) has had a varied collection of motives. One of them has been the wish to lay bare the logical relations among statements. A formalized language which is analytic to a high degree is obviously one way of realizing this aim.

B. *Four traditions*

A deeper understanding of the role of formalized languages may be acquired by studying the motives which historically drove men to the creation of such languages. The motives have varied from circle to circle and from time to time. One can roughly speak about a Leibniz–Boole tradition, a Peano tradition, a Frege–Russell tradition, and a Hilbert tradition, each of which has a different dominant motive. (These traditions have intersected and converged in a complicated manner which cannot be described here.)

The Leibniz–Boole tradition

In an effective calculus the process of inference has a mechanical character. If the calculus is also decidable, then the question whether or not a sentence is a theorem of the calculus can be answered mechanically. When Leibniz dreamed about his *characteristica universalis*, and when he sketched his many fragmentary logical calculuses, he seems to have had in mind the notion of an effective and perhaps also decidable calculus. He wished to create a situation where philosophers, instead of speculating and disputing, would engage in exact calculations. Leibniz's own logical calculuses constitute, roughly speaking, generalizations of Aristotle's syllogistic calculus, which itself offers a method of calculation. With his epoch-making work, *The Mathematical Analysis of Logic, Being an Essay toward a calculus of Deductive Reasoning* (1847), the Englishman George Boole (1815–64) initiated a logico-algebraic tradition to which belong nineteenth-century logicians like Augustus De Morgan (1806–71), Hugh McColl (1837–1909), Charles Saunders Peirce (1839–1914), W. S. Jevons (1835–82), and Ernst Schröder (1841–1902). Characteristic of this tradition was its great interest in developing methods of calculation in an area which can be described as an extension of Aristotle's syllogistic calculus. Lively attention was given to the algebraic problem of solving logical equations.

The Peano tradition

The Italian mathematician Giuseppe Peano (1858–1932) was primarily interested in creating for mathematics a precise notation with a fixed formal interpretation, and in axiomatizing mathematics. His axioms for the theory of the non-negative integers, known as "Peano's axioms" (although they were anticipated by Dedekind), have become classical. On the other hand, the idea of an effective calculus plays a less prominent role in Peano's work. Results of the research of Peano and his disciples were collected in the encyclopaedic work *Formulaires de Mathématiques* (1894–1908).

The Frege-Russell tradition

Formalization was for Frege, as we have seen, an element in his epistemologically motivated attempt to derive arithmetic from an axiomatized logic. Whitehead's and Russell's *Principia Mathematica* belongs to this tradition. A more recent work in the same tradition is the American logician W. V. O. Quine's *Mathematical Logic* (1940, 2nd edn. revised 1951).

The Hilbert tradition

Frege conceived his formalized system of logic in a naïve spirit, in the sense that he was unaware of the very real risk of contradictions. His system was in fact shown by Russell to be contradictory. The many contradictions which were found at the turn of the century on the basis of apparently correct mathematical reasoning, and of which the so-called Russell paradox is one, seemed to make it an urgent task for mathematicians to establish, if possible, guaranteed consistent foundations for mathematics. The contradictions struck most directly at the set theory developed by Georg Cantor (1845–1918). Russell's theory of types (1908) was an early attempt to place set theory on a firm foundation. Another contemporaneous attempt was Ernst Zermelo's (1871–1953) axiomatization of set theory (1908). The great German mathematician David Hilbert (1862–1943) was the one who most clearly saw the problem as a question of expressing mathematical theories in calculuses and proving the consistency of these calculuses. Hilbert and the school of logicians he inspired (Paul Bernays, Wilhelm Ackermann, John von Neumann, Gerhard Gentzen, Jacques Herbrand, and many others) initially concentrated their efforts on obtaining a consistency proof for a calculus embodying Peano's arithmetic.

C. *Instrumentalist views on the value of formalization*

The instrumentalist conception of language, which we met in Carnap, has interesting consequences with regard to the value of formalization. The bearing of instrumentalism is perhaps most readily seen when it is contrasted with, for example, Bolzano's view. The logical rules which hold for sentences, must, from Bolzano's perspective, be derived from the logical rules which hold for the propositions-in-themselves expressed by the sentences. According to one version of instrumentalism, propositions-in-themselves, and all their conceptual relatives, are a metaphysical illusion. The meanings of sentences are not, according to this kind of instrumentalism, entities which determine the logical rules holding for the sentences. On the contrary, the logical rules themselves constitute to a large degree the "meaning" of the sentences. To clarify the meaning that sentences have, is for an instrumentalist essentially to codify the logical rules which govern them. The best way to do this has often been thought to be the creation of a formalized language.

Another instrumentalist argument for formalization, which can be found in the literature (in Carnap, *inter alios*), can be formulated as follows.

In our customary non-formalized thought we are guided by "meanings" which we associate with the words. But meanings are generally vague, unclear, and changeable, and their lack of definition is carried into our reasoning. Meanings cannot be used in establishing a workable criterion of the correctness of inferences. The vagueness disappears, or is at least diminished, if we use a formalized language and let our inferences be guided by its formal rules. The transition from non-formalized, meaning-dependent thought to formalized language implies no scientific impoverishment, if only the formalized language is coupled to our observations (making possible explanations and predictions of observable events) to the same degree as our non-formalized thinking is.

D. *Formalized and natural languages: some misleading views*

From time to time, exaggerated claims have been made as to the superiority of formalized languages over non-formalized ones. Although today they have an antiquated ring, it may still be worth while to take notice of them.

In the already quoted work "The Concept of Truth in Formalized Languages" ("Der Wahrheitsbegriff in den formalisierten Sprachen"), Tarski suggests that ordinary language is contradictory because of its universal character ("if we can talk meaningfully at all about anything, we can speak about it in ordinary language"), provided that the normal laws of logic hold in ordinary language. One reason for this suggestion is the possibility of constructing the ancient paradox of "The Liar" in ordinary language. Tarski's suggestion is, however, misleading. It presupposes that ordinary language can be regarded as some sort of calculus with fixed postulates and fixed relations of inference; yet one of the characteristics of ordinary language is that nothing in it is fixed. It can be indefinitely extended (its universality!), it can change its sense, and in contradistinction to a formalized calculus is not tied to definite patterns of thought (for example postulates and rules of inference).

Another idea which has often been expressed is that the grammar of ordinary language tolerates meaningless sentences, and that this is a reason for preferring formalized languages. This idea, which can be traced back to Russell's theory of types, was often maintained by Carnap and other logical empiricists in the 1930s, and also occurs in Tarski's work cited above. It seems, however, to be, if not wrong, at least deceptive. It is probably correct to say that nonsense sentences can be constructed in ordinary English without violating its grammar. But one must remember that grammar is the work, not of God, but of grammarians, and what does not violate one grammar book may violate another. One must further remember that what is meaningless in the mouth of one person need not be meaningless in the mouth of another. Besides, one should recall that formalized languages are also human products, that they usually acquire their meaning by some sort of translation into a language which we think we already understand, and that we can never have a guarantee from above that we have given them a good meaning throughout. Finally, one ought to remember that no one has yet clarified, in a satisfactory manner, the intended distinction between the meaningful and the meaningless.

E. *The dream of a universal language*

The dream of some sort of universal formalized language can be traced back to Leibniz's idea of a *characteristica universalis*. The man who has most strongly sustained the dream in modern times is Carnap. His mathematico-phenomenological language in *The Logical Structure of the World* (*Der logische Aufbau der Welt*, 1928), his mathematico-physicalistic language in *The Logical Syntax of Language* (*Logische Syntax der Sprache*, 1934), and his empiricist languages in *Testability and Meaning* (1936–7) and several later publications, are all designed to constitute, in some sense or other, "universal" languages for science. Carnap has never made it clear what his claims to universality actually amount to. In order to avoid doing him an injustice, let us say that he dreamed of drawing the blueprint for a language that would be, as far as possible, both formalized and co-extensive with the scope of empirical science.

It is of interest to observe that in a precisely defined sense, no exact notation N with a fixed formal interpretation can be universal. Let us assume that a denumerable sequence of arithmetical functions:

(i) $f_1, f_2, f_3, \ldots,$

are represented by expressions in N. (For every non-negative integer x, $f_i(x)$ is also such an integer.) Through Cantor's well-known diagonal procedure, we can then define a new arithmetical function which is not represented by any expression in N:

(ii) $f(x) = f_x(x) + 1.$

If this function f were identical with any of the functions in (i), say with f_j, then it would be the case that:

(iii) $f(j) = f_j(j) = f_j(j) + 1,$

which is impossible. Notation N is thus, in an obvious sense, not "universal". Can an exact notation with this unavoidable arithmetical incompleteness yet be, to repeat the previous phrase, "coextensive with the scope of empirical science"? The question obviously coincides with the obscure and baffling question whether "empirical science" can, once and for all, desist from utilizing certain mathematical notions.

F. *The dream of a logically perfect language*

The dream of a universal language has a twin, the dream of a logically perfect language. Leibniz was the first to dream the latter dream as well as the former. The man in our time who has been most strongly captivated by the latter is Bertrand Russell. Wittgenstein, who in the *Tractatus* was enchanted by this dream, became, during his later phase, one of its most vigorous opponents. In *The Philosophy of Logical Atomism* (1918), Russell expresses the idea as follows:

I propose now to consider what sort of language a logically perfect language would be. In a logically perfect language the words in a proposition [sentence] would correspond one by one with the components of the corresponding fact, with the exception of such words as "or", "not", "if", ,'then", which have a different function. In a logically perfect language, there will be one word and no more for every simple object, and everything that is not simple will be expressed by a combination of words, by a combination derived, of course, from the words for the simple things that enter in, one word for each simple component. A language of that sort will be completely analytic, and will show at a glance the logical structure of the fact asserted or derived. The language which is set forth in *Principia Mathematica* is intended to be a language of that sort. It is a language which has only syntax [logical signs] and no [extra-logical] vocabulary whatsoever. Barring the omission of a vocabulary I maintain that it is quite a nice language. It aims at being that sort of a language that, if you add a vocabulary, would be a logically perfect language.[5]

The description of a "logically perfect", or "perfectly analytical" language in Russell's sense suffers from a serious vagueness, which depends on the indefiniteness of such concepts as "component of a fact", "simple component", and "structure" of a fact". Perhaps these concepts admit of a clarification that will make Russell's idea of a perfect language an interesting and fruitful philosophical notion. But

[5] Russell, B., *Logic and Knowledge* (London: George Allen & Unwin, 1956), pp. 197-8.

until such clarification has been achieved, there is no way of judging his idea that *Principia Mathematica*, enlarged by a suitable extra-logical vocabulary, might be a perfect language.

G. Formalized languages and computers

In this age of computers, formalized languages have acquired a new use which is not in any traditional sense philosophical. We have seen that the set of proofs in an effective calculus is effective, and that a computer can always, in principle, find a proof of a given sentence in an effective calculus, provided that there is such a proof. The rapid development of technology has brought about a situation whereby this theoretical possibility is on its way to being translated into actual fact. Perhaps the day will soon be here when computers can compete with mathematicians, not only in the practical handling of computations, but also in the matter of proving interesting mathematical theorems (within given calculuses).

Formalized languages are also the type of language in which conversation with computers is suitably conducted.

39. FORMALIZED LANGUAGES AS OBJECTS OF STUDY

A formalized language, presented as an exact notation, an effective calculus, or something like it, is a structure of the sort with which modern pure mathematics so often deals. Such structures can be studied mathematically from enormously many different points of view, which defy the attempt to sum them up. No attempt at a survey can hope to have any validity for the future. Here, I will merely touch upon some important points of view which have already been pursued and which have philosophical relevance.

It should be mentioned that the purely linguistic aspect of formalized languages does not play any role whatsoever in the proof-theoretical and semantical studies of these languages. In both cases formalized languages are studied as systems of expression-forms, and these forms can, as we have seen, be identified with their Gödel numbers. Proof-theory can, therefore, be regarded as a purely arithmetical study. Semantics can be considered to be a study of certain relations which obtain between the language as a numerical structure and certain other structures. In both cases the result can be applied to the linguistic manifestations, if any, of the numbers. In the study of formalized languages it is often interesting and fruitful to suspend the limiting conventions which are dictated by the intended use of the language as a language, and to allow structures which in principle transcend the boundaries of possible linguistic manifestation; for example languages with a non-denumerable alphabet, with terms, sentences, or proofs of infinite length, etc.

A. *Proof theory*

The original problem for the proof theory founded by David Hilbert was, as noted, the clothing of mathematical theories in calculuses whose construction would rule out the possibility of contradictions. Or, more precisely: the problem was to prove the consistency of formalized mathematical theories, starting with Peano's arithmetic and then proceeding, it was hoped, to more comprehensive mathematical theories (analysis, set theory). Since the set of proofs in a calculus is a precisely delimited set of sequences of sentences, it can be made the object of exact mathematical study.

The proof-theoretical study of a mathematical theory is usually called metamathematics. The proof-theoretical study of some logical theory is usually called metalogic, and instead of talking about the proof theory for a theory A one often talks about the metatheory of A. While 'metamathematics' is often considered to be restricted to the so-called finitistic method recommended by Hilbert, no such restriction is customarily placed on 'metatheory'. The expressions "object language" and "metalanguage" have become widespread, primarily through their use by Carnap. When someone investigates the properties of a formalized language, that language, the object of study, is the so-called object language, while the language which the investigator uses is the so-called metalanguage. The passage from an object language to a metalanguage is, in Carnap's terminology, the beginning of a series which can be prolonged indefinitely: object language, metalanguage, meta-metalanguage, and so on. (The American logician H. B. Curry has raised several noteworthy objections against Carnap's terminology. He notes that the language which the investigator uses in studying a formalized language is, in general, simply the investigator's normal language, possibly enriched with some technical vocabulary for the current purpose. For this language Curry proposes the term "U-language". Curry also holds that regarding the object language as a linguistic entity is mathematically unnecessary.)

The problem of showing that arithmetic as a calculus is consistent, coincides, as Hilbert noted, with the problem of showing that:

(i) There is no proof in the calculus of the sentence "$0 \neq 0$".

The metamathematical proof of (i) must itself be carried out within some mathematical theory. Let A be the arithmetical theory whose consistency is to be proved, and let MA be the mathematical theory within which the proof of consistency is to be carried out. In order for a consistency proof to have any epistemological value, obviously the consistency of MA must be less doubtful that the consistency of A. If MA itself were an inconsistent theory, the proof within MA of the consistency of A would be worthless. Hilbert chose for his MA a "finitary" mathematical approach whose possibilities he indicated without exactly defining them. The known paradoxes all deal with the conception of "actually infinite" sets. When adopting the finite approach one avoids working with that conception. Only finite sets, which can have what Aristotle called a "potential infinity", are considered. An early summary of the results of Hilbert's proof theory is given in Hilbert's and his collaborator Paul Bernay's *Grundlagen der Mathematik* (1934–9, 2nd revised edn. 1968–70).

A significant year in the history of proof theory was 1931, when the Austrian Kurt Gödel (b. 1906) published his paper "On Formally Undecidable Propositions of Principia Mathematica and Related Systems". Roughly speaking, he showed first that every consistent formalization of a certain elementary arithmetical theory is necessarily incomplete. (Not the theory M stated in section 38, but a theory very much richer in content!) Second, he showed that if the consistency of such a formalization A can be proved in a theory *MA*, then *MA* is included in *A* only if *A* is inconsistent. If one can prove within *MA* taken to be the finitary approach, the consistency of *A* in an epistemologically relevant way, then the finitary approach must hence allow certain arguments which do not occur in *A* itself but which are (nevertheless) less suspect than *A*. In 1936, Gerhard Gentzen (1909–45) presented what can be taken to be the first proof of this sort.

How important epistemologically is the consistency of mathematics? One can distinguish between (i) the absolute set of proofs and theorems of a theory (or calculus), that is all the proofs which in principle could be constructed and all the theorems which in principle could be proved, and (ii) the set given to man, that is, all the proofs and theorems which men (roughly: on earth, in a reasonable historical perspective) will ever encounter. Even if there were an inconsistency in the absolute set, it need never show itself in the set given to man. The shortest proof of a contradiction could be of astronomical length! Even if a contradiction did appear in the set given to man, we might, as the later Wittgenstein occasionally proposes, as it were, cut it off, go around it, and make it harmless for the application of the theory. What ought one say about a contradiction of this practically harmless sort? If one regards mathematics, in a Platonic spirit, as a description of ideal objects or, in the spirit of conceptualism and mathematical intuitionism, as a description of mental constructions, then even a harmless inconsistency is an abomination. The inconsistency then shows that the theory gives an incorrect picture of these ideal objects or mental constructions. An inconsistent mathematics is from this point of view like a map which shows palm groves at the North Pole! If, on the contrary, one maintains that mathematics ought to be regarded as a calculatory instrument for empirical science, i.e. if practical usefulness is made into the ultimate criterion of the value of a mathematical theory, then the harmless inconsistency is seen in another light: To give consistency proofs for mathematical theories remains an interesting form of mathematics, but is no longer unconditionally an epistemological task of the first magnitude.

Another problem which occupied Hilbert's proof-theoretical school was the problem of finding a decision procedure for the fundamental logical theory known as the "first order predicate calculus". All of classical mathematics can be formulated in this calculus. In a paper in 1931 Gödel proved this calculus to be complete, in a sense implying that the two propositions:

(ii) Sentence Y is a consequence of sentences $X_1, \ldots, X_n$,

and:

(iii) A theorem of the form, "If X_1 and $\ldots$ and X_n, then Y", is provable in the calculus.

are equivalent, provided, of course, that $X_1, \ldots, X_n$, and Y are all formulated in the language of the calculus. A decision procedure for the calculus would be a method by which one could always mechanically decide whether or not a given sentence, in the language of the calculus, is a theorem of the calculus. If sentences $X_1, \ldots, X_n$ are the axioms of a theory, formulated in the calculus, then a decision method of this sort would enable us to decide whether or not an arbitrarily given sentence Y is a consequence of these axioms. A decision procedure for the first order predicate calculus would thus, in principle, free mathematicians from the job of searching for proofs. A significant negative result in proof theory was the demonstration presented by the American logician Alonzo Church in 1936 that no decision procedure for first order predicate calculus exists.

The proof theory of mathematics has, in recent decades, developed very rapidly. Accounts of the status of proof theory at the middle of the century are given in such works as S. C. Kleene's *Introduction to Metamathematics* (1952), K. Schütte's *Beweistheorie* (1960), and A. Mostowski's *Thirty Years of Foundational Studies* (1965).

B. *Semantics*

In modern philosophy and logic, concepts relating to the connection between linguistic signs and what they signify, are usually called "semantic concepts", and by "semantics" is understood a study in which these concepts play an essential role. There is an empirical semantics, which deals with semantic properties of natural languages, and a logical semantics, which deals with formalized languages and which has an abstract, axiomatic character. Observations and lines of thought which at least in part have an empirical semantic character have already been encountered in Bolzano, Frege, and Russell, and will be met in Moore, and the later Wittgenstein.

Logico-semantic ideas occur early in modern mathematico-logical literature: Hilbert's proof-theoretical school, for example, took a lively interest in certain semantic problems. But, as a systematic discipline with precisely defined concepts, logical semantics dates from Tarski's work "The Concept of Truth in Formalized Languages" (Der Wahrheitsbegriff in den formalisierten Sprachen"). In this work Tarski defined the concept of truth (more precisely: a concept of truth) for a particular formalized language, at the same time showing how the concept can be analogously defined for a comprehensive class of formalized languages. Utilizing the same basic ideas, Tarski later defined a semantic concept of consequence. During the 1950s, with the so-called theory of models, Tarski created a new form of logical semantics, which has shown itself to be a very fruitful mathematical discipline. Tarski's early semantic ideas were enthusiastically accepted by Carnap. In *Introduction to Semantics* (1942), *Meaning and Necessity* (1947), and *Logical Foundations of Probability* (1950), he defined semantic concepts like 'truth', 'logical truth' ('analytic'), 'intension' and 'extension' (analogues of Frege's 'sense' and 'reference'), and 'probability' for certain formalized languages.

A deeper understanding of logical semantics is hardly possible without an acquaintance with the formalized languages being discussed. I shall here present only a few very general considerations concerning Tarski's original definition of truth.

(1) *Tarski defines 'truth' as a predicate applicable to sentences.* It is doubtful whether in daily speech the predicate

'true' (and its synonyms 'correct', 'right', etc.) is ever applied to sentences. We say:

It is true that snow is white,

but we hardly ever say:

The sentence "Snow is white" is true.

However, we can obviously apply a concept, which may be called "truth", to sentences in a way which makes sense even if we thereby modify or extend the current usage of the word. If the sentence "Snow is white" means that snow is white, we may decide to characterize that sentence itself as true.

(2) *Tarski regards the class of true sentence instances as a formally defined class.* He assumes, i.e., that if a concrete sentence X is true and X and Y have the same form, then Y is also true. This assumption does not hold for natural languages. While the instance of the sentence-form "This snow is white", which is uttered on 10 December 1965 in Stockholm, happens to express a truth, the instance of the same form uttered next day when the snow has altered its colour expresses a falsehood. This, of course, depends on the fact that the interpretation of natural languages is not formal. Since Tarski deals only with formalized languages having a formal interpretation, his class of true concrete sentences is formally determined. If X expresses a truth under a given formal interpretation, and if X and Y have the same form, then Y expresses the same truth under that interpretation.

(3) *Tarski defines 'truth' as a predicate applicable to sentence-forms.* This is an example of the previously mentioned transposition of formally determined concepts from "*la parole*" to "*la langue*".

(4) *Tarski defines 'truth' as an absolute property.* In Tarski's theory, a statement predicating truth of a given sentence does not have the form:

(iv) Sentence X is true for person P at t,

or:

(v) Sentence X is true under interpretation I,

or something of that sort. Instead, it has the simple, absolute form:

(vi)   Sentence *X* is true.

This feature of Tarski's definition again depends on his pre-supposing a fixed formal interpretation of the language for which he defines truth. Since the formal interpretation is fixed, a sentence of the language *either* expresses a truth and is true *or* expresses a falsehood and is false. Naturally, there is nothing to stop us from not making Tarski's assumption: if we abandon it, we may be led to define some relative concept of truth like (iv) or (v).

(5) *The form of the definition, and the requirement of extensional identity.* The definition that Tarski is looking for will thus be of the form:

(vii)   Sentence *X* is true if and only if . . . *X* . . . ,

where ". . . *X* . . ." states some condition or other. Whatever else we may demand of an acceptable definition (vii) of truth, we must, of course, always require that (vii) be a correct statement, i.e. that the set of those sentences *X* which *are* true in the indicated sense, exactly coincides with the set of those sentences *X* which satisfy the right-hand condition of (vii). We may call this requirement the requirement of extensional identity.

(6) *The language for which Tarski defines 'truth' is part of the language in which he defines it.* Let us suppose that "Snow is white" (Tarski's own example) belongs to the formalized language for which the definition of truth is given. If this language is a part of the language which I speak when framing the definition, I can obviously state:

(viii)   "Snow is white" says that snow is white,

and therefore also:

(ix)   "Snow is white" is true if and only if snow is white.

Tarski assumes this situation to obtain with respect to the formalized language that he studies.

(7) *Tarski's demand that the definition be materially adequate.* Thereby we get the criterion of "material adequacy"

which Tarski requires his definition to satisfy: a definition of truth is "materially adequate" if and only if every statement of the same type as (ix), thus every statement:

(x) The sentence "(write a sentence here)" is true if and only if (write the same sentence here),

can be derived from the definition.

Here again Tarski has chosen one among several possible roads. The set of those sentences of a formalized language that are true in the indicated sense may in many cases be correctly defined in ways that are not "materially adequate" in Tarski's sense. In languages where truth is axiomatizable, truth can, for example, be defined by means of a system of axioms. There are, I think, two reasons for Tarski's choice here. One is his view that a "materially adequate" definition has the virtue of agreeing with the classical Aristotelian definition of truth. The other is that his procedure of definition is applicable to such a wide range of formalized languages.

(8) *Tarski's demand on the vocabulary used in the definiens.* Besides the concepts occurring in the formalized language for which the definition is given, there must occur in the *definiens* only well-known notions from logic and mathematics. Provided that the formalized language studied has a purely logico-mathematical content, Tarski's definition of truth thus acquires a purely logico-mathematical character, and it will meet mathematical standards of rigour. If the formalized language studied has a non-mathematical content and perhaps suffers from some degree of vagueness, the definition will be vague only to the same degree.

Summing up, we may say that Tarski considers a formalized language with a formal interpretation. Here certain sentence-forms are true in an absolute sense (i.e. express true assertions under the interpretation). What he wants to achieve—and does achieve—is to characterize, or define, this set by means of merely the ideas occurring in the language plus generally accepted logico-mathematical ideas and in a manner which meets his particular demand for what he calls "material adequacy". Unless the formalized language had a (formal) interpretation, there would be no basis for such a definition of truth. The whole enterprise would, Tarski says, be meaningless.

Tarski's definition itself, which is a model of precision, cannot be reproduced here. Philosophers have vigorously debated whether the definition solves, or casts new light, on the question sometimes vaguely designated as the philosophical problem of truth. As I see it, this problem includes a number of difficult epistemological questions which Tarski's definition does not touch at all. With Tarski's method one can define truth for theoretical languages, concerning which many philosophers would say, in another sense, and with fairly good reasons, that they contain no truth! (Compare, for example, certain positivists' view of the language of theoretical physics, or certain nominalists' views of the language of mathematics.) The epistemological relevance of logical semantics must be said to be highly problematic at present.

Tarski's follower Carnap also introduced some very problematic ideas into logical semantics. For Tarski, the language for which he defines the concept of truth already possesses an interpretation, independently of the definition, and his definition claims to be correct with respect to that interpretation. Carnap has given currency to the idea that to present a truth-condition:

(x) The sentence X is true if and only if . . . ,

is to *explain* the meaning of X, or to *give* a meaning to X. To present a semantical theory for a language L that implies a truth condition (x) for any sentence X of L, is, accordingly, on Carnap's frequently repeated view, to *give* an interpretation to L. He also thought that the notion of logical truth, or analyticity, i.e. truth by virtue of meaning, can be explained by reference to truth conditions. If we lay down the truth condition (x) for X then X is logically true, or analytic, he assumed, if and only if the truth of X can be inferred from (x). These ideas of Carnap's which have exerted a certain influence, are, of course, entirely mistaken. The truth-condition (x) says nothing about the meaning of X. If (x) is correct when X expresses the assertion p, it will remain correct if we let X express any assertion q that is equivalent to p. A correct truth-condition is, for instance, this:

(xi) The sentence "Charles XII died in 1718" is true if and only if $1 < 2$ or it is not the case that $1 < 2$,

but it says nothing about the meaning of the sentence with which it is concerned. From (xi) we can infer the truth of that sentence, but the sentence is certainly not logically true, or analytic.

Philosophers who are doing logical semantics today, are largely concentrating their efforts on non-extensional languages. They endeavour to lay down truth-conditions such as (x) for such languages in extensional metalanguages. The philosophical ideas that guide them in this activity, have, strangely enough, never been clearly articulated.

C. *Formalized languages as theoretical models of natural languages*

Carnap proposed the idea that the best way to describe certain aspects of natural languages is to construct and study formalized languages with a similar pattern. Through Carnap's work this idea was at one time widely disseminated among philosophers interested in formalization. With reference to "the unbelievably complicated word-languages", Carnap wrote, in *The Logical Syntax of Language* (1934):

The direct analysis of these, which has been prevalent hitherto, must inevitably fail, just as a physicist would be frustrated were he from the outset to attempt to relate his laws to natural things—trees, stones, and so on. In the first place, the physicist relates his laws to the simplest of constructed forms; to a thin straight lever, to a simple pendulum, to punctiform masses, etc. Then, with the help of the laws relating to thse constructed forms, he is later in a position to analyze into suitable elements the complicated behaviour of real bodies, and thus to control them. One more comparison: the complicated configurations of mountain chains, rivers, frontiers, and the like are most easily represented and investigated by the help of geographical co-ordinates—or, in other words, by constructed lines not given in nature. In the same way, the syntactical property of a particular word-language, such as English, or of particular classes of word-languages, or of a particular sub-language of a word-language, is best represented and investigated by comparison with a constructed language which serves as a system of reference.[6]

[6] Carnap, R., *The Logical Syntax of Language* (London: Kegan Paul, Trench, Trubner, & Co, 1937), p. 8.

Using the word "model" in one of the many current fashions, we may say that, according to Carnap, the use of formalized languages as theoretical models is a very helpful if not necessary device in the study of natural languages.

The pessimistic view of the "direct" study of natural languages which the above quotation, taken literally expresses, seems strange considering the rich development of linguistics. However, Carnap's words ought not to be understood literally. At the time when the passage was written, a syntactic description of a language was expected by Carnap preeminently to describe the relations of derivability among the sentences of the language. To be more precise, he expected a description of these relations in purely formal terms. Since the sense of the concrete sentences in a natural language is not determined by their form, and since the relations of derivability between given concrete sentences are, in *one* importance sense, determined by their senses, Carnap's goal of 1934 cannot possibly be realized, and his pessimism was thus undoubtedly well founded.

The desire to characterize formally the relations of derivability in a natural language may seem as unreasonable as, say, a wish to determine people's sex by the colour of their shoes. Is it really so? The reason for an affirmative answer has already been indicated. The dubious reasons for a negative answer would be approximately the following. In practice, it has been found that persons can be taught to translate, with fairly great accuracy, statements of their natural language into an artificial formalized language, and that, by the aid of the formalization, they can then obtain a clearer insight into the logical relations of statements. (Naturally, this holds only for certain persons and only for certain statements of their natural language.) This, however, is a matter of employing a formalized language as a tool rather than of making it an object for study.

The research programme which he put forth in *The Logical Syntax of Language*, Carnap later expanded to include not only the syntactic but also the semantic properties of natural language. If we wish to clarify concepts like 'truth', 'analyticity', 'consequence', and 'probability', Carnap advises us to construct formalized languages and define the concepts for *them*, not directly for any natural language. The rationality of this procedure, understood as an element in the description of natural language, is open to the same doubts as the original programme of *The Logical Syntax of Language*.

The idea of using formalized languages as theoretical models of natural languages actually has a very limited application. The study of formalized languages undoubtedly has a relevance for the study of natural languages, but it is mainly of another sort. Types of concepts which were first developed within the study of formalized languages, appear to be "directly" applicable also to natural languages. Noam Chomsky's generative grammars for natural languages are an example. When Carnap, and those contemporary philosophers and logicians who work in his spirit, replace a natural language L and a conceptual apparatus B, designed for the description of L, by formalized language L^* and a corresponding conceptual apparatus B^*, when they thus go from $\langle L, B \rangle$ to $\langle L^*, B^* \rangle$, what they do is to abandon an empirical phenomenon which is difficult to analyse, the language L, and certain concepts B, which are perhaps somewhat indefinite, in favour of an abstract and easily analysable construction $\langle L^*, B^* \rangle$. The latter can have more or less similarity to $\langle L, B \rangle$, it can in itself be theoretically interesting, and it can, if brought down into the sense-world, be as good as or better than $\langle L, B \rangle$ for certain purposes. The problem of understanding L itself and clarifying the conceptual apparatus B, is, however, a different problem. This latter problem remains unsolved after the formalist has left $\langle L, B \rangle$ behind in the empirical world, and ascended to $\langle L^*, B^* \rangle$ in the realm of intellectual constructions.

VIII

Common Sense and Analysis:
George Edward Moore

40. GEORGE EDWARD MOORE

Idealistic speculation with roots in German romanticism,
not least in Hegel, played a dominant role in British philosophy (Bradley, Green, and others) toward the end of the
nineteenth century. The reaction against idealism, which
began around the turn of the century, found two of its
leaders in the Cambridge philosophers Bertrand Russell and
George Edward Moore (1873–1958). Moore, as well as
Russell, was deeply influenced by the ideas of classical
British empiricism, and through him and Russell these ideas
experienced a renaissance in England at the beginning of the
present century.

Moore's philosophical interests were always much narrower
than Russell's. He has said, with some exaggeration, that
neither the world nor science ever directly inspired him to
philosophical reflection. He found his philosophical problems,
he said, in what other philosophers had said, and these
problems were of two sorts: What does the philosopher
so-and-so actually mean by his assertion so-and-so? Is what he
means correct? Above all, Moore was concerned with
problems of ethics and with that tangle of problems which
were touched upon in the chapter about "Experience and the
external world" (vol. II, ch. VI).

In ethics Moore belonged to the utilitarian tradition. In
Principia Ethica (1903) and *Ethics* (1912) he stated his own
version of utilitarianism, which in the precision of its definitions is superior to earlier versions. In his catalogue of what is
positively, or negatively, valuable for its own sake, he includes
much more than the "pain" and "pleasure" of earlier utili-
tarians. Moore's ethics has not only exercised a strong
influence on academic moral philosophy, but it also became
(as J. M. Keynes, among others, has testified) an ideal of life

for the so-called Bloomsbury Group (E. M. Forster, Virginia Woolf, and others).

Moore also sought to clarify such problems concerning perceptual knowledge and sense-data as those already discussed by the classical British empiricists. He formulated and discussed a large number of hypotheses concerning the epistemological and ontological status of sense-data, without ever taking a definitive stand himself. Russell's speculations about sense-data and sensibilia ("possible sense-data") with which we earlier became acquainted, were to no small extent inspired by Moore's reflections. Russell chose one among the major conceivable alternatives which Moore distinguished very early (for example in the lectures delivered in 1910–11, and published in 1953 under the title *Some Main Problems of Philosophy*). Moore's instinctive sympathies lay with some form of naïve realism, but he was sensitive to the classical objections to naïve realism (especially what I have called the Argument from Variation). He was inclined to a critical realism somewhat in the spirit of Locke, but he also reckoned with the possibility that an even further retreat from naïve realism might be necessary.

The evaluation of Moore's work has gradually changed. At an early stage it was above all his specific doctrines that attracted attention: his ethical theory, his critique of idealism and his defence of realism, and his theory of sense-data. Today his own theories are on the whole considered dated in the English philosophical world. What is still felt to be of vital philosophical interest is his philosophical method. The two corner-stones of this method are the common-sense position and the philosophical, or logical, analysis. Through them Moore is an ancestor of the philosophy of the later Wittgenstein and of current (1965) Oxford philosophy. Since it is from this point of view that I will discuss Moore here, I shall focus my attention on his method.

One sometimes meets a serious misinterpretation of Moore's philosophy. The importance which Moore attaches to common sense and analysis is now and then interpreted as though he stood apart from what is customarily called philosophical speculation. But this is by no means the case. Moore's philosophical analysis is rather a very special form of speculative philosophy. Theories which in other philosophers would without doubt be called "metaphysical", are, as we shall see, encountered in Moore in the guise of hypothetical "analyses". Moore's insistence on an analysis that verifies common sense, far from ruling out metaphysical speculation, is rather a kind of boundary condition which he demands that any speculative theory should fulfil, a boundary condition with a rather indefinite, and in Moore's practice very liberal, content.

Perhaps it is for neither his doctrines nor his method, but for his moral attitude as a thinker, that posterity will come to see his true greatness. The philosopher Moore is as scrupulous with ideas and words as the conscientious clerk is with his figures. All his statements bear the mark of being the result of intense and prolonged reflection. Their truth and correct formulation is for Moore a matter of vital personal importance. He thinks with a passionate common sense which makes him into a kind of naïve genius.

41. COMMON SENSE, CERTAINTY, AND ORDINARY USAGE

The three concepts "common sense", "certainty", and "ordinary usage" are closely tied to each other in Moore's thought. In many of his philosophical essays Moore asserts statements of the form:

(1) I [G. E. Moore] know with certainty that p.

In place of "p" there occur statements which are formulated in non-technical ordinary language, and Moore assumes that the knowledge of p is to some degree common property, that it belongs, as he says, to common sense.

In "A Defence of Common Sense" (1925) he gives a long list of statements p of which (1) is claimed to hold. The list begins:

There exists at present a living human body, which is *my* body. This body was born at a certain time in the past, and has existed continuously ever since, though not without undergoing changes; it was, for instance, much smaller when it was born, and for some time afterwards, than it is now.[1]

Moore proceeds to list statements to the effect that his body

[1] Moore, G. E., "A Defence of Common Sense". In Moore, G. E., *Philosophical Papers* (London: George Allen & Unwin, 1959), p. 33.

has always existed in the vicinity of the earth, that in its environment there have been and are material objects, among which are the bodies of other persons; that the earth and human beings have existed for many years; that he is a human being who has had many experiences, who has had perceptions, expectations, thoughts, dreams, and feelings of many sorts; and that all this is also true of the human beings to which other human bodies belong. Finally, Moore asserts that the very many other human beings have similar knowledge about themselves. In the papers "Proof of an External World" (1939), "Four Forms of Scepticism" (from the beginning of the 1940s), and "Certainty" (1941), assertions of type (1) play a decisive role. Holding up both his hands in front of himself and looking at them, Moore asserts in "Proof of an External World":

(2)   Here is a hand, and here is another.

and:

(3)   I [Moore] know with certainty that (2).

The article "Certainty" is in part an attempt to clarify the type of certainty in question. Moore insists that (1) is entirely different in sense from the statement:

(4)   I feel certain that p.

An important difference between (1) and (4) is that p's being the case follows from (1), while (4) is compatible with p's not being the case. (1) also has a content different from this statement:

(5)   I feel certain that p, and p is the case.

(5) can be true without (1) being true: a blind conviction, which happens to be correct, is not yet knowledge. However, we shall see that statements of type (1) have the same status in Moore's philosophy as the statements p in (1) have: they are common-sense statements, which are formulated in ordinary language and which are objects of certain knowledge, but the analysis of which constitutes a problem. When Moore makes assertions of type (1), he does not apply any given definition of "certain knowledge" ("know with certainty"), but puts his trust in ordinary language.

There are primarily two features of statements of type (1) which ought to be noted.

(a) When Moore makes them, he consciously uses what he calls "ordinary language", by which he means the non-technical language which we all (more precisely: all educated Englishmen—a class to which the present author does not belong!) use in daily life. Instead of "ordinary language" he occasionally uses phrases such as "good English", "good natural English", "correct English", "properly expressed English", and so on. Although in many contexts Moore shows himself to be conscious of the ambiguity of ordinary words and sentences, he has at the same time great confidence in the possibility of unambiguously communicating certain ideas, in certain situations, with the help of ordinary language. One of the propositions of type (1) which Moore asserts is:

(6) I [Moore] know with certainty that the earth has existed for many years.

There are, he says in "A Defence of Common Sense", philosophers who say that the truth of statement "The earth has existed for many years", depends entirely on what is meant by "the earth", "exists", and "years". Against them Moore affirms that the statement is "the very type of an unambiguous expression, the meaning of which we all understand."[2]

(b) The knowledge, which Moore claims to possess through assertions of type (1), belongs to what he calls common sense. Naturally, he does not mean that everything which he knows is also common-sense knowledge. But, for his philosophical purposes he is especially interested in pointing out just such items of knowledge that he possesses which also belong to common sense. Moore has hardly given any good general explanation of what he means by 'common sense'. When he says that knowledge of *p* belongs to common sense, he seems to imply that either (i) all men, or in any case a very large number of men, have this knowledge, or (ii) this knowledge is of a kind such that all men, or in any case a very large number of men, have knowledge of this kind. Common-sense knowledge is thus knowledge which is not

[2] Ibid., pp. 36–7.

based on complex scientific evidence and theories, but is provided by normal everyday experience and can be formulated in everyday language.

42. COMMON SENSE AND THE PHILOSOPHERS

The items of common-sense knowledge which Moore claims to possess, might seem philosophically pointless. However, philosophers have considered statements of the following sort to be important philosophical truths:

(7)   No material objects exist.
(8)   Time is unreal.
(9)   Space is unreal.
(10)   The self is unreal.
(11)   No one ever perceives a material object.
(12)   We can know nothing with certainty about other minds.
(13)   We can know nothing with certainty about material objects.

Now let us confront, for example, statement (7) with the common-sense knowledge:

(a)   Here is one hand, and here is another,

which I have when I hold my hands before me and look at them and see that they are two hands. If 'material object' is used in an ordinary way, then from (a) follows:

(b)   Here is one material object, and here is another.

from which follows in turn:

(c)   There are at least two material objects.

This simple inference is, according to Moore, a conclusive refutation of (7). What one can expect of a proof is above all (i) that the premisses of the proof are true and are objects of knowledge, (ii) that the conclusion which is to be proved does not occur among the premisses, and (iii) that the conclusion follows logically from the premisses. All these demands are fulfilled, Moore insists, by the deduction of (a)–(c). In an analogous way the remaining theses in the above list, and innumerable similar theses, can be refuted

by an appeal to common sense. Let us look at (8), an assertion made by the idealist Bradley. The proposition is vaguely
formulated, but it certainly implies, Moore claims, that
nothing has temporal properties or stands in temporal relations, for example that nothing ever changes or is created or
destroyed, that one event never succeeds another, and so on.
But, as an item of common-sense knowledge, I can state,
for example:

(d)   I shaved before sitting down at my desk.

From (d) follows:

(e)   There have been at least two events, of which one
occurred before the other,

and if (8) is interpreted in the proposed way, then from (e)
follows:

(f)   Time is real.

This is a conclusive refutation of (8). At this point the reader
can no doubt easily figure out for himself how, in Moore's
spirit, one can refute (9)–(13) and many similar assertions.

Moore appends a number of significant remarks to these
refutations of what I shall here call "wild" philosophical
theories.

(i) Could we not, through philosophical and scientific
reflection, encounter propositions which contradict common
sense, yet which are even more certain than common sense
and which would, hence, force us to surrender certain parts
of common sense? The answer naturally depends on how
"common sense" is defined. If, however, we cautiously
satisfy ourselves with a partial definition of common sense
like Moore's list of propositions in "A Defence of Common
Sense", then Moore's answer is a confident *no*. The listed
commonsensical propositions have, according to Moore, a
higher degree of certainty that any competing philosophical
or scientific theories could ever attain.

(ii) Philosophers who support theses like (7)–(13), which
militate against common sense, can be reproached not only
for making obviously false statements, but also for making

statements which oppose what they themselves *know* to be true. The reason is that what they assert goes against common sense of which the philosophers themselves partake.

(iii) To the degree that we can draw a boundary between the "philosophy" of a philosopher, and the rest of his thoughts, the opposition between his philosophy and his common sense need not imply that his philosophy is in itself inconsistent. But the wall between a philosopher's philosophy and his common-sense knowledge is seldom watertight, according to Moore; the common sense is liable to seep into the philosophy and actually make the latter inconsistent. One who doubts the existence of the external world may adduce, say, facts of optics to justify his doubt. A solipsist will perhaps cite other solipsists in support of his contention that there is no other thinking being than himself, and thus that there are no other solipsists.

The type of common-sense critique of "wild" philosophical theories which Moore has put forward so many times can seem both inescapable and liberating. It is easy to learn the technique. But at the same time it is obvious that this sort of critique can easily become sophistical. Moore's refutation of (7) presupposes a particular interpretation of (7), namely an interpretation such that if (7) is true, there are no hands. Generally criticism *à la* Moore presupposes that the philosophical theory under attack has so simple and manifest a significance that it is in open conflict with trivial everyday insights. That may sometimes be the case, but we cannot take for granted that it is always so. It is, for example, very doubtful whether Berkeley's denial of material substance is affected by Moore's refutation (a)–(c).[3]

The assertion (10) might, for example, be directed against a Cartesian theory of mind.[4] And so on. Moore would surely

---

[3] Moore himself sometimes reckons with this possibility, for example, in the essay "Some Judgements of Perception". The later Wittgenstein was inclined to consider Moore's critique as, on the whole, invalid against those philosophical theories which apparently contradict common sense. Sometimes Wittgenstein stated his own view in the form that solipsists, for instance, play another language-game than that of common sense, although they may not themselves be clearly aware of this fact.

[4] While in "A Defence of Common Sense" (1925) Moore considers the existence of the self as a piece of indubitable common-sense knowledge, he admits

not wish to deny this. He would probably say that his criticism (a)–(c) refutes proposition (7), *provided* that it is understood in a natural sense. If someone asserts (7) in some *other* sense with the result that (7) is not affected by the critique, the critique has nevertheless, Moore could add, the value that it challenges him who asserts (7) to make his own meaning quite clear.

Another question raised by Moore's critical technique is obviously: How can I decide, for a given *p*, whether I know *p* with certainty? How easily we make mistakes even in everyday questions! How unnoticeable is the passage from the justified and true conviction to the unjustified, and from this to the false. If sound common sense trickles into philosophical speculation, the converse is probably also the case: speculation trickles into common sense (or what resembles common sense, supposing that only the genuine article deserves the name). Moore provides no criterion which could help us to keep account of where in the quagmire we are.

43. PHILOSOPHICAL ANALYSIS

Common-sense knowledge is philosophically relevant from Moore's point of view, not only as a basis for the refutation of wild philosophical theories, but also as material for philosophical analysis.

Moore's discussion of philosophical analysis is intimately related to Russell's, which we encountered earlier, and also to Wittgenstein's in the *Tractatus*. An example which Moore occasionally produces to clarify what he means by analysis is the assertion:

   (14)   Brother = male sibling,

or:

   (14*) The concept 'brother' is identical with the concept 'male sibling'.

Let us try to discern the properties in (14) which, according

in "The Status of Sense-data" (1913–14) that possibly "there is no entity which deserves to be called 'I'". (It is possible that Moore would have explained this sceptical utterance as directed, not against common sense, but against a specific analysis thereof.)

to Moore, are essential to an analysis in his sense. To simplify the discussion we can agree to regard the very linguistic expression (14), *with* the meaning it has here, as an analysis. Moore would prefer to say that it is what is said by the linguistic expression which is an analysis; but this terminology seems to lead to the so-called paradox of analysis. It makes it well nigh impossible to talk sensibly about analysis.

(14) is a statement asserting identity between concepts. As a condition which, according to Moore, any analysis must satisfy, we can lay down:

(A1) An analysis is an assertion of identity beween concepts or propositions.

One must distinguish an analysis from an assertion of identity between linguistic expressions. For instance, (14) and (14*) are completely different from the false statement:

(15) The expression "brother" is identical with the expression "male sibling".

In (14) the expression "brother" is synonymous with the expression "male sibling". A second demand which Moore places on an analysis is this:

(A2) Those expressions which stand on the two sides of the sign of identity in a correct analysis are synonymous.[5]

---

[5] According to principle (A3) below, if:

(i)   Brother = male sibling,

is a correct analysis, then (i) is synonymous with:

(ii)   Brother = brother.

C. H. Langford, who was the first to point out this puzzle (1942), known as "the paradox of analysis", says that since (ii) is trivial, (i) is also trivial. He then presupposes something which is not trivial, namely that if two sentences are synonymous and one of them is trivial, then the other is also trivial. In his reply to Langford, Moore suggests that since (i) is an analysis and (i) and (ii) say the same, then perhaps (ii) also ought to be an analysis—which (ii) is *not*! If it is not the sentence (i) but rather what the sentence says, which is the analysis, then one cannot (in any case according to Moore's position) escape the conclusion that (ii) is also an analysis. But if it is the sentence (i) itself, with its meaning, which is the analysis, then Moore's suggestion is groundless unless we assume that if two sentences say the same and one is an analysis, the other is also an analysis. The absurdity of this assumption is immediately apparent when one confronts it with the conditions, stated in the text, which a correct analysis must satisfy according to Moore.

The concept of synonymy is understood by Moore to be such that the following holds:

(A3)   If a part of an expression (sentence) is replaced with a synonymous part, the newly formed expression (sentence) is synonymous with the original.

As corollaries to the condition just stated one can conceive of a series of conditions, which Moore either formulates explicitly or assumes in practice:

(A4)   If $p = q$ is a correct analysis then the following is the case:
      (i) p is true if and only if q is true.
      (ii)   I know (believe, assert, etc.) that p, if and only if I know (believe, assert, etc.) that q.
      (iii)   I verify that p, if and only if I verify that q.
      (iv) r logically follows from p, if and only if r logically follows from q.
      (v) r contradicts p, if and only if r contradicts q.
      and so on.

When Moore wishes to refute a proposed analysis '$p = q$' of a proposition p, he often exploits some of these corollaries. The analysis is incorrect if, for instance, p is true and q false, or if we know that p but we do not know that q, or if some proposition follows from p and does not follow from q, and so on.

(14) is not symmetrical. Let us call the term to the left, the expression "brother", the "analysandum", and the term to the right, the expression "male sibling", the "analysans". The analysans explicitly names the two concepts 'male' and 'sibling', which are not explicitly named by the analysandum. A fourth property which Moore demands from an analysis is the following:

(A5)   The analysans in a correct analysis explicitly names concepts (or propositions) which are not explicitly named by the analysandum.

The analysans must have (as it were) a linguistic structure which is more refined than the linguistic structure of the analysandum. (It should be mentioned that (A5) is very problematic for Moore, and that in certain cases he is prepared to renounce it.)

Moore also demands of an analysis that it not be circular:

(A6)   The analysandum must not occur as a constituent of the analysans.

Moore's ideas about analysis are intertwined with his Platonistic view of concepts and propositions. The theory of propositions, which Moore presented most explicitly, and with least hesitation, in *Some Main Problems of Philosophy* (Chapter III), is closely related to Bolzano's doctrine of propositions-in-themselves and Frege's doctrine of thoughts. When I hear the word "brother" and understand it, then I am conscious of both the word and the concept 'brother' for which it stands. When I hear and understand the sentence "The sun is shining", I am analogously conscious not only of the sentence, but also of the proposition (the mental content) 'that the sun is shining' which the sentence expresses. According to Moore, we are able to think of concepts and propositions without simultaneously conceiving them as clothed in any linguistic expression. When I hear and understand "The sun is shining", then I have a "direct awareness" of the proposition that the sun is shining. Moore raises the question whether this "direct awareness" is of the same nature as the "direct awareness" of sense-data which occurs in perception. Although Moore is sometimes inclined to the view that this Platonistic talk about concepts and propositions is merely a *façon de parler* (for example in Chapter XIV of *Some Main Problems of Philosophy*), Platonism permeates the terminology in which he states his ideas.

(A7)   In a correct analysis, analysandum and analysans designate the same concept or express the same proposition.

To find an analysis of a concept or a proposition is to discern a structure in the concept or proposition, to notice a number of parts and the manner in which they are combined. Moore often expresses himself as though the analyst must concentrate his attention, and meticulously inspect the "directly experienced" concept or proposition in order to discover its analysis—approximately in the way one must inspect a painting to distinguish all that it contains. There are simple concepts, which cannot be analysed because of their simplicity. *Principia Ethica* grants this status to the concept "(ethical) good".

Russell, during his period of logical atomism, and Wittgenstein in the *Tractatus*, spoke about "the complete analysis" of a given fact or a given sentence. Russell thought that the analysis can be pushed further and further, and that at last one comes to a point beyond which analysis is no longer possible. To the best of my knowledge this idea does not explicitly occur in Moore. According to Russell, there are generally several equally correct analyses of a given fact. Moore never took a clear stand on this question. He occasionally writes about "an analysis" of something, as if there could be several, and occasionally about "the analysis", as if there were only one. (Is Moore's idea about "the analysis" related to Russell's and Wittgenstein's idea about "the complete analysis"?)

Moore's philosophical analysis is also different from Russell's in that it lacks a direction. Russell's analysis is directional in the sense that he has a more or less clear notion of the language of analysis within which all analyses ought ultimately to be formulated. If an analysis is regarded as a definition and a system of analyses as a chain of definitions, then the language of analysis is that vocabulary which constitutes the ultimate basis of the chain. Moore, however, seems not to be concerned with the notion of a language of analysis.

44. PHILOSOPHICAL ANALYSIS OF COMMON SENSE

Moore probably held that there are pieces of common-sense knowledge that are not in need of philosophical analysis, and also that philosophical analysis can be practised on propositions and concepts that do not belong to common sense. However, the analysis of certain common-sense beliefs expressed in "good natural English" occupies a central place in Moore's thought. In his ethical writings he wishes to analyse propositions like:

This is (ethically) good [bad].
This action is (ethically) right [wrong].

This action is my duty.

This thing is beautiful.

In his many epistemological papers he endeavoured above all to analyse propositions like:

I seen a pen (a hand, an inkstand, etc.),

This is a pen (a hand, an inkstand, etc.),

uttered by a person who now sees a pen (a hand, an inkstand etc). To give the analyses of concepts and propositions which belong to common sense is an important philosophical task for Moore, although by no means the only philosophical task. It often happens that someone knows with certainty that p, without knowing how p ought to be analysed philosophically. To know p without knowing the (an) analysis of p is to know less about the world than to know that p and simultaneously know the (an) analysis of p. The analysis of common sense is also philosophically urgent for Moore because, in his eyes, common sense constitutes a touchstone for many speculative philosophical theories about the world. Although their authors usually overlook it, these theories often imply certain analyses of common sense, and by testing the validity of these analyses one can then test the theories themselves.

If, as Moore likes to think, concepts and propositions are entities of which we are "directly aware" much as in perception we are "directly aware" of sense-data, then it might seem that the analysis of concepts and propositions ought to be a fairly easy matter. What is needed, then, is for us carefully to "inspect" (Moore's expression) these entities which we directly apprehend. We are hardly ever completely unaware of the structure of what we directly perceive, and by analogy it would seem that we always ought to have some awareness of the structure (the analysis) of those concepts and propositions which we experience. Must not common sense, one might ask, know something about the structure (the analysis) of p when common sense knows with certainty that p? One argument against a proposed analysis of a common sense proposition p which Moore occasionally uses is that the anlysis in question gives a "Pickwickian" interpretation of p. When doing so, Moore thinks that he, or we, have "a strong tendency to believe" that we know (assert, believe) some proposition q, when we know (assert, believe) p. And he calls the recommended analysis of p "Pickwickian" because the analysis implies that we do *not* know (assert, believe) q when we do know (assert, believe) p. When Moore reproaches a proposed analysis with being "Pickwickian", he seems to credit himself and us with a certain sound feeling for the correct analysis. But he often argues as if he and common sense know offhand little or nothing about the analysis of those propositions which he and common sense know with certainty to be true. It seems that his position on this matter became more sceptical with the years. A series of esoteric philosophical theories about the nature of matter, which in *Some Main Problems of Philosophy* (Chapter VII) are rejected as opposing common sense, are listed in later writings as possible analyses of common sense.

As an example, let us consider Moore's repeated attempt to analyse the "perceptual judgement":

   (i) This is a hand,

uttered by a person who holds up his hand and looks at it and sees it is a hand. According to Moore, that person is then directly aware of sense-datum, which we shall call s.[6] All that Moore claims to be able to establish with absolute certainty about the analysis of (i) is that (i) is a proposition about s. A correct analysis[7] of (i) thus ought to have the form:

   (ii) . . . s . . . .

What is it then that we are asserting about s in (i)? Moore thinks it obvious that s is not a hand, and thus (i), which the

[6] Concerning the concept "sense-datum" cf. the earlier discussion of classical British empiricism in vol. II. According to Moore, we directly experience a "sense-datum" (or a "sensible") in every "sensory experience". Among sensory experiences, in addition to our normal waking perceptions, he includes dreams, hallucinations, the awarenss of so-called after-images, and visual fantasies. The term "sense-datum" (and "sensible") generally acquires in Moore the broader meaning of an entity which is of the same kind as that which is directly experienced in this type of experience, even if *in fact* it does not happen to be so experienced. Thus, Moore's term "sense-datum" ("sensible") often becomes nearly synonymous with Russell's "sensible".

[7] For the sake of brevity I shall write here "a correct analysis" when according to terminology introduced earlier I ought properly to say "an *analysans* in a correct analysis".

person knows to be true, cannot express that *s* is a hand. Moore considers the possibility of analysing (i) as follows:

(iii) There is exactly one thing such that it is a hand and *s* is part of its surface.

Whoever wishes to defend (iii) must answer all the classical arguments against naïve realism. Of them it is the Argument from Variation, which carries most weight with Moore. The arguments do not constitute for Moore a conclusive refutation of (iii), but they are sufficiently serious to compel him to try out other analyses.[8]

Another line of analysis which Moore considers is:

(iv) There is exactly one thing such that it is a hand and a part of its surface has relation *R* to *s*,

where *R* is not identity. One possibility would be to regard *R* as a causal relation of some special sort, or as a unique and unanalysable relation of "manifestation". Moore tends to think that both possibilities are illusory because he is not aware of any such relations that would fit into (iv).

Moore seems to think that almost every philosophical theory about "the nature of the matter" implies a certain analysis of (i), and of similar propositions. He also seems to maintain that a good way of testing such a theory is to investigate whether the analysis of (i) which the theory implies is tenable. From this point of view Moore discusses among other things what I have called Berkeley's "hypothetical" interpretation, Russell's theory of material objects as sets of sensibilia, the spiritualistic hypothesis that a material object is mental in nature (for example, a mind, or an assembly of minds), and a critical realism in the spirit of Locke. All these theories except Locke's have the disadvantage of giving a Pickwickian sense to (i). But Moore does not definitively reject any of them. Unfortunately, Moore's

---

[8] The Argument from Variation is discussed especially in "The Nature and Reality of Objects of Perception", chapter II of *Some Main Problems of Philosophy*, "Some Judgements of Perception", and "A Defence of Common Sense". In the latter two articles Moore proposes an idea by which the argument might be circumvented, at least in some cases. In his book *The Mind and its Place in Nature*, C. D. Broad has further developed this idea under the label "the multiple relation theory of appearing".

discussion on this point is very sketchy. He neither explicitly formulates which analysis of (i) he assumes to be implied by a given philosophical theory about the nature of matter, nor does he clarify exactly why he assumes that the theory in question implies the analysis in question.

"The entire question about the nature of material things" is, according to Moore, tied up with the question of how propositions of type (i) ought to be analysed. There are here two related but not identical trains of thought in Moore. In "Some Judgements of Perception" he says:

". . . I cannot help thinking that assumptions as to the nature of material things have too often been made, without its even occurring to those who made them to ask, what, if they were true, we could be judging when we make such judgements as those [for example (i)] ; and that, if this question had been asked, it would have become evident that those assumptions were far less certain than they appeared to be".[9]

Here the thought seems to be that a theory about the nature of material things (usually/often) implies an analysis of propositions like (i), and that the validity of the theory can be tested by testing the analysis. This is what I had in mind when saying (p. 297) that the demand for an analysis that verifies common sense is a boundary condition which Moore insists that a philosophical theory must satisfy. That the condition is very indefinite should be obvious from our previous discussion.

In "A Defence of Common Sense" we read:

It is the analysis of propositions of the latter kind [the kind exemplified by (i)] which seems to me to present such great difficulties, while nevertheless the whole question as to the *nature* of material things obviously depends upon their analysis. It seems to me a surprising thing that so few philosophers, while saying a great deal as to what material things *are* and as to what it is to perceive them, have attempted to give a clear account as to what precisely they suppose themselves to *know* (or to *judge*, in case they have held that we don't *know* any such propositions to be true, or even that no such propositions *are* true) when they know or judge such things as 'This is a hand', 'That is the sun', 'This is a dog', etc. etc. etc.[10]

[9] Moore, G. E. *Philosophical Studies* (London: Routledge & Kegal Paul, 1922), p. 225.
[10] Moore, G. E., "A Defence of Common Sense", pp. 53-4.;

Here Moore seems to entertain the idea that the analysis of (i) conversely implies something decisive for the question of the nature of material things, perhaps even that the analysis implies some theory of matter. The analysis of (i) would then not only make it possible to refute incorrect theories about the nature of the matter, but also open an overlooked short cut to the correct theory.

The optimism about the importance of the results of analysis, which now and then appears in Moore, stands in marked contrast to his doubts as to the possibility of finding the correct analysis of common sense. While Moore, the evangelist of common sense, can seem tinged with dogmatism, Moore, the analyst of common sense, comes close to a defeatist scepticism. At the same time that he adheres rigidly to the set of propositions which he considers to be parts of the common-sense picture of the world, he thinks that he knows with certainty very little, indeed, practically nothing, about how these propositions ought to be analysed. He acknowledges that their analysis may be utterly Pickwickian and paradoxical. The demand that an acceptable philosophical theory about the world be coupled to an acceptable analysis of these propositions, is hardly, then, the test of or clue for speculation which Moore occasionally sees it as. Moore himself acknowledges that he is "completely puzzled" by the task of philosophically analysing (i).

IX

Linguistic Philosophy:
The Later Wittgenstein

45. MOTIVES AND METHOD

Interest in language is prominent in all the philosophers discussed in this survey of a line of development in the philosophy of the last 150 years. But most of them are not exponents of linguistic philosophy in the narrower sense of a philosophy that considers the study of everyday language (Moore: "good natural English", Oxford philosophers: "ordinary language") to be a central philosophical task. Some of Moore's ideas plainly foreshadow characteristic ideas of the later Wittgenstein and contemporary Oxford philosophy. Although it can be tempting to classify Moore as a linguistic philosopher, he is, more accurately, to be looked upon as a precursor of linguistic philosophy. Its foremost representative is the later Wittgenstein, the author of *Philosophical Investigations* (*Philosophische Untersuchungen*, completed in 1945, published posthumously in 1953). The Oxford philosophers whose ideas are more or less closely related to those of the later Wittgenstein also belong here: Gilbert Ryle, John L. Austin, H. L. A. Hart, H. P. Grice, P. F. Strawson, J. O. Urmson, David Pears, Stuart Hampshire, G. J. Warnock, Michael Dummett, Elizabeth Anscombe, R. M. Hare, Anthony Quinton, and many others.

Linguistic philosophy clearly belongs to the Socratic tradition. If Socrates' question "What is justice" is transformed into "What does 'justice' mean", we get a question of the sort that engages the interest of linguistic philosophers. Of the motives which were found (Vol. I, Ch. IV) to have nourished interest in conceptual analysis in antiquity, motives I, II, and III have also played a large role for modern linguistic philosophy (although for 'definition' one should substitute a less technical term like 'analysis of meaning' or 'analysis of usage'). Motives IV, V, and VI are, on the other hand, peculiar to the ancient, Platonic–Aristotelian pattern of thought. Motive VII outlived antiquity, and can be found, for example, in Leibniz, Bolzano, and Russell. This motive is sustained by the idea that to define is to discern the components of something complex. The idea also occurs in Moore, but he hardly shows any desire to reach what is simple and so, according to the present view of definition, indefinable.

The modern interest in the analysis of ordinary language is also nurtured by a number of motives that were unknown in antiquity. In an unavoidably schematic way I shall try to state some of them (christening them to make them easier to recall). Although I do not include Moore among the linguistic philosophers, it seems appropriate to pay attention to some of his notions in this chapter, notions that have exercised a powerful influence on the linguistic philosophers properly so called.

Moore's first motive. There is a common-sense knowledge more certain than any philosophical theories, a knowledge of which most of us partake and which has found expression in ordinary language. The philosopher who seeks certainty ought to contemplate this knowledge with care and respect. This idea, which was stated so forcefully by Moore, plays a large role in the later Wittgenstein and the Oxford philosophers.

Moore's second motive. Philosophical theories which fly in the face of our common-sense knowledge are false. By invoking this knowledge we can therefore refute many wild philosophical theories, avoid mistakes, and free ourselves from pseudo-problems. This thought, first set forth by Moore, recurs in modified form in the later Wittgenstein and the Oxford philosophers.

Moore's third motive. By analysing our common-sense knowledge we can hope to solve, or get important clues to the solution of, metaphysical problems like, for example, the question of "the nature of matter" (choosing between such competing theories as Leibniz's monadology, Locke's critical realism, Berkeley's phenomenalism, etc.). This thought of Moore's does not occur in an equally clear form in the work of the other philosophers mentioned above, but it is not entirely foreign to them. Ryle's *The Concept of Mind* (1949), for example, is an attempt to refute the "Cartesian myth" of a "thinking substance" and to clarify the true nature of mind largely through a study of the psychological vocabulary of ordinary language.

Wittgenstein's first motive. In his analyses of common sense Moore assumes a certain view of the function of language, a view he took over from a tradition inaugurated by Aristotle: that when we understand a linguistic expression, we associate with it an idea of what it signifies, or there occurs in us a mental act by which we apprehend what is signified. In Wittgenstein's eyes this theory of language is a web of errors, involving: (i) the illusion that linguistic expressions have a common function of "naming" or "meaning"; (ii) the illusion of Platonic entities (for not all expressions name something concrete and tangible); and (iii) the illusion of mental acts as components of the understanding of language. Through his own study of ordinary language Wittgenstein wishes to refute the type of philosophy of language which Moore takes for granted, and to present another, more adequate view, a view which can be roughly characterized as instrumentalistic, anti-Platonistic, and semi-behaviouristic. The same is true, in large measure, of the Oxford philosophers. (Since there are so many of the latter, this assertion naturally requires very many reservations and modifications.)

Wittgenstein's second motive. In the later Wittgenstein's opinion, all philosophy is based on a misconception of ordinary language and/or consists in the actual misuse of this language. Through his own unprejudiced study of ordinary language (and to some extent also the language of science, at least that of mathematics) Wittgenstein wanted to put an end to philosophy. Sometimes he refused to label his own study of language "philosophy", considering it instead as one of the activities which ought to replace philosophy. Oxford philosophers have sometimes entertained similar ideas.

Austin's first motive. Ordinary language has developed on the basis of the experiences of many generations and their attempts to communicate effectively. On the whole it is therefore safe to assume that ordinary language codifies more subtle observations, finer and more essential distinctions than the philosopher can think up during a few hours at his desk. This is particularly true when it comes to such matters as have concerned and do concern men in their everyday life. Through a meticulous study of ordinary language with an eye on those phenomena which it describes, philosophy can hope to achieve basic insights regarding, say, perception and moral evaluation. In this sense Austin occasionally speaks about his philosophy as a "linguistic phenomenology". The same thought occurs, although less prominently, in Wittgenstein. It is shared, I think, by most of the so-called linguistic Oxford philosophers.

Austin's second motive. Austin hoped to lay the foundation for a future science of language, subtler and more realistic than the present. I mention this idea only in passing since, to the best of my knowledge, Austin never gave substance to it.

Some other features are also common to many of the linguistic philosophers. One is the attitude towards the construction of formalized languages, formal logic, and the entire mathematical mode of thought which has infiltrated so many areas of modern philosophy. Their attitude is generally critical or negative, although criticism and negation assume different forms. Moore said that laziness kept him from following Russell's advice to learn the calculus, and that he was uncertain whether it would have done him any good. The later Wittgenstein combated the thought he met in Frege and Russell that a task of philosophy is to replace ordinary language with a logical formalism. According to Wittgenstein ordinary language is perfectly in order as it is, and to abandon it for a formalized language would be, say, like giving up croquet and taking up chess. Similar opinions occur among leading Oxford philosophers. Wittgenstein relegated the study of formalized languages and formal logic from philosophy to mathematics. Oxford philosophers (for example Strawson, Warnock) have also reproached formal logic for forcing an unnatural meaning upon the idioms of ordinary language.

It is a fact that the linguistic philosophers have been little interested in the philosophical problems to which the natural sciences give rise, and, on the whole, in problems which demand for their treatment scientific insights of a more advanced kind. Moore was entirely unfamiliar with non-humanistic research—he had been trained in the classics. Wittgenstein, although originally a student of science and technology, wished to establish a watertight barrier between philosophy and science on the basis of motives which seem to have been particularly complicated. The scope of "science" was, in the *Tractatus*, coextensive with the realm of material truth, and even of sense. Philosophy, then, became either a mystical insight into the logic of the world, or nonsense, or a therapy for the philosophizing intellect. As Wittgenstein grew older, he also seems to have developed a highly personal indifference to science. Oxford philosophers have shown a similar tendency to separate philosophy from science, especially natural science.

Philosophers usually have the feeling of working on deep and difficult problems, of seeking a truth which is hidden. The Oslo group around Arne Naess had occasionally called its position "trivialism", thereby expressing its wish to "de-dramatize" philosophical problems. Moore was certainly not a trivialist, his thought always remained metaphysically open. But the word "trivialism" is a good characterization of one aspect of the thought of the later Wittgenstein and of many Oxford philosophers. One fundamental attitude of theirs is that philosophy cannot reveal new truths: it can only, for one purpose or another, remind us of what is familiar.

In a correct analysis of Moore's kind, $p = q$, the analysans q should say the same as the analysandum p, and thus in a sense q should be a translation of p. Moorean analysis has therefore been described as "analysis through translation". When Wittgenstein and the Oxford philosophers enquire as to the meaning of a linguistic expression, they usually do not want a translation but a description of the rules according to which the expression is correctly used. They wish to lay bare what they call the "logic", "grammar", or "logical grammar", of the expression. (Not the least part of this logic is a phenomenological description of situations where the expression is correctly used, according to linguistic custom.) On this point there is an interesting similarity, yet also a dissimilarity, between the later Wittgenstein and the Oxford philosophers on the one hand, and Carnap and the logical empiricists on the other. Both parties are interested in the rules of language. While Carnap lays down the rules for formalized languages that, he hopes, may replace portions of natural language, Wittgenstein and the Oxford philosophers try to register the actual rules of natural language (English). While the interest in the syntactical aspects of language and the sentence–sentence relations plays such a prominent role with Carnap, the linguistic philosophers have, I think, focused their interest rather on the relations between sentences and situations of use.

The linguistic philosophers mentioned in this chapter have on the whole employed the armchair method in their study of ordinary language. When a linguistic philosopher of the Oxford kind studies the logical grammar of, say, the verb "see", he considers himself to be in the same situation as that of an expert dancer asked to explain how a dance is performed: he dances it and observes what he does. Similarly, the Oxford philosopher activates his ability to use the verb "see" correctly and records how he does it. (This simile comes from R. M. Hare.) Austin also recommended the use of good dictionaries. From the point of view of method, the study of language as pursued by the later Wittgenstein and the Oxford philosophers cannot be acquitted of the charge of a certain primitiveness.

46. THE LATER WITTGENSTEIN

A. *General characteristics*

The *Tractatus*, the only philosophical book that Wittgenstein published during his lifetime, was a farewell to philosophy. The book claimed to give the definitive solutions to the great problems of philosophy. At the same time it argued that sense and science are coextensive, and hence that philosophical statements are bound to be nonsense. To continue as a philosophical author with these convictions would be something of a paradox. For a long time the farewell appeared to be final. During the greater part of the 1920s Wittgenstein devoted himself to activities far removed from philosophy in the academic sense. However, in 1929 he returned to Cambridge in England, where he had studied under Russell before the war, and therewith also to philosophy. From 1939 to 1947 he occupied the professorship which G. E. Moore had previously held. During the last two decades of his life—he died in 1951 at the age of 62—Wittgenstein developed a philosophy, or at least a way of philosophizing, which is in many respects in sharp contrast with the work of his youth. The difference between the *Tractatus* and the philosophy which he now evolved is on many scores so deep that it is customary to speak of "the early Wittgenstein" and "the later Wittgenstein" almost as if they were two philosophers. But, of course, there is also a continuity. Not only do attitudes and opinions from his youth remain in a more or less modified shape; but also and perhaps more importantly, much of what the later Wittgenstein says becomes fully understandable only when seen as a reaction against the views of the early Wittgenstein.

For both Wittgensteins, language is the focus of interest. Both wish in some way to clarify "the essence of language". In the *Tractatus* language is looked upon as a "picture" of reality. This is a view which the later Wittgenstein never tires of attacking. The nature of language, he thinks, can be more adequately described by such analogies as that language is a game ("language game") played by a group of people, that it is an instrument for doing something, that it is a machine of which words and sentences are parts, or that it is the form of life of a community.

Both the early and the later Wittgenstein draw a sharp distinction between philosophy and science. Scientific problems are material questions to be answered through a study of facts, whereas philosophical problems are nonsense questions solved only by realizing that they are nonsense. Both the early and the later Wittgenstein say that philosophers get entangled in nonsense by misunderstanding, or violating, the "logical syntax" or "logical grammar" of language. But while the early Wittgenstein seems to assume the existence of a universal grammar, the later Wittgenstein insists that *different* grammars apply to *different* areas of language. This is tied up with another shift in Wittgenstein's position. While the *Tractatus* shows a tendency to identify language with some formalized language (an amended version of Frege's and Russell's formalisms), and while the interest in the *Tractatus* in ordinary language is faint, it is the latter on which the later Wittgenstein's interest is focused. The philosophical problems which primarily concern him are non-technical problems formulated in ordinary language.

In order to see clearly here, it is necessary to study the conditions under which ordinary language functions meaningfully. The contrast: philosophy/science, which was so dominant in the *Tractatus* is, in the later Wittgenstein coupled or even replaced with by the contrast: philosophy/ordinary usage. Although Wittgenstein does not defend "common sense" as explicitly and as unambiguously as did Moore, the contrast: philosophy/common sense, implicitly plays a great role in his thinking as well. Like Moore he often rejects philosophical theories and dispels philosophical doubts by citing everyday facts, expressed in everyday language.

The notion that philosophy is nonsense placed the young Wittgenstein in a puzzling situation: the philosophy of which this notion was a part was itself judged to be nonsense. The young Wittgenstein had the paradoxical courage to accept the consequence. The later Wittgenstein thought he could eschew it. What he pursues is *not* philosophy, but one of the studies which are to replace it, viz. the logical grammar of ordinary language. Besides, he does not consider himself to be presenting *theories* about language, theories which could run the risk of being philosophical nonsense. What he does is merely to describe well known linguistic situations, to make us see what we already know but did not properly attend to. While the *Tractatus* is marked by a rich and esoteric technical vocabulary, the later Wittgenstein is at pains to describe ordinary language in terms which this language knows and accepts. (In the *Philosophical Investigations* the terms which have a technical character of a sort can be counted on one's fingers' "language-game", "rule", "family resemblance", "use", "mental processes", and a few others.)

There is a clear difference between the two Wittgenstein's on the matter of general world-views. What the "world" of which the *Tractatus* has so much to say really is, remains ambiguous in a way that stirs the imagination. Sometimes it appears to be a subjective world of experience— Schopenhauer's *Welt als Vorstellung*—and the young Wittgenstein then seems to be a kind of solipsist. The later Wittgenstein definitely and radically rejects epistemological idealism. In *The Blue Book* he often speaks as though only material objects exist, or at least as though material objects alone can be bearers of names. There is undoubtedly a materialistic tendency in the later Wittgenstein, even if it is misleading to say that he is a materialist. Of course he does not maintain any materialistic theses—since all philosophical theses are nonsense to him! In the later Wittgenstein there is also a strong tendency to think in more or less behaviouristic terms. Wittgenstein's thinking about language in the *Tractatus* was dominated by the conceptual scheme (L),

(L)

where the world is the original, of which language and thought are two pictures, and where also the last two are pictures of each other. To every meaningful sentence there corresponds, according to this scheme, a thought as well as a possible state of affairs in the world, and the sentence is a picture of both. For the later Wittgenstein, on the other hand, language is essentially a part of human behaviour. He is inclined to deny, ignore, or minimize the role of thoughts, experiences, and consciousness, in the handling of language.

While the early Wittgenstein wrote like one who had, with the help of logic, penetrated deeply beneath the surface of things, the later Wittgenstein speaks like one who, with a philosophically unbiased view, sees and describes what lies in plain view for all to see and who besides knows that the depth below is an illusion. In contrast with the brooding prophetic gravity of the *Tractatus*, the *Philosophical*

Investigations is marked by a kind of lightness and mobility of thought.

The *Tractatus* can be read with real understanding only by a person acquainted both with the situation in mathematical logic at the turn of the century (especially with the works of Frege and Russell) and with Russell's logical atomism. The *Philosophical Investigations* can, on the whole, be read with a great measure of understanding without particular specialist knowledge. Nevertheless, both works are, ultimately, equally difficult to understand. When I attempt in what follows to collect some of the ideas of the later Wittgenstein under a number of rough headings, I do so with the reservation that my interpretation must of necessity be highly subjective. It might reasonably be claimed that a summary of the sort which I shall try to give must be misleading in principle. The later Wittgenstein did not *want* to defend a philosophical doctrine, yet nevertheless I shall attempt to find in his writings something like a doctrine. In the preface of the *Philosophical Investigations* Wittgenstein says that he has traversed an intellectual landscape in many directions, and that his book is a collection of landscape sketches made during these meandering travels. One way to study the later Wittgenstein would be merely to follow him on his travels—without being anxious about the route, about the coherence of the ideas, about a general doctrine. However, there is concealed behind Wittgenstein's many loosely-joined aphorisms something which resembles a common basic outlook. It is this outlook which has influenced contemporary philosophy more than his views on any particular questions, and it is this outlook which I shall try to get hold of, for better or for worse.

During his second creative period Wittgenstein prepared, time and again, more or less finished manuscripts, presenting his new philosophical insights. They circulated among his friends and disciples, but he could never persuade himself to publish. After his death a number of volumes of his *Nachlass* have been printed. The most important posthumous work is the *Philosophical Investigations*, a work which Wittgenstein regarded as his philosophical testament. Other important works now in print are *The Blue and Brown*

Books, Remarks on the Foundations of Mathematics, Philosophical Remarks, Zettel, Philosophical Grammar, Proto-Tractatus, and *On Certainty.*

B. *The nature of language*

In order to illuminate the nature of our language Wittgenstein imagines a number of simpler languages. The simplest of them, "language (2)", he describes as follows:

> The language is meant to serve for communication between a builder A and an assistant B. A is building with building-stones: there are blocks, pillars, slabs and beams. B has to pass the stones, and that in the order in which A needs them. For this purpose they use a language consisting of the words "block", "pillar", "slab", "beam". A calls them out; B brings the stone which he has learnt to bring at such-and-such a call. Conceive this as a complete primitive language.[1]

Wittgenstein then expands language (2) into "language (8)", which contains, in addition to the vocabulary of (2), the letters of the alphabet, the two words 'there' and 'this', and colour samples:

> A gives an order like: "*d*—slab—there". At the same time he shews the assistant a colour sample, and when he says "there" he points to a place on the building site. From the stock of slabs B takes one for each letter of the alphabet up to "*d*", of the same colour as the sample, and brings them to the place indicated by A.—On other occasions A gives the order "this—there". At "this" he points to a building stone. And so on.[2]

Concerning languages of this sort Wittgenstein says that we can compare them with "those games through which children learn their mother tongue":

> I will call these games "language-games" and will sometimes speak of a primitive language as a language-game.
>
> And the processes of naming the stones and of repeating words after someone might also be called language-games. Think of much of the use of words in games like ring-a-ring-a-roses.
>
> I shall also call the whole, consisting of language and the actions into which it is woven, the "language-game".[3]

The expression "language-game" which Wittgenstein

---

[1] Wittgenstein, L., *Philosophical Investigations* (Oxford, 1958), I § 2.
[2] Ibid., I § 8.
[3] Ibid., I § 7.

introduces in this passage, stands for one of the most important points of view in the *Philosophical Investigations*. A language like English can, according to Wittgenstein, be considered to be a language-game or, perhaps more accurately, a large number of interwoven language-games. I believe that one can discern at least five different reasons why Wittgenstein thinks the term language-game to be so apt.

(1) With a few exceptions such as solitaire, a game is something which is played by several persons. It is a social activity, and normally language is so, too. One of the targets of Wittgenstein's criticism in the *Philosophical Investigations* is the notion of a "private language", a language which deals with things that only I experience, and which I alone understand. This notion is a natural consequence of certain rather common philosophical views. We can arrive at it, for example, if we assume that linguistic expressions as used by me represent my experiences ("ideas", "sense-data", etc.) and that no two subjects can share exactly the same experience.

(2) A game is bound by certain rules. The rules of a game are arbitrary in the sense that we can decide to change them and so play another game. However, as long as we wish to play just this game, we must follow just these rules. The same holds for language.

(3) It is impossible to conceive of a perfect or complete game. Every game can be changed, and to every game can be added new rules, new pieces, and so on. The same is true of language: there cannot be a perfect or complete language such as Leibniz, Russell, the young Wittgenstein, and the logical empiricists dreamt of.

(4) To play a game is normally (unless one plays blind chess with oneself) to perform certain outward actions together with other persons, to move about oneself, to move things, to say things, and so on. What one thinks or feels when playing croquet is irrelevant strictly from the point of view of the game. Wittgenstein is inclined to think that something similar is true of language-games. Just as a person knows a game if he does the proper thing at the proper time, so he knows a language if he can handle it correctly.

(5) There is no common feature which belongs to all

games and to nothing but games. The class of games is like a "family" held together by "family resemblances". The family resemblances within a family are like the fibres in a thread: "And the strength of the thread does not reside in the fact that some one fibre runs through its whole length, but in the overlapping of many fibres."[4] The same is true of language-games: the particular language-games of which our language consists, have many features in common, and these common features overlap, but there is nothing like "the essence of a language-game" to be captured in an exact definition.

Wittgenstein also compares words and sentences to different sorts of tools. Some of the similarities he sees are these:

(1) A tool is something which we use to obtain a certain result, for instance to build a house. In the languages (2) and (8), which we have just encountered, A uses certain words in order to make B do something. Wittgenstein tends to conceive of a language as a collection of tools of which we avail ourselves in our intercourse with other people.

(2) A hammer, pair of pliers, a saw, a screwdriver, a foot-rule, a glue-pot, a nail, and so on, are all tools, but they have completely different functions. Wittgenstein insists that diferent sorts of words and sentences have just as different functions as these tools. In language-game (8) the names ('block', 'pillar', and so on) have one function, the letters of the alphabet used as numerals have another function, 'there' and 'this' have a third function, the colour samples a fourth; and there is no function which they all have in common.

(3) In many cases the same result can be reached by using different tools. The same holds for language. In a language-game analogous to (8), A could for instance say "slab, column, brick" whereupon B would react by first pulling out a slab, second a column, and finally a brick. The order of the words would indicate the order of execution. But A could also use special ordering words, for example "first, second, third, . . .", and say "second, column; first, slab; third, brick!" with the same effect as before.[5]

[4] Ibid., I §67.
[5] Wittgenstein, L., *The Blue and Brown Books* (Oxford, 1958), p. 83

(4) Carnap, too, as we have learnt, saw an instrument in language. A similarity that Carnap wished to stress was that the choice of language, like that of an instrument, is a practical question, a "decision" which does not commit us to any "conviction", "opinion", or "belief", and that it cannot be "correct" or "incorrect", only more or less "expedient". Wittgenstein occasionally makes remarks which can be interpreted in the same vein. In *The Blue Book* he says that philosophers who discuss perception in terms of sense-data, introduce a "new phraseology", a new language, but that they are mistaken when they believe that they have discovered a new type of object in the world or that they are putting forward a philosophical theory.[6] The *Philosophical Investigations* says that idealists, solipsists, and realists misunderstand their own debate: what they are defending and attacking are forms of expression, not statements.[7] In Carnap the comparison of language with an instrument is coupled with an exhortation for linguistic tolerance, something which is not to the same extent true of the later Wittgenstein.

Sometimes Wittgenstein compares language to a machine. A machine can be at work or run idle. When our language runs idle the result can be philosophy. Occasionally he also speaks of language as a form of life.

All these comparisons which the later Wittgenstein employs are vague and ambiguous, but they all unmistakably express a view of language that is very different from the picture theory of the *Tractatus*.

C. *Some semantic illusions*

In the history of philosophy, it has commonly been assumed that, on the whole, the expressions of language bear certain characteristic relations to extra-linguistic entities. In Russell's philosophy of language and in the *Tractatus*, the relation:

(N) x is a name of y,

---

[6] Ibid., p. 70.
[7] Wittgenstein, L., *Philosophical Investigations*, I §402.

is such a relation. With regard, for example, to language (8), Russell might say:

> (i) "Block" is a name of the property of being a block.
> "a" (used as a numeral) is a name of the number 1.
> "This", whenever uttered, is a name of that which the speaker points to.

According to the later Wittgenstein, (i) gives a basically false notion of language (8). The uses of "block", "a", and "this" in (8) are entirely different. There is no common function of naming which they all fulfil.

For common sense the relation:

(M) *x* means *y*,

is perhaps a more universal linguistic relation than (N). A French–English dictionary can, for instance, be read by an English-speaking person as a collection of bits of information about this relation:

> (ii) *chat* means *cat*,
> *marcher* means *walk*,
> *ne-pas* means *not*,
> *un* means *one*,
> and so on.

We certainly *can* say (ii), and these statements fulfil a definite function in our language. The information which they provide, could, Wittgenstein seems to mean, be conveyed just as well by the following statements:

> (iii) *chat* in French fulfils the same function as "cat" in English,
> *marcher* in French fulfils the same function as "walk" in English,
> and so on.

Statements of type (ii) become misleading if they induce us to ask, for example, "What is this *not*, which *ne-pas* means? Is it a Platonic idea, or a thought in someone's consciousness, or what?" *Chat, marcher, ne-pas,* and *un* have different functions in French, and the lexical information in (ii), correctly understood does not ascribe to them a common function of meaning.

According to Aristotle, the word is a symbol for a *thought*, which in its turn is, or may be, a picture of a thing. According to a medieval line of thought which we have met in Ockham, the spoken or written sign stands, by arbitrary convention, for a mental sign which in a natural way, non-arbitrarily, refers to its object. Locke said that words primarily stand for ideas. The later Wittgenstein turns sharply against the philosophical tradition of which these theories are examples. In *The Blue Book* he describes the traditional view as the view that to speak is to *translate* from the mental into the verbal language.[8] Some of his many objections to this position are the following: (1) The notion of a "mental language", like that of "mental processes", is obscure. (2) Even if there were mental processes, their presence or absence would be irrelevant. Language-games (2) and (8), for example, could, in principle, function equally well even if neither person A nor person B had any mental processes. (3) The philosophical belief in mental processes depends on a misunderstanding, the mechanism of which we can understand. It is correct to say that those who participate in a well-functioning language-game must understand the linguistic expressions which are used. But to understand is here the same as to handle the expressions correctly, to master the "technique" of the game. Philosophers err when thinking that an expression used with understanding is an expression accompanied by a special "process of understanding", or "act of understanding". An unbiased study of the facts shows us no such processes or acts, and the supposition that they exist is saved by calling them "mental": "the word 'mental' indicating that we mustn't expect to understand how these things work", says *The Blue Book*.[9]

D. *Meaning and Use*

To the extent that Wittgenstein is willing to talk about the "meaning" of expressions, he prefers to identify that meaning with what he calls the use or the function. An expression is meaningful only if it has some use in a working language, and its meaning is that use. What Wittgenstein

[8] Wittgenstein, L., *The Blue and Brown Books*, p. 41.
[9] Ibid., p. 39.

includes in the "use" is not very clear. The notion of use in Wittgenstein doubtless has a certain connection with the verification principle of logical empiricism: when considering the use of a word or a sentence, he *often* thinks of the conditions under which it can be correctly uttered according to linguistic usage, or those observations which would justify our uttering it. (Wittgenstein makes an amusing use of the verification principle when he says that the statement, "The earth has existed for millions of years", makes clearer sense than the statement, "The earth has existed in the last five minutes." Concerning the former, but not the latter, we know what observations count as evidence for it.[10]) But the verifying conditions or observations are only a special case of what the later Wittgenstein intends by the use. The greeting "Good-day" has a use but naturally is not verifiable.

There is a connection between what Wittgenstein means by the use of an expression and what he means by the rules for, or the logical grammar of, the language-game to which the expression belongs. The use is something which is anticipated or determined by the rules, the grammar.

The rules of logical grammar as Wittgenstein conceives them do not coincide with the rules of traditional grammar.

(i) Sentences which ordinary grammar allows may be rejected by logical grammar. Examples which Wittgenstein mentions are: "It is five o'clock on the sun", "I have n friends and $n^2 + 2n + 2 = 0$".[11]

(ii) While customary grammatical rules speak only about the possible combinations of the elements of language, Wittgenstein's logical grammar speaks also of the way in which the expressions are integrated into the whole net of activities which the language-game includes. The logical grammar for language (8) might contain, for example, the rule that B counts, or should count, one block for a, another for b, still another for c, and also for d, when A says "d—block".

Are Wittgenstein's rules of logical grammar to be understood

---

[10] Wittgenstein, L., *Philosophical Investigations*, II p. 221.
[11] Ibid., I §§ 350, 513.

as descriptive or normative? The use he talks of, is it the actual use, which we all know to be highly irregular, or is it that use which, from some grammarian's point of view, is the correct one? Wittgenstein seems to think that the rules have both aspects. As it is inconceivable that all chess players should constantly violate the rules of chess, so it is inconceivable that all those who use a language should constantly violate the rules of its grammar. The rules of language, like those of chess, are based on a general (although not exceptionless) regularity in human conduct, and they can be regarded as descriptions of this regularity. But just as the person who wishes to play chess must (ought to, should) follow the rules of chess, so the person who wishes to speak the English language must (ought to, should) follow its rules. No more than other apostles of linguistic correctness can Wittgenstein be acquitted of the charge of a measure of conservatism in his language policy.

One of Wittgenstein's maxims is that when searching for the (correct) use of an expression one ought to go back to the language-game which is its "original home".[12] The maxim hardly gives any clue to the understanding of how Wittgenstein conceives (correct) use—what kind of "originality" does the maxim refer to? In his attempts to clarify the use of different expressions, he sometimes studies how we initially learn to use them. His own discussion of what one could call the process of generalization shows that his practice contains a problem. We learn to use an expression in those cases which occur in the learning process—we could call them the learning cases—but we have actually learned how to use it when we can use it also in new cases. The learning cases are examples of the grammatical rule which determines the use of the expression, but the rule covers a boundless multitude of further cases. In the *Philosophical Investigations* Wittgenstein discusses how the generalization takes place. Obviously the generalization must also be a methodological problem for a linguistic theoretician like Wittgenstein when he tries to clarify the use (the rule) through a study of the learning.

[12] Ibid., I § 116.

E. *Meaning and family resemblance*

The concept 'family resemblance, together with the concepts 'family' and 'family of meanings', plays a major role in the later Wittgenstein's philosophy of language. He never defines his terms, and he probably would have rejected an attempt to give to these terms a sharply circumscribed use. If the following definitions are not taken too seriously, they can nevertheless serve to make his thought more accessible. Let us consider a set S of objects, and let us suppose that $P = \{A, B, C, \ldots\}$ is a set of properties ("resemblances") which can belong or not belong to the objects in S. Let us say that two objects in S are connected, if one can pass from the one to the other via a series of intervening objects in S, in such a way that at each passage from one object to another, some property from P occurs in both objects. One could then say, I think, that the set P is a set of family resemblances for S, in Wittgenstein's sense, if any two objects in S are connected by P—and perhaps also, to avoid redundancy, that any property in P belongs to at least two objects in S.

One could suggest, therefore that a set of objects S constitutes a family, in Wittgenstein's sense, as long as both of the following conditions are fulfilled: (i) there is a set of family resemblances for S, and (ii) there is no one property which belongs to all the objects in S. The family resemblances of a family overlap in about the same manner as the fibres in a thread. Doubt may be raised as to whether conditions (i) and (ii) are compatible: if $P = \{A, B, C, \ldots\}$ is a set of family resemblances for S, is not the disjunctive property 'A or B or C or $\ldots$' a property which belongs to all objects in S? Wittgenstein's answer reads: "Now you are only playing with words. One might as well say: 'Something runs through the whole thread—namely the continuous overlapping of those fibres'."[13] We may take it that Wittgenstein understands the word "resemblance" here in such a fashion that a disjunction of resemblances does not qualify as a resemblance.

What has now been said in explication of Wittgenstein's notions requires at least two important qualifications. First, when Wittgenstein talks about a set as a family, he generally

[13] Ibid., I §67.

assumes it to be a set without definite boundaries, which in turn implies that the associated set of family resemblances also lacks definite boundaries. For special purposes one can fix the boundaries of a family, but one need not do so. According to Wittgenstein, games form a family in this sense; also, the different kinds of numbers in mathematics constitute a family. Sentences and languages are families, and Wittgenstein holds that many terms of ordinary language stand for families. Second, both a family and its associated set of family resemblances are for Wittgenstein sets whose membership may change in the course of time: new kinds of numbers are invented in mathematics, new games and new languages are devised or grow, etc.

A family of meanings in Wittgenstein's sense is a family whose several members are meanings. Apparently Wittgenstein thinks that the words of ordinary language, to a large extent, are associated, not with single meanings, but with families of meanings.

F. *The status of ordinary language*

Wittgenstein's respect for ordinary language is one of the most characteristic features of the *Philosophical Investigations*. One way of summing up his view is to formulate some of the philosophical errors about ordinary language which he is anxious to correct.

(1) *The error of logical analysis.* According to this erroneous idea, the sentences of ordinary language state in an unanalysed form what can be stated in analysed form through the sentences of a *Begriffsschrift*, a "logically perfect" language. This idea, which we have met in the logical atomist Russell and in the young Wittgenstein, is, according to the *Philosophical Investigations*, incorrect on several scores. The belief in logical analysis, in Russell's and the young Wittgenstein's sense, is, for example, historically tied up with the belief that there are "meanings" which sentences have, and that the same "meaning" can be expressed with different degrees of analysis by different sentences. In the *Philosophical Investigations* Wittgenstein rejects the belief in "meaning" in this sense. He draws a further argument against

analysis from his view that languages are games: a *Begriffs-schrift* would be *another* game from ordinary language, not a clearer version of it.

The idea of a logically perfect language is certainly obscure, and few philosophers today accept it without reserva-tion. Also the notion of analysis as a decomposition of meanings is far from clear. If Wittgenstein's critique of analysis is directed against formalization in general, it seems, however, to overshoot the target. To replace a segment of ordinary language, say *X*, with a certain formalized linguistic structure, say *Y*, need not be just to replace one game with another. The same game can be played with pieces whose appearance clearly shows their role in the game (a new pack of cards), or with pieces whose appearance does not (a very worn-out pack). The difference between *Y* and *X* could be of this nature. It could also be the case that *Y* is a more developed, more refined, and more interesting "variant" of *X*.

(2) *The illusion of logical precision.* The terms of ordinary language often have a vague, fuzzy, obscure meaning, and therefore, so the illusion goes, they need to be defined, clarified, or replaced by other terms which do not suffer from these defects. Against (2) Wittgenstein argues that ordinary language is a perfectly satisfactory instrument for the purposes for which it is used.

Here, too, Wittgenstein's position seems rather vulnerable. It is undeniably a fact that for many purposes one must define, clarify, or coin new expressions. Striving for increased precision is not always unwarranted, and increased precision is not always impossible to reach, even if absolute precision may be utopian. There is no evidence that Wittgenstein held the search for terminological precision in the sciences to be misplaced, unjustified, or doomed to failure, but apparently he considers it to be so in philosophy. But why? He never makes his reasons clear and convincing.

Concerning the language that he himself uses in his study of ordinary language he says, in his characteristically enigma-tic way:

When I talk about language (words, sentences, etc) I must speak the language of every day. Is this language somehow too coarse and material

for what we want to say? *Then how is another one to be constructed?*
—And how strange that we should be able to do anything at all with
the one we have.

In giving explanations I already have to use language full-blown (not
some sort of preparatory, provisional one); this by itself shews that I
can adduce only exterior facts about language.[14]

(3) *The sceptical error.* Philosophers have often held whole
categories of assertions that we make unproblematically in
everyday life to be in principle incorrect. Against the everyday
assertion "I know for a certainty that the book is on the shelf",
the philosopher holds that "we never know anything for
certain". Against the everyday observation "the book is
green", another philosopher objects that "material objects
have no colours". Against "I know that the sun will rise
tomorrow", a third philosopher holds "we can never know
anything about the future". Against the everyday "he put his
soul into the work", a fourth philosopher holds "there is no
soul". And so on.

Moore, we know, thought he could refute various philosophical theories of this sceptical nature by simply citing
items of common-sense knowledge with which the theories
are, so he assumed, incompatible. Wittgenstein's attitude
toward this argument of Moore's is extraordinarily complex
and ambivalent. On the one hand, Wittgenstein is inclined,
just like Moore, to reject philosophical views that go against
our simple everyday certainties as expressed in our everyday
language. In many scattered aphorisms, Wittgenstein also
supplements Moore's argument with additional considerations. A language-game such as our ordinary language cannot
function unless the application of certain words to certain
things is simply accepted, without questioning. Only thereby
does the game acquire its meaning. A philosophical theory
that questions such application thus undermines the very
rules of the game.[15] Or, doubting and being certain (taking
for granted) are themselves activities for which the language-
game lays down the rules, and they make sense only when
conforming to these rules.[16]

[14] Ibid., I § 120.
[15] Wittgenstein, L., *On Certainty* (Oxford, 1969), for example, §§ 114, 369,
370, 374, 401, 446, 448, 449, 455, 509, 519, 522, 779,
[16] Ibid., §§ 24, 105, 310 ff., 457, 458.

On the other hand, alternative language-games are always possible. Couldn't it be that those philosophers who apparently contradict common sense have chosen to play other language-games of their own, or to use other "notations"? Their error is then only that they take their disagreement with common sense to be of the same kind as the scientist's disagreement, which is founded on more subtle knowledge and analysis of facts. When the same words and sentences occur both in the language of such philosophers and in that of common sense, they are nevertheless used differently and thus have different sense in the two contexts. Moore's argument is therefore also a mistake:

> There is no common sense answer to a philosophical problem. One can defend common sense against attacks of philosophers only by solving their puzzles, i.e., by curing them of the temptation to attack common sense; not by restating the views of common sense.[17]

The cure that Wittgenstein has in mind here will presumably consist in making it clear to the philosopher both that he has adopted a new language-game, and, perhaps also, what the needs are that have made him do so.

If this line of thought is taken seriously, couldn't a philosophy that verbally contradicts common sense possibly be judged just as legitimate as common sense? Since different languages may, after all, talk, wholly or in part, of different things, isn't it even possible that the anti-commonsensical philosophy may be a valuable complement to common sense? Wittgenstein seems inclined to reply in the negative to such questions. Of the solipsist, whose "notation" differs from ordinary language, he even says, in *The Blue Book*, that "he is not stating an opinion", he is merely "irresistibly tempted to use a certain form of expression".[18] In the *Philosophical Investigations*, he speaks of solipsists in a similar vein, together with idealists and realists.[19]

Wittgenstein's dominant negative view of philosophies that are not in consonance with ordinary usage and common sense is expressed in many well-known dicta: philosophical

---

[17] Wittgenstein, L., *The Blue and Brown Books*, pp. 58–9.
[18] Ibid., p. 60.
[19] Wittgenstein, L., *Philosophical Investigations*, I § 402.

problems arise when language is running idle; they are due to a misunderstanding of the forms of our language; their depth is the depth of a grammatical pun; they are to be treated like diseases; words should be brought back from their metaphysical to their everyday use; philosophy must not interfere with the actual use of a language; etc., etc.

G. *Mental processes, behaviourism, and the psychological vocabulary of ordinary language*

Wittgenstein's position in the *Philosophical Investigations* as well as in his other later works contains a strong element of behaviourism. The behaviouristic mode of thought which again and again appears in his aphorisms is a logical behaviourism akin to that of the logical empiricists in the 1930s. Wittgenstein does not dispute the psychological assertions which we commonly make about ourselves and our fellow men. He only interprets their meaning, and his interpretation has a behaviouristic tint. Further, his behaviourism is of the so-called molar kind: our psychological assertions are construed as assertions about observable behaviour.

"Well, one might say this: If one sees the behaviour of a living thing, one sees its soul."[20] The allusive character of so many of Wittgenstein's utterances makes it difficult to determine with certainty the extent of his behaviourism. The indeterminacy is, in this case, deeply rooted in his entire way of thinking: he simply cannot formulate any behaviouristic theory, since he distrusts all theory.

A behaviouristic interpretation of our everyday psychological vocabulary could be presented by first establishing a certain behaviouristic vocabulary and then showing that the former can be translated into the latter. The later Wittgenstein's aversion to philosophical analysis obviously closes this way to him.

A behaviouristic interpretation could be necessitated by a philosophical position according to which, while there are no mental processes, our everyday psychological statements are, in principle, correct. In the *Philosophical Investigations* Wittgenstein sometimes speaks about "mental", "inner", or "non-bodily" processes as if he meant to say:

[20] Ibid., I § 357.

(i) There are no mental processes.

Are you not really a behaviourist in disguise? Aren't you at bottom really saying that everything except human behaviour is a fiction?—If I do speak of a fiction, then it is of a *grammatical* fiction.[21]

However, for Wittgenstein (i) must be a case of what I have called the sceptical error, and he is bound to criticize (i) just as he criticizes other cases of this error.

Why should I deny that there is a mental process? But 'There has just taken place in me the mental process of remembering . . . .' means nothing more than: 'I have just remembered . . . .' To deny the mental process would mean to deny the remembering; to deny that anyone ever remembers anything.[22]

Far from subscribing to (i), Wittgenstein thus maintains approximately the following:

(ii) The facts which we describe with the psychological vocabulary of ordinary language imply the occurrence of mental processes. That a mental process occurs simply means that a fact so described occurs.

A position which Wittgenstein occasionally seems inclined to adopt is this:

(iii) There are mental processes of the sensory kind (sense-impressions, sensations of pain, etc.), it is true, but there are no such processes of a non-sensory intellectual kind (thoughts, understanding of language, memory, expectation, etc.).

Try not to think of understanding as a 'mental process' at all.—For *that* is the expression which confuses you. But ask yourself: in what sort of case, in what kind of circumstances, do we say, 'Now I know how to go on', when, that is, the formula *has* occurred to me?

In the sense in which there are processes (including mental processes) which are characteristic of understanding, understanding is not a mental process.

(A pain's growing more or less; the hearing of a tune or a sentence: these are mental processes.)[23]

When I think in language, there aren't 'meanings' going through my

---

[21] Ibid., I § 307.   [22] Ibid., I § 306.   [23] Ibid., I § 154

mind in addition to the verbal expressions: the language is itself the vehicle of thought.[24]

The words with which I express my memory are my memory-reaction.[25]

Remembering has no experiential content.[26]

Wittgenstein also expressed a very large number of less far-reaching ideas about the everyday psychological vocabulary. Sometimes he intimates that many so-called psychological statements assert, not only (if at all) the occurrence of mental processes, but also (what is equally important) something about overt behaviour. Occasionally he maintains that there must be observable, behaviouristic "criteria" for the application of psychological concepts. He also says that a psychological utterance in the first person singular, like, for example, "I am in pain", is not a description of the speaker's condition, but a substitute for some other component in his "pain" behaviour, for instance a scream, or that such an utterance is not a statement but a "signal". These ideas are only loosely outlined, and at this point we must leave them.

[24] Ibid., I § 329.   [25] Ibid., I § 343.   [26] Ibid., I p. 231.

Index

340   *Index*